Cultural Cabaret

Cultural Cabaret

Russian and American Essays for Richard Stites

Edited by David Goldfrank
and Pavel Lyssakov

NAP NEW ACADEMIA
PUBLISHING

Washington, DC

Printed in the United States of America

Library of Congress Control Number: 2012946218
ISBN 978-0-9855698-9-1 paperback (alk. paper)

New Academia Publishing
P.O. Box 24720, Washington, DC 20038-7420
info@newacademia.com - www.newacademia.com

All pictures are in the public domain unless otherwise indicated.

Richard,
come to the cabaret, dear friend...
come to the cabaret!

Contents

Preface-Tribute

by Pavel Lyssakov

I do not remember exactly how I met Richard Stites, but I remember our last meeting very well. I think we first met in St. Petersburg where he came to give a lecture in 2000 or 2001. I knew the name, of course, since I spent the 1990s in the United States and received my Ph.D. at Columbia University. I remember more clearly his next visit; he gave a lecture on Russian serf theatre in the 18th century, based on the research he was doing for *Serfdom, Society, and the Arts in Imperial Russia* (2005).[1] It was the time when the volume *Cultural Studies (Kul'tural'nye issledovaniia*, finally published in 2006)[2] was under preparation. As one of the editors, I was in charge of editing or translating our American contributors into Russian and translated his article "Petersburg as a Cultural Capital."[3] Richard wanted to take a look at my translation and we met in the afternoon, a couple hours before his lecture. He liked the text, but made two or three comments, and I still remember one of them. I translated "capital" as "stolitsa" ("kul'turnaia stolitsa" is a fixed expression in the Russian language applied to St. Petersburg) and he said that in the title he meant both "city" and "wealth," so I had to resort to "kul'turnaia stolitsa i kul'turnyi kapital," which is clumsier, but this is all you can do, since these meanings are expressed in Russian by two different words.

Richard had a good sense of humor; every time we met he would tell a couple new jokes. Next time I saw him was in Stock-

holm at the seminar of the network for Russian Cultural Studies
funded by the Council of the Ministries of Nordic Countries, where
we both presented papers. A colleague from Finland was reading
a paper on Soviet consumption patterns in the 1930s. On one of the
pictures from that period that he showed, there was a man standing
in the hall of a department store. He was shown from the side, one
could not see his other hand, and there was something on his other
side in the back of the hall; it was emerging above his head and
on the flat picture it really looked like an antenna of a cell phone
pressed to his ear (many cell phones still had little antennas until
the early 2000s). Richard, who knew the speaker, asked him, "Is it a
Nokia or is it a Sony-Ericsson?"

Richard came to Stockholm from Helsinki where his second
home was located. He liked Finland and was very much attached
to the Finnish National Library (which is at the same time the University of Helsinki Library). In the days of the Russian Empire it
used to be one of Russia's Imperial libraries; it has a very good and
well preserved collection of books and archives from the Imperial
period. We met in Helsinki twice in the summer of 2006. We had
corresponded by e-mail and I brought him copies of *Cultural Studies* with his article. I traveled in Europe for two weeks and on the
way back to St. Petersburg stopped in Helsinki again. I stayed in
the University area. I took a walk and as I was passing by the Library I saw Richard standing outside the entrance smoking. He, of
course, was working there, which he did almost every day when in
Helsinki.

In November, 2007, I was at the AASSS conference, which was
held in New Orleans that year. It was a nice evening, the temperature was in the 60s and everybody was thinking about seafood. I
was going to a restaurant with my friends. Somebody called me; it
was Richard standing on the sidewalk, talking to a colleague. We
exchanged a couple words, but unfortunately my friends and I had
to go because we had a reservation at a rather busy place. I thought
I would see him during the remaining days of the conference, but it
did not happen. That was the last time I saw him.

Many words have been said during Richard's lifetime and after
his death about his research interests and his ability to find new
outlooks and discuss previously ignored or dismissed subjects. His

works such as *The Women's Liberation Movement in Russia: Feminism, Nihilism, and Bolshevism, 1860-1930* (1978), *Revolutionary Dreams: Utopian Vision and Experimental Life in the Russian Revolution* (1989), *Russian Popular Culture: Entertainment and Society Since 1900* (1992), and *Serfdom, Society, and the Arts in Imperial Russia* (2005) brought to light many aspects of Russian history and culture, which at the time of publishing had not been explored by his colleagues in the profession–not only in the West but also in the USSR and post-Soviet Russia. His books are said to be of interest to specialists and to the general-interest readers alike; they are also a great aid in teaching. I use excerpts from *Russian Popular Culture* and his article on the Bolshevik search for new cultural rituals from the volume *Russia in the Era of NEP* (which he also edited)[4] in my film classes.

Richard Stites had much to say to the world of Russian studies. It would not be an overestimation to say that he had much to say to the world.

Notes

1   For precise bibliographic entries for this and Richard's other three monographs, see below, Anton Fedyashin, "'I'm a Classic'," note 2.

2   Complete bibliographic data: Aleksandr Etkind, Pavel Lys(s)-akov, eds., *Kul'tural'nye issledovaniia: sbornik nauchnykh rabot* (St. Petersburg: European University/Moscow: Letnii sad, 2006).

3   The English version appeared as "Cultural Capital and Cultural Heritage: St. Petersburg and the Arts of Imperial Russia," in Helena Goscilo, Stephen M. Norris, eds. *Preserving Petersburg: History, Memory, Nostalgia*. (Bloomington-Indianapolis: Indiana University Press, 2008), 182-96; rpt: *Passion and Perception. Essays in Russian Culture by Richard Stites*, ed., David Goldfrank (Washington DC: New Academia, 2010), 499-514.

4   Complete bibliographic data: Richard Stites, "Bolshevik Ritual Building in the 1920s," in Sheila Fitzpatrick, Alexander Rabinowitch, and Richard Stites, eds., *Russia in the Era of NEP: Explorations in Soviet Society and Culture* (Bloomington-Indianapolis: Indiana University Press, 1991), 295-309; rpt. *Passion and Perception*, 165-83.

Introduction

by David Goldfrank

I have already presented Richard Stites's unusual and productive life, works, and impact in two introductions. For the late 2010 re-publication of his essays on culture, I reviewed his professional life and scholarship,[1] and for a three-part, former students' memorial festschrift to be issued over 2012-13, I sketched his career at George-town and his relationship with the individual contributors, all of whom I had all also taught and advised.[2] Still, it is worth repeating here that Richard rose out of childhood poverty, had passions all of his life for culture, both highbrow and popular, fell in love with Russia upon his first serious encounter, and was an irrepressible entertainer and comedian. But at the same time he was a singu-larly attentive listener, and wherever he taught, he was viewed as a master—at all college and university levels. Likewise, a creative, clever, sensitive and effective writer, he inspired, encouraged, and fortified professional colleagues at Georgetown and elsewhere to pursue their intellectual passions, to venture into new areas of re-search, and to exceed their own expectations for themselves. He was certainly more responsible than anyone else for my own suc-cess in developing a second, modern research field and for my feel-ing at liberty to employ biting or humorous chapter and section titles and turns of speech. Accordingly, the irreverent title of my contribution to the first festschrift in his honor served as my medi-evalist's tribute to him,[3] and he continues to be an inspiration when

I encourage and aid younger scholars to loosen up a bit and liberate themselves from any stodgy restraints on their creativity. He will, moreover, become more of an inspiration for all of us, when his posthumous study of the Decembrists in the light of the preceding Spanish, Neapolitan, and Greek revolutions, *The Four Horsemen: Riding to Liberty in Post-Napoleonic Europe*, appears in print.[4] Like his four published monographs mentioned in the Preface by co-editor Pavel Lyssakov, this one too will become a standard and a classic of a type with a special vision connecting to developments in Russia and Mediterranean Europe.[5]

The subjects of the contributions to this memorial project—itself the brainchild of Pavel Lyssakov and a product of the type of Russian-American cooperation, which Stites worked so hard to promote—range from the most sophisticated theoretical linguistics to the lowest life Soviet gulag criminal tattoos, and from a well respected Imperial Russian writer to contemporary Reality TV.

We commence, in rough chronological order, with an offering by the last student to start history PhD work under Richard's guidance, Anita Kondoyanidi. Her "Noblewomen, Courtesans, and Merchant Women: P.D. Boborykin's Literary Photographs" reflects the burning interest Richard evinced in his own PhD research and first monograph, as well as his love of reading. The quite individualist Boborykin (1836-1921), the early propagator of the term intelligentsia whose revealing interchange with Lev Tolstoy Kondoyanidi retells, stands as a *sui generis* precursor of Stites and his pioneering, sympathetic study of Russia's "woman question"—a phenomenon which so astounded our colleagues.[6]

Russia's vibrant provinces[7] and the international nature of culture[8] figured heavily in Richard's work, and our other pre-Revolutionary contribution, Boris Gasparov's "Евразийские корни фонологи-ческой теории: Бодуэн де Куртенэ в Казани" touches on both of these phenomena. More than that, Gasparov advances an original hypothesis, that the anti-Positivist, psychophonetic notions of Baudouin de Courtenay[9] had much in common with those of the conservative, Slavophile-influenced, Orthodoxy-promoting, but pro-native language educator of Russia's Turkic and Finno-Ugrian peoples, Nikolai Il'minskii, as well as that these views were influenced by the overall milieu of Kazan at the time both men resided there. Stites, as we know, always encouraged such bold thinking and delighted in surprising conclusions.

"A vast activity deserving of special study" is how Richard Stites characterized sports in the USSR,[9] and so we welcome our first post-Revolution contribution, Bob Edelman's "Soviet Football, 1917-1941." Composed with the verve of a sportswriter, this essay places us squarely within the celebrated Dinamo-Spartak rivalry, as it developed, with all of the characteristics normally associated with professional sport. The author shows, moreover, how here, as elsewhere, such spectator sport made for "enclaves of autonomy" where "mass audiences" can evade "the goals of those who seek to control them."[10]

"Sing a song, tell a joke, and smile," said Andrei Stites on the occasion of the Georgetown memorial service in April 2010, recalling his father's advice to all of us. Indeed, Richard was legendary for his repertoire of jokes, and he considered them important sociocultural artifacts.[11] Though he was partially, as well, a product of rigorous, old-fashioned Roman Catholic schooling, I do not know how he would have reacted to my present claim that punch lines are at heart maxims, and hence subject to Aristotle's treatment of such aphorisms as premises or conclusions to syllogisms, where the listener provides the missing elements.[12] But this is what we see in our fourth presentation, "The Image of Stalin in the Kremlin: One Life-Death Joke from the 1930s," where Boris Briker creates a wide-ranging and model fusion of logic and politically contextual literary criticism, as he methodically seeks true meaning. We shall stop here and allow the author himself to present the biting punch line to his essay.

Like many good writers, Richard Stites also crafted clever, satirical sketches and cartoons.[13] Hence it is fitting that our next contribution to this volume, Steve Norris's "Laughter's Weapon and Pandora's Box: Boris Efimov in the Khrushchev Era," analyzes the cartoons along with the life-odyssey and the reflections composed in the 1960s of one of Soviet Russia's greatest political cartoonists, and certainly the longest-lived (108 years!). Privileged to have met the still sharp Efimov when he was 106, Norris employs these reflections and his subject's use of the Pandora's box metaphor as a prisms for grasping an essential aspect of intellectual life during the Khrushchev era and the Thaw.

At a memorial at Washington, D.C.'s Martin's Tavern to celebrate a plaque there in Stites's honor several months after he died, the organizers passed out "You Dirty Rat" pins—a testimonial to his life-long passion for films, well reflected in his scholarship,[14] and his irrepressible and frequent imitations of Jimmy Cagny. Richard, in fact, was a pioneer in introducing Russian cinema to the history classroom,[15] and our film-specialist and novelist publisher, Anna Lawton, thus pays tribute to him in our sixth article, "Fiction in the Service of History: A Tale of How *Brief Encounters* Ended Up on the Shelf," on one of Kira Muratova's suppressed movies. In a *sui generis*, creative recalling of classical historiography's placing of appropriate words in the characters' mouths, Lawton consciously extends the unavoidable fictional aspect of narrative history to its logical extreme with her invented "Tale." Stites also introduced creative historical drama into our Russian history teaching,[16] and here Lawton has produced as a byproduct an excellent script for such a classroom play, as well as a plausible explanation of the workings of Soviet censorship in a specific case.

Many of us, in different ways, have written about Stites's impact. My introduction to *Passion and Perception* contains reflections of fourteen other scholars and a retired US Army officer, while the introduction and testimonials in *Beyond Revolutionary Dreams* will present thirty-three from active scholars and former students— only one appearing in both books.[17] Several obituaries have also appeared. But nothing else so far approaches our seventh essay, Sergei Zhuk's "Richard Stites, the Soviet West, Media, and Soviet Americanists," for the sweep of its analysis and conclusions, which boldly claim and substantiate for Richard a historic "role in changing intellectual landscape in both American and post-Soviet space." So this may turn out to be the singularly most important piece ever written about him.

Conspicuous commodity consumption was utterly alien to Richard's way of life, though he avidly collected books, and film videos, owned catchy posters and other cultural artifacts, and of course possessed such basic necessary items as a refrigerator. His prize personal item may have been his upright piano for his improvising show tunes and other songs. As for his car, he proved to be the ultimate economic urban rationalist, just as Soviet authorities would have loved for their own populace. For once he moved to Washington in 1987, he switched to bumming rides or paying for taxis. Yet his famed Cagny and Brando imitations (besides "You dirty rat," "I could have been the champ") indicate that inwardly he thrived on at least the entertainment value of macho bravado, which expresses itself in motorcycles and hotrods, as well as competitive sports. And so our eighth contribution, Lewis Siegelbaum's "Cars and the Particularities of 'Personal Property' in the Brezhnev Era," which uses comparisons with refrigerators and pianos to identify the significance of the growth of automobile ownership in late Soviet society, intersects profoundly with Richard's sense that American and Soviet people shared far more values than not.

"Prison is prison," Stites said to me one day in the 1980s, as we were reviewing the horrors of different types of confinement. Indeed, he had grounds to know a thing or two of such matters, since his own father lived on the edge of the law as a bookie, sometimes threatening to employ force to collect debts. Likewise, serving time was a normal occurrence for people from his youthful milieu. So being possessed of a sense of the codes of the underworld, as well as fascinated by images and their decoding, Richard would surely have welcomed our ninth essay by Helena Goscilo, "Texting the Body: Soviet Criminal Tattoos." She gifts us with sophisticated and well grounded elucidation of how this alternative society generated its own socially and culturally meaningful symbols, which now may be undergoing post-Soviet changes, parallel to the rest of the country.

"Why would anyone want to study that crap? That's gotta be real garbage!" This is how one no-nonsense American aficionada of NBC Nightly News, "Dancing with the Stars," and HGTV reacted upon learning of our final article by co-editor Pavel Lyssakov, "Reality-TV: Реальность или ТВ?" But another American not at all ignorant of the US television scene, also a graduate student in Russian history who had once studied with Stites, immediately grasped the utility for understanding economy, society, and popular culture of analyzing the stages of what we might term Russia's «так наз. Reality TV»—a twenty-first century adapted and domesticated import. Lyssakov, of course, sees through the false consciousness (to use a no longer fashionable term—and one which

Stites avoided in principle) generated by such нереальность, as do, we must suspect, most Russian viewers and their counterparts elsewhere, who turn to these shows chiefly for their entertainment and escape values.

So here we have a potpourri of Russia for you, Richard: a male feminist; Eurasianism and linguistics; Moscow soccer; an anti-Stalin joke; a legendary cartoonist; a banned film; your own impact; private cars; criminal tattoos; and Reality TV. As with the North African freedman and Roman comic playwright Terence almost 2300 years ago, "nothing human" was "alien to" you![18]

We conclude this memorial festschrift with "'I'm a Classic:' In Memory of Richard Stites," a slight revision of an eloquent obituary published in 2011 by his former student Anton Fedyashin.[19] He beautifully sums up the man, the teacher, and the scholar, to whose cherished memory all of the contributors happily dedicate their contributions to this volume.

Notes

1   *Passion and Perception*, pp, xii-xxxix: I will be happy to furnish electronic copies of these introductions to anyone who lacks access to them.

2   Sandra Pujals, ed., *Beyond Revolutionary Dreams: Essays in Memory of Richard Stites = Canadian-American Slavic Studies*, 46, no. 3 (2012), 1-24. Thirteen of the fifteen contributors were among the sixteen Georgetown Ph.Ds, who wrote their dissertations under his mentorship.

3   "Burn, Baby, Burn: Popular Culture and Heresy in Late Medieval Russia," *Journal of Popular Culture,* 31.4 (Spring 1988): 17-32.

4   Oxford University Press will publish the finished manuscript, as edited by our Georgetown colleagues Catherine Evtuhov and John McNeill.

5   See below, Anton Fedyashin, "'I'm a Classic'," 254.

6   See Helena Goscilo's comment to this effect in my Introduction to *Passion and Perception*, xv-xvi: "I recall when I first encountered his superlative book on the women's movement, which impressed me not only by its excellence, but also by its meticulous scholarship and the sheer fact that a MAN had devoted so much intelligent attention to the topic."

7   For example, "The Creative Provinces in Nineteenth Century Russia," in Natalia Baschmakoff and Paul Fryer, eds., *Modernization in the*

Russian Provinces = Studia Slavica Finlandensia, XVII (March 2000), 306-23; rpt., *Passion and Perception*, 451-68; and a goody half of *Serfdom, Society, and the Arts in Imperial Russia* is devoted to the provinces.

8   Note here Natsascha Baschmakoff: "Editing and reading closely his articles, though, it amazed me how fluent he was IN DETAILS over the whole map of European and Russian culture – marrying events that happened at a same epoch far away from each others:" (personal email, summer 2010).

9   Lest this name confuse a reader, please note that due to an ancestor's immigration to Poland in the mid 18th century, Jan Niecisław Ignacy (aka Ivan Aleksandrovich) Baudouin de Courtenay was an Imperial Russian subject from the Kongresówka.

10   "Soviet Popular Culture in the Gorbachev Era," in *Harriman Institute Forum* 2, no. 3 (1989); rpt. *Passion and Perception*, 239.

11   Anna Lawton, "A Meaningful Montage," in *Passion and Perception*, 532. For a representative selection, see *Passion and Perception*, 34, 174, 214, 218, 230, 287, 335, 343, 393, 399 (n24), 413, 483; the originals are: "On the Border with the Soviet Avant-garde," *Soviet Observer* (Harvard University, Sept. 1988); "Soviet Popular Culture in the Gorbachev Era," *Harriman Institute Forum*, March 1989; "Bolshevik Ritual Building in the 1920s; "Cultural History and Russian Studies," in Daniel Orlovsky, ed. *Beyond Soviet Studies* (Washington DC/Baltimore: Wilson Center Press/Johns Hopkins University Press, 1995); "Frontline Entertainment" in Richard Stites, ed., *Culture and Entertainment in Wartime Russia* (Bloomington IN: Indiana University Press, 1995); "Days and Nights in Wartime Russia," in Aviel Roshwald and Richard Stites, ed., *European Culture in the Great War: The Arts, Entertainment, and Propaganda, 1914-1918* (Cambridge, UK: Cambridge University Press, 1999); "Soviet Russian Wartime Culture: Freedom and Control, Spontaneity and Consciousness," in Robert Thurston, ed. *A People's War: Popular Responses to World War II in the Soviet Union*. Urbana-Champaign: University of Illinois Press, 2000); "The Misanthrope, the Orphan, and the Magpie: Imported Melodrama in the Twilight of Serfdom," in Louise McReynolds and Joan Neuberger, eds. *Imitations of Life: 200 Years of Russia Melodrama* (Durham, NC: Duke University Press, 2002).

12   "Maxims are the premises or conclusions of enthymemes without the syllogism:" Aristotle, *Technes Rhetorikes*, II.xxi.2 (1394a), in John Henry Freese, ed. with trans., *Aristotle: The "Art" of Rheotoric*, Loeb Classical Library (New York: Putnam, 1926), 278-79; see on these, David Goldfrank, "Adversus Haereticos Novgorodensos: Iosif Volotskii's Rhetorical Syllogisms," to be published by Slavica in a forthcoming festschrift to Donald Ostrowski. Indeed, if you have even been dissatisfied with the logic of a joke and then recast the lead up to the punch line, you have affirmed my approach here.

13   See Goldfrank, "Introduction," in *Beyond Revolutionary Dreams*, 3.

14   For a survey of Stites's writings on cinema, see Goldfrank, "Introduction," in *Passion and Perception*, xxviii-xxix; these are: "Soviet Movies for the Masses and for Historians," *Historical Journal of Film, Radio, and Television*, 9, no. 2 (June 1991): 185-94, rpt. *Passion and Perception* , 273-87; "Doing Film History in the Soviet Union: a Research Note," *Russian Review*, 50, no. 4 (Oct. 1991): 481-83; "Dusky Images of Imperial Russia: Pre-revolutionary Cinema," *Russian* Review, 53, no. 2 (Apr. 1994): 285-95, rpt. *Passion and Perception*, 289-305; "To the Virgin Lands. The Epic and the Idyll in the Cinematic Representation of Khrushchev's Great Adventure," ed., David Goldfrank, in *Passion and Perception*, 307-18; "*The Pawnbroker*: Holocaust, Memory, and Film," in American Historical Society, *Perspectives on History*, 46, no. 1 (Jan. 2008): 30-31.

15   See Goldfrank, "Introduction," in *Beyond Revolutionary Dreams*, 5, 6, 19, 22.

16   We actually did this together, but he was the initiator and the "maestro:" see Goldfrank, "Introduction," in *Beyond Revolutionary Dreams*, 5.

17   *Canadian-American Slavic Studies* plans to issue the three-part *Beyond Revolutionary Dreams*, which was completed by late 2011, over the period 2012-13, with the last volume containing the testimonials gathered by Paul du Quenoy and also the short speech that Tom Barrett delivered at our Georgetown University memorial service in April 2010. (Both Paul and Tom did their PhD's under Richard and are contributors to that memorial project).

18   Cf. the original in the first person present: "Homo sum: humani nihil a me alienum puto."

19   *Russian Review*, 70, no. 1(Jan. 2011): 175-78. Fedyashin was one of a large number of our graduate students who wrote their dissertations under another mentor, but profited immensely from Richard's teaching, critical reading, and overall guidance.

1

Noblewomen, Courtesans, and Merchant Women: P. D. Boborykin's Literary Photographs

by Anita Kondoyanidi*

Peter Boborykin's life and career were full of paradoxes. Born in the village of Ankudinovka near Nizhnii Novgorod in 1836, he spent his entire life in Europe's major cities—London, Paris, Vienna, Madrid, Rome, St. Petersburg, and Moscow—through which he absorbed the intellectual, political, scientific, and theatrical trends of his time. In Derpt, he performed as an actor and turned into a prodigious playwright, but his plays fell into oblivion—where they remain to this day—after Soviet theatres stopped staging them in 1920. Boborykin failed as the owner of private theatres and a journal (*The Library for Reading*), but he consistently organized popular groups and societies to discuss current ideas. Living the life of the mind, he divided his intellectual passion and aspirations between chemistry and belles-lettres. On the surface, the writer's calling prevailed. When he moved to St. Petersburg in 1860 after studying science at Derpt University, Boborykin chose writing as his vocation and spent his long life—he died at 85 in 1921—submitting novels and essays to the most prominent thick journals such as *Herald of Europe* and *Russian Thought*. However, his scientific training constantly manifested itself in the way he approached his subjects. He observed the gestures, jargon, habits, dress, behavior, and homes of various Russian social groups with astonishing care, for which his admirers praised him. His meticulous eye and prolific pen discov-

*I am grateful to Richard Stites and Angela Stent who advised me on this paper when I was a student at Georgetown's Center for Eurasian, Russian, and East European Studies in 2007.

P. D. Boborykin (1836-1921)

ered and preserved for Russia's reading public numerous descriptions of women's daily lives abroad and at home. His critics, however, said that Boborykin failed to delve into his protagonists' inner worlds by drowning the reader in details and creating characters with facial expressions but without features.

The vicissitudes of Boborykin's life—among them an unexpected inheritance that he lost through numerous business failures—forced him to write for a living, which is why his output was so impressive, but yielded no masterpieces. Nevertheless, his indefatigable spirit, hunger for learning, and literary voyeurism made him persevere toward his goal of becoming an eminent chronicler of his society and its dominant intellectual trends. Perhaps Boborykin's true calling was that of an historian.

From this perspective, Boborykin's novels represent priceless snapshots of Russian life at the end of the 19th and the beginning of the 20th centuries because Boborykin approached every plot and character with "scientific" precision. For this reason, it is not surprising that Boborykin always chose to write about the dominant intellectual themes of the day. He wrote about nihilism at the same time as Ivan Turgenev, delved into the lives of the "the insulted and demeaned" before Dostoevsky, was the first to coin the term *intelligentsia*, and published a novel about adultery, *Victim of the Night*, in 1868, nine years before Tolstoy.

Women's role in society always interested Boborykin. Inspired by George Sand's and George Eliot's writings, he studied women by analyzing their behavior, dress, and interests. In his novels *Victim of the Night* (*Zhertva vecherniaia*), *Kitai-gorod*,[1] and the novella, *Without Husbands* (*Bez muzhei*), Boborykin created a colorful gamut of female characters, wealthy gentry women in St. Petersburg, poor noblewomen in the Crimea, merchant women in Moscow, and courtesans. Their searches for a niche in life met with failure more often than success. In these portraits, Boborykin accentuated, that in the 1860s and 1870s, women without money depended solely on finding affluent husbands. A good marriage meant a decent income and a respectable position in society. Noblewomen's lives revolved around the household. However, with the advent of industrialization and increasing urbanization, professional women who were educated and had a sense of responsibility became more successful. His observations led him to believe that Russian women merchants could take control of their lives and could achieve independence and professional recognition in society.

The biography of a literary photographer

Boborykin as a young boy had a great desire to learn. In order to keep him close to home, his parents sent him to the gymnasium in Nizhnii Novgorod. Like his classmates, he dreamt of becoming a university student, which they considered a rite of passage to adulthood with the right to wear a sword and cocked hat. Although during the years of Nicholas I the spirit of military grandeur reigned in Russian society, Boborykin never aspired to join the army.[2] As a gymnasium student, he fell in love with reading for which he had a lot of free time. The teachers were not demanding and the program was not rigorous, although the school was prestigious and offered its graduates direct entrance into Kazan' University, one of the best in Russia at the time. In hindsight, Boborykin appreciated the fact that students from different strata of Russian society attended the school. This exposure prevented him from thinking in terms of estates and made him interested in the lives of different social groups.[3]

Boborykin's favorite subject was philology. In sixth grade, his teachers considered his first humorous story, "The Frock," one of the best essays written in the province. As a result, he earned the reputation of a "lively pen."[4] He began to research his stories painstakingly and spent much time at the library reading journals, novels, and sketches. He perused Alexander Dumas, Walter Scott, James Fennimore Cooper, Charles Dickens, William Makepeace Thackeray, and Honoré de Balzac. In gymnasium, he came to love Georges Sand, and as a university student smuggled her forbidden novels to his female friends by hiding the books under his cocked hat. Alexei Pisemskii, Ivan Goncharov, and Dmitrii Grigorovich attracted him more than did Ivan Turgenev. He already knew very well Alexander Pushkin's *Eugene Onegin, The Captain's Daughter, Belkin's Novellas,* Nikolai Gogol's *Arabesques* and *Dead Souls,* and Mikhail Lermontov's *The Hero of Our Time.*[5] His family supported his intellectual aspirations and encouraged him to learn German and French, to study music and science. Although he did not develop his body physically, he invested hours in the cultivation of his mind. He found the motivation to learn at home, the natural source of mental stimulation under a political regime notorious for its discouragement of independent intellectual exploration.[6]

In 1853, Boborykin entered Kazan University where he majored in mathematics and chemistry, but two years later, he decided to leave for Derpt, a "scientific El Dorado," to study at its renowned Sciences Department.[7] Derpt's professors read lectures in German, which Boborykin wanted to master. The transfer from Kazan to Derpt also expanded Boborykin's horizons—foreign cultures fascinated him. In hindsight, he wrote that the Derpt period contributed immensely to his intellectual evolution and moral development. Throughout his life, Boborykin believed in a well-rounded education—the Renaissance idea of *universitas.* At Derpt, he studied not only chemistry, but also philosophy, rhetoric, poetry, science, medicine, and mechanics. He noted that his German *alma mater* was conducive to students who sought a European education.

In the summers, Boborykin visited home. These vacations served as good material for his future books. The thick Russian journals fed his curiosity and enhanced his desire to write. His first play *Windbags* and *The Smallholder* were successful. In 1860, Alexei

Pisemskii published Boborykin's *The Smallholder* in *The Library for Reading*, after which Boborykin decided to become a playwright.[8] In Derpt, Boborykin changed his plans to take his medical qualification exams and spent the remaining time at the university writing plays—he was prolific and finished four by the end of 1860. Soon thereafter *The Library for Reading* published "Old Evil" and "Century." The Malyi Theater in Moscow staged "Old Evil" under the title "Huge Apartments."[9] Boborykin moved to St. Petersburg at the end of December 1860.

While adapting to his new life in the capital, he found out that he had inherited two of his grandfather's estates in Nizhnii Novgorod Province, which made him an affluent landowner of the Lukoianovsk District with a hundred newly emancipated peasants on his lands. Having received a university diploma and an inheritance, he could have joined any ministry and made a brilliant career, but Boborykin treasured the freedom he had as a writer.[10] Instead, he replaced Pisemskii as the editor of *The Library for Reading*.

Boborykin arrived in St. Petersburg as a young man with established values and beliefs rooted in German freethinking. The intelligentsia of the capital had just begun reading Ludwig Büchner's materialistic *Force and Matter* and *The Whirlpool of Life*, but Boborykin knew these works already from Derpt. While studying medicine and chemistry, he had become interested in psychology, logic, and the history of philosophical systems. Boborykin knew well the history of European literature, particularly German literature and criticism, Shakespeare, and contemporary British and French literature. He immersed himself in Russian thick journals and empathized with Nikolai Chernyshevskii's anthropological principle, which Russia's eminent social critic described in his article on the philosophy of history. However, Boborykin never operated from a nihilist paradigm or used his writing as a platform for social denunciation. Nor did he ever participate in the coed communal experiments that were so popular among the nihilist youth.[11] The life of a revolutionary did not attract him. Charles Fourier's, Pierre Leroux's, and Pierre Proudhon's search for the "social El Dorado" did not inspire him. When he could afford it, he bought copies of Alexander Herzen's *Bell*, but the journal did not impress him as much as it did the "progressive youth" or "radical" St. Petersburg bureaucrats.[12]

Boborykin's failed editorship of *The Library for Reading* hardened him as a writer and an individual. He spent his adulthood paying off his debts. After he closed the journal, Boborykin wanted to take time off in order to find himself and come up with a plan to emerge from bankruptcy. He spent part of the summer of 1865 at his father's estate. During the rest of the year, he vacationed at the spa resort of Lipetsk where he met scientist and writer Gregory Vyrubov who later published the journal *Philosophie Positive* in Paris. One of Boborykin's Moscow relatives loaned him 600 rubles for his trip to Europe, so he went to Paris where he settled down in the Latin Quarter, the students' part of the city. He attended lectures at the Sorbonne, participated in Vyrubov's discussion circle, and became a convert to Auguste Comte's positivism. It is no wonder that Boborykin, whose initial education was in the sciences, upheld Comte's theory. The scientific ferment served him well even in writing novels, plays, memoirs, and reviews. He always paid a lot of attention to the minuscule details of the epoch he described—from tableware to philosophical trends. He did not create psychological portraits, but absorbed the minutiae of the day as an historian would and produced one literary photo album after another.

In Paris, Boborykin connected with international culture and history, which he decided to explore and serve for the rest of his life. In his view, one had to be a firm and stubborn Russophile to resist becoming a deep admirer and worshipper of western culture.[13] Boborykin attended lectures at the Sorbonne and the Collège de France where he listened to law professor Eduard Laboulé's speak of Montesquieu. The auditorium was always full. To Boborykin's surprise, the Collège de France allocated the best seats in the auditorium near the pulpit to women. He basked in Paris' intellectual and philosophically stimulating atmosphere. It restored the balance in his life, re-inspired him as a writer, and helped him to forget a Russian journalist's misfortunes.[14] Earning his income by serving as a foreign correspondent for *Herald of Europe* and *Russian Thought*, Boborykin traveled to London, Rome, Vienna, and Madrid.

Approaching 30, Russian men's cut-off age for marrying well, Boborykin did not give it a second thought. He preferred to study women in different parts of the world by analyzing their behavior, dress, and interests. In his own words, he was "a ladies' friend" who was afraid of relations with "easy" women who did not "speak to his soul."[15] In Paris, he socialized mostly with actresses, but in London he studied courtesans in the streets and visited George Eliot's literary salon in which men were overrepresented. She struck him as a true Englishwoman—respectable and reserved. As hostess of a literary salon, George Eliot was very modest, but when a phrase or an issue interested her, she interfered in a discussion and demonstrated great erudition and intelligence.[16] Western women struck Boborykin as more progressive and interesting than their Russian counterparts. Moreover, his observations led him to believe that Russian women had less style than the French or British. Inspired by George Sand's and George Eliot's writings, Boborykin contemplated the women question until his last days to which his final novel's title testified: *Confession of a Professional Woman* (1920). He undertook his first serious attempt at analyzing women's issues in 1868 when he wrote *Victim of the Night.*

Vera Fedorovna Komissarzhevskaia (1864-1910) playing Princess Olga Gorbatova in Boborykin's comedy *Scum* (Nakip').

Noblewomen

When *Victim of the Night* first appeared in 1868, it caused an un-precedented literary scandal because Boborykin exposed St. Petersburg's high society and accused its members of leading a double life. Neither the editor of *Worldwide Labor* (*Vsemirnyi trud*), Emmanuil Khan, nor the author suspected that the novel would have such an effect.[17] While the public perused *Victim of the Night* and exchanged tattered copies, an anonymous critic, most likely Mikhail Saltykov-Shchedrin, wrote a scathing review in *Notes of the Fatherland*, calling the novel rubbish. His opening remarks started with a question: "Could empty and worthless people be of interest to our literature?" He gave some credit to the rising writer, but with the caveat that although the novel was easy to read and well written, Boborykin only succeeded at avoiding a neophyte's mistake because of the novel's scandalous content. Saltykov-Shchedrin believed that *Victim of the Night* did not stimulate thought. The narrative flowed well and the prose was not repetitive because there was nothing to repeat. The detailed descriptions of nymphomania stimulated the reader's imagination, but they could only impress and excite the flesh. For him, *Victim of the Night* symbolized bad pornography that would confuse Russian women and mar their development. The censors banned the novel from being published as a separate volume, but a special committee chaired by Tsar Alexander II himself cancelled the ban.[18] Reconstructing *Victim of the Night's* publication history in his memoirs in 1906, Boborykin proudly wrote that it was Alexander II who sided with the minority in the committee and supported the novel.[19] Nor did Boborykin's notoriety spoil his relations with the editor of *Notes of the Fatherland*, Nikolai Nekrasov, who turned to him in a few months with a request for further submissions. The scandal and the accusations of writing pornography did not seem to bother Boborykin. "I always believed that the idea and issues which drove *Victim of the Night* had nothing to do with pornographic literature," he wrote in his memoirs: "this novel contained a bitter lesson and a merciless portrayal of high society's empty life which brought the main heroine to complete moral bankruptcy."[20] Who were these women and men described by Boborykin as leading double lives?

The novel's heroine, Mariia Mikhailovna, is born into a provincial gentry family. Petite and pretty, but uneducated, she attracts a young adjutant when her family takes her to a resort in order to find her a good husband. Nikolai comes from an affluent noble family, but dies soon after Mariia Mikhailovna gives birth to a son. As a widow, she becomes head of the household and receives 50,000 rubles a year. Until she meets a literary celebrity, Vasilii Dombrovich, life in St. Petersburg bores her. Her only entertainment is the Saturday benefit performances, which she finds hysterically funny. Petersburg's gloomy weather and her little son, Volodia, depress her. Although she envies her girlfriends who spend amorous nights in lovers' embraces, she does not want to remarry. For her, all Russian men—ministers, officers, or ambassadors—are idiots and animals who laugh like horses at stupid jokes. Interesting young men like her cousin, Stepan, shun Petersburg's high society and flee to Europe to study while the dim-witted noblemen, officers, and hussars fill the capital's ballrooms.[21]

At one of St. Petersburg's salons, Mariia Mikhailovna meets a literary celebrity, Vasilii Pavlovich Dombrovich, who impresses her with his good manners and mastery of Russian and French. At the end of the evening, he says: "Thousands of men told you that you are beautiful, but I am sure none of them knows what your beauty is about."[22] After he recites a part of his novel, Mariia Mikhailovna stops doubting his intelligence and his work conquers her mind and heart. Essentially, he turns into her mentor and secret lover. According to Vasilii Pavlovich, the key to a good life in St. Petersburg is to enjoy the balls and to give in to the play of hearts. Mariia Mikhailovna follows Dombrovich's teachings diligently and begins attending masquerades and balls, which break her cycle of boredom. Dombrovich takes all the necessary precautions not to disclose their secret relationship and not to jeopardize "their reputations."

When the season of masquerades ends before Lent and the Orthodox begin to fast, Dombrovich organizes evening meetings at his friend's apartment on the outskirts of town to which three noblemen friends of his invite their mistresses, countess Dodo Rybinskaia, baroness Schpies, and countess Varkulova. All three have reputations of irreproachable wives, good mothers, and prudes. Baroness Schpies devotes herself to charity and children, and everyone knows the countess Dodo Rybinskaia as a senile fool's wife who spends all her time babysitting her husband. Although Mariia Mikhailovna is pleasantly surprised to see this trio, she does not judge them. She endorses their trysts because they do not seem to suffer from these affairs. For these women adultery was analogous to comedy. The matter of fact manner with which these women referred to these nocturnal escapades is astonishing. Countess Varkulova explains to Mariia Mikhailovna that High Society is in great need of good comedy and clever women realize this quickly.[23] These noblewomen were not afraid of jeopardizing their reputations or hurting their families. Leading a double life did not affect their consciousness. Boborykin demonstrates that for them infidelity was an escape from dullness of St. Petersburg High Society. Since noblewomen do not pretend that they suffer from having affairs with such men, Mariia Mikhailovna endorses their trysts. The nights are full of music, champagne, gossip, embraces, cabaret, and laughter. These gatherings culminate in a sexual orgy, which ends with Mariia Mikhailovna's fainting caused by her cousin Stepan's appearance. Ashamed of herself, she severs her relations with Dombrovich and, under the influence of Stepan who had studied science in Europe, she decides to educate herself in order to bring up her son properly.

Boborykin did not invent the sexual orgy. Many people were aware that such "literary evenings" took place frequently in St. Petersburg. In the 1880s, Fyodor Dostoevsky's friend Nikolai Strakhov wrote about a literary salon, which he attended with Dostoevsky and writers Vsevolod Krestovskii and Dmitrii Minaev. Strakhov was surprised that no one paid attention to the physical excesses that took place that night. People who prided themselves on high morals talked about sexual orgies as common entertainment. They judged spiritual ugliness harshly, but overlooked the excesses of the flesh. This strange form of emancipation had bad repercussions: some men died or went mad because of guilt.[24] Strakhov did not delve into the details, but Boborykin, who was also aware of these "sexual escapades," described them in *Victim of the Night* in minute detail, making Dombrovich a typical landowner of the 1840s who did not have any qualms about using women.

In his memoirs, Boborykin also identified men who had led double lives. Writer Alexander Druzhinin was famous for organizing orgies, which he called "evenings in Athens." He not only planned annual New Year's Eve orgies that he referred to as "Family Saunas," but also organized various erotic experiments at home. Boborykin could not believe that this pedantic and reserved gentleman was a champion of erotic gatherings.[25] His friends, Ivan Turgenev and Nikolai Nekrasov, also had the old gentry's proclivity for telling dirty jokes, reciting indecent poems, and writing lewd short stories. Boborykin was iritated by Nekrasov's long poem about the customs of priests and annoyed by Turgenev's licentious story which he told once at breakfast with young Russian writers during the International Congress of Literary Critics. Boborykin compared the Russian writers' habits to the French authors' love to share inappropriate conversations about women after dessert.[26] Moreover, Boborykin lived what he preached, while Tolstoy, Turgenev, and Dostoevsky condemned the pretentiousness of St. Petersburg's high society and harshly judged immorality in their writings but in reality had lovers, gambled, and participated in sexual orgies. Boborykin's treatment of sexual deviance is objective. Unlike Tolstoy and Dostoevsky, he never used Christian principles either to pardon or explain his characters' immorality. He also never employed religious imagery or referred to the Church in his novels. His scientific approach to the philosophy of life manifested itself distinctly in his exclusive choice of real subjects.

As for infidelity in the late 19th century, it was rampant in Russia. E. J. Dillon, a regular contributor to *The Contemporary Review* and Russian correspondent for *The London Daily Telegraph*, wrote that "sexual immorality in Russia… is not accompanied by the same misgivings, succeeded by the same pricks of remorse, nor socially punished with the same obloquy and ostracism as elsewhere. It is one of the ordinary incidents of an unchequered life, like marriage or the measles."[27] A keen observer of Russia, Dillon wrote extensively about its daily life and politics in the heyday of European Imperialism. Even Russian dignitaries, such as Sergei Witte, considered his writings a reliable and accurate representation of Russia. In his memoirs, Witte wrote: "Of the foreign correspondents I knew Dr. Dillon, a prominent and able English publicist and a man of honor and sincerity, known to fame both in England and America... He speaks and writes Russian very well and his familiarity with Russian conditions, especially recent, is very great indeed."[28]

However, Dillon's impressions of Russia were not at all flattering. A reserved Englishman, he was shocked at the excesses of sexual frivolity and freedom and lack of moral education. In his articles, Dillon depicted how the educators of youth walked in broad daylight in public places with "their mistresses on their arms, although provided with lawful wives."[29] Compliments, small talk, and scandal constituted the daily bread of the nobles' minds. "Intrigues, underhand negotiations, treacherous plots, are also engaged in at times; but these are the nobler efforts, the loftier flights of men and women whose natural element is contented stagnation. These people never dream of the glorious potentialities of human nature; they have no fixed standard of right and wrong; the furniture of their souls contains nothing answering to the words of poisonous conventionality infinitely removed from the natural."[30] A Russian journalist once said to Dillon that spiritual ideals or interests did not exist in Russia and they were alluded to as mental aberrations. To his surprise, Dillon found out that neither Russian men nor women had lofty aspirations or ideals. While interrogating a talented woman of noble descent "with the eye and talent of an artist, and uncommonly good looks," he discovered that even she did not set high ideals or aims in life because to the people with whom she consorted her talents meant nothing. "Why should [she] cultivate [talents]? For what and for whom?"[31] She confessed to Dillon that sometimes she was conscious of a yearning for other and better things, but she suppressed it. "Why encourage selfish dissatisfaction with one's lot?" she asked him.[32]

Dillon, a highly educated man and a product of Western civilization, concluded that the Russians' barbarous nature was to blame for the lack of morals. Moreover, neither the Church nor the government actively punished misdeeds. Russians looked lightly upon marriage as an alliance entailing no obligation whatsoever. It cost them nothing to abandon each other. As conservative paper *Grazhdanin* wrote in 1889: "Whithersoever you turn, you meet with such shipwrecked families, the husband going one way, the wife going another. Their position in society is not one jot the worse on this account; no one dreams of censoring their conduct."[33]

Echoing Dillon, Vladimir Mikhnevich wrote in his book, *St. Petersburg's Ulcers*, that out of 538,041 inhabitants in St. Petersburg, only 226,270 were married. Furthermore, only 68,000 married men and women lived with their husbands and wives. Mikhnevich believed that infidelity was rampant in St. Petersburg because there were so many single people or married people who preferred to live separately.[34] Boborykin went a step further than Dillon and Mikhnevich. He not only described sexual orgies and wrote about the infidelity of noblewomen, but also explored their causes from a woman's perspective. What did marriage mean for a 19th-century noblewoman? What did a girl's marriage mean for her family?

In Boborykin's famous novella *Without Husbands* written in the 1890s, Mariia Denisovna, a young and poor noblewoman, spends several years with her mother visiting various resorts in search of a good husband. According to Barbara Engel, a mother's active role in relation to her daughter usually began after the girl turned sixteen. Essentially, to marry daughters well became the mother's responsibility.[35] In Boborykin's novella, Olga Evgrafovna explains to her daughters that marrying well means acquiring a good annual income for the entire family. Since they are poor, Olga Evgrafovna hopes that her daughters' husbands will cover their debts and provide for them in the future. As Barbara Engel and William Wagner have noted, through the 19th and into the 20th century, family and community needs took precedence over individual preferences in the making of most marriages.[36] When Mariia's younger sister, Lily, becomes engaged to an old general whom she despises, no one suspects that she will commit suicide several days before the wedding day. Mariia envies Lily's courage in standing up to their mother.[37] The irony of it is, of course, that Lily does so only in death.

In this novella, Boborykin created an account of a woman's struggle to realize herself emotionally and to resist the weight of patriarchal authority. According to Engel, women's memoirs are indicative of female resistance. To this category belong the memoirs of Vera Tretiakova and Ekaterina Andreeva-Balmont who were raised in educated and eminent merchant families. Both experienced numerous impediments before they could marry men whom they loved, but both won in the end. Vera Tretiakova had to resort to a spell of hysterical blindness and fits before her father agreed to her marriage to the musician Aleksander Ziloti, a noble by birth. Ekaterina Andreeva had to overcome similar barriers before she could marry Konstantin Balmont whose divorced status made him disagreeable to her parents. Anna Volkova, a merchant daughter and a feminist author, wrote in her diaries about a merchant girl who in 1894 committed suicide before her wedding day rather than marry the man her father had chosen for her. In her memoirs, Volkova accentuated the conflict between parents and children when parents made a decision that would be advantageous to the entire family without considering their children's feelings and needs.[38]

Boborykin suggested that unless a noblewoman inherited much money, she could only earn income by marrying well. Even then, the noblewomen had to maintain their social image by either appearing at balls and masquerades or running literary salons. In a highly stratified society, they had to be invited to social events by well-established families to be noticed. Having an affluent and titled husband always helped because his name was on these guest lists. Failure to find a husband meant miserable existence and hatred of the family. Mariia Denisovna in *Without Husbands*, fails to find herself a husband and thereby enraged her mother. Boborykin let his readers contemplate her destiny. Historians believe that if a gentry woman did not marry, society looked down upon her. As Richard Stites has written, the saying went *"ne zhenat, ne chelovek...* not married, not human. And though the saying refers to bachelorhood, the object of real pity in Russian society, as in most, was the unmarried female rather than the male."[39] In her memoirs, noblewoman Elizaveta Popova described a case when a mother forced her daughter to marry by simply threatening to withdraw her help in marrying her off. According to Popova, some woman who had a twenty-two or twenty-three-year-old daughter told her that if she did not marry the man her mother had chosen, she would give up on her as an old maid and concentrate on a younger daughter. The young girl capitulated and married a man she barely knew.[40]

Another potential point of concern in making a good marriage for Russian noblewomen were French women. Russian officers and noblemen preferred French femme fatales who were skillful seductresses and refined ladies. "How did Blanche and Clémence charm Russian men? Why did they have so much fun with these French courtesans and leave their Russian wives for them?"[41] In *Victim of the Night*, Mariia Mikhailovna decides to study French women because she can not believe that Russian noblewomen are incapable of cultivating similar skills. On the male market, Russian noblewomen also competed against native female dancers of low social status. Mariia Mikhailovna considers it beneath herself to write about their manners and education. "What language did they use when they speak to men? They know only a little French. Even Russian noblewomen fail to think in Russian, not to mention these corps de ballet girls. But what is annoying, wherever one goes, one hears conversations about them."[42] One of the characters, wealthy nobleman Prince Peter lives with a dancer for fifteen years and finally severs his relations with her to marry a noblewoman. Yet, Russian officers enjoy the dancers' company, love them passionately, and occasionally marry them.

With marriage came children, but parents kept them at a distance. Despite a noblewoman's subordination to her husband, memoirs suggest that responsibilities made the mother a positive role model for her daughters and sons, even as they kept her from being as intimately involved with infants and small children as were middle-class mothers in the West. As Engel has noted, motherhood was an important social role in Russia, but it meant something different from motherhood as the European and American middle classes construed it. Childrearing was not the central focus of a noblewoman's life as it was for the Western middle-class woman who had ceased to participate in her husband's business and was expected to embellish the domestic sphere and devote herself to her offspring. In Engel's words: "among the various duties a Russian noblewoman performed, childcare occupied a relatively insignificant place."[43] Noblewomen bore their children, then turned their attention elsewhere, leaving them for others to raise. Before Emancipation, serf women were attentive and loving substitutes for the biological mother. If the family was sufficiently wealthy, the child passed from nurse to governess to tutor and then to school. One of the prerogatives of wealth seems to have been freedom from the daily responsibilities of childcare. The more conscientious mother might assume a supervisory role, but most seemed satisfied to inspect their children in the morning and evening and receive reports from a nurse, a governess, or a tutor. "Relations between parents and children were defined quite precisely," recalled the daughter of a noble family of modest means. "Children kissed their parents' hand in the morning, thanked them for dinner and supper, and took leave of them before going to bed. Every governess spent most of her time trying to keep the children as much as possible from bothering the parents."[44] Girls and boys entered their mothers' and fathers' worlds when they matured. "Perhaps the most important task a woman faced after actual childbirth," wrote Jessica Tovrov, was to see to it that her daughters were properly married."[45] Mothers occupied the central role in the family even though other female figures mediated their relationships with their children.

Mariia Mikhailovna neglects her son most of the time, letting her English governess, Miss Phlebs, bring up little Volodia. After Stepan discovers her at Dombrovich's sexual orgy and she begins to seek meaning in her life, she finally becomes serious about her son. Mariia Mikhailovna decides to educate herself so she could in turn teach Volodia math, languages, and art. The boy who always depressed her becomes an indispensable part of her life. At the end of the novel, she dies and leaves him in the hands of Stepan's friend, a man she loved but of whom she thought herself unworthy. This transfer reflected the socially accepted pattern. Fathers usually became responsible for their boys' education after they reached adolescence. In Tovrov's words: "After the boy was transferred to the male sphere, ideally, and usually in fact, the mother and son had few activities or concerns in common and encountered each other only in fairly limited contexts."[46]

Leaving a child in male hands was a traditional practice, but committing suicide and failing one's son was a terrible sin. Neither Mariia Mikhailovna's cousin nor his friend, Aleksandr Krotkov, can help her. As a man of the 1860s, Stepan attempts to educate Mariia Mikhailovna by reading books together, writing, and discussing the latest ideas. Mariia Mikhailovna, however, can not change the perception of herself as a sinful woman. In her mind, this image does not differ from the image she has of prostitutes whom she has tried to rescue.

In her search for meaning, she works for a social activist and poor noblewoman Lizaveta Petrovna. They attempt to rescue courtesans by talking them into leaving bordellos for the sake of universal love. Mariia Mikhailovna buys an apartment and tries to introduce them to literature and languages, but the courtesans decline these offers and implore Mariia Mikhailovna to set them free to pursue the lifestyle they have chosen. In her groundbreaking book on prostitution, Laurie Bernstein has argued that it was fashionable to rescue fallen women. In her words: "At the turn of the century, feminists, society ladies and gentlemen, moral crusaders, and other members of the Russian privileged classes devoted thousands of volunteer hours and rubles to this goal."[47] But these efforts often floundered because Salvationists, who were usually sincere in their desire to help, tended to be too naïve. Boborykin's Stepan introduces Mariia Mikhailovna to Lizaveta Petrovna in order to show her that the problem of prostitution is social and economic: in this way Boborykin attempted to capture the debate about the causes of prostitution which dominated St. Petersburg society at the time. By describing the squalor in which prostitutes lived, their dead-end lives, and their desire to continue this vocation, he depicted two main trends in the social debate of the 19th century. According to I. Golosenko, there were two schools of thought about prostitution in Russia—anthropological and sociological. On the one hand, V. Taranovskii, A. Fedorova, and N. Krainskii argued that some women were genetically predisposed to prostitution. The other school believed that social and economic conditions played a vital role in prostitutes' choices.[48]

At the end of the novel, Mariia Mikhailovna, lost in her own world, commits suicide. In his memoirs, Boborykin blamed St. Petersburg's high society for the death of this weak character. Although she has money and is beautiful, Mariia Mikhailovna lives in a society that does not expect her to hold strong opinions acquired through education. Being in the dark, she fails to stand up to Dombrovich and recognize who he is in reality. Focusing only on her inner world and neglecting her child, she also gives in to social pressure. After her nocturnal escapades with Dombrovich, Mariia Mikhailovna's cousin, Stepan, who was educated in Europe, tries to rescue her by educating her about life through math and philosophy, but his efforts are in vain. Unlike Tolstoy or Dostoevsky, Boborykin viewed education, not prayer, as the ultimate path to salvation in a modern world driven by science.

Fourteen years later, Boborykin created his masterpiece, *Kitai-gorod*, in which the main protagonist, Anna Serafimovna Stanitsyna, is the exact opposite of Mariia Mikhailovna. In the 1880s, Boborykin became interested in the lives of the merchants. Observing their rapid ascent to economic and social prominence in Moscow, he wrote *Kitai-gorod*, which became the first detailed fictional novel about the merchants' daily lives. In his memoirs, *Merchants' Moscow*, Pavel Buryshkin, who was born into a prominent merchant family and had to emigrate after the Bolshevik Revolution, wrote that Boborykin created photographic snapshots of the merchants' houses, funerals, and benefit performances in his novel.[49] Buryshkin further noted that unlike Nikolai Ostrovsky, Boborykin did not depict his merchants as ignoramuses and fops, but still looked down upon most, although not his main heroine, Stanitsyna, whom he modeled on a real person, Varvara Morozova.[50]

Stanitsyna is an educated, independent, attractive, and intelligent woman born into a wealthy merchant family. Her husband is a profligate landed nobleman who has mistresses in Europe and Russia. She divorces him and takes direct control of the factories belonging to herself and her dissipated husband. Boborykin draws a complex portrait of his heroine. Although she is a capable businesswoman who knows the textile business well and is respected by her workers, she spends nights crying because of the pain her husband causes her. Growing up in a merchant family, she receives a good education and learns French, but is always shy to speak it in front of her husband who always looks down upon her because of her social background. In spite of her ability, beauty, and character, Boborykin's heroine is acutely self-conscious of her origins. She chooses a wrong fabric for her dress, which reveals her background. "She contemplated: this sandy color cries out loud a *merchant woman*. ...Why did I choose these colors? Undoubtedly, it is the most merchant color. Well, the fabric looked so good and would not show stains. Why must I have chic? I do not want to become a noblewoman. Nevertheless, I should have style and taste."[51] Andrei Paltusov, the main male protagonist of the novel, a nobleman educated in Europe, studies merchants to enter their business circles and notices Anna Serafimovna's faux pas. Her dress' bright yellow color blinds him, but he is too fascinated with her poise, character, and beauty to let it distract him. Paltusov admires Stanitsyna's professionalism and willingness to educate her workers. Anna Serafimovna runs special schools, organizes housing for her employees, and is the first businesswoman to hire a Russian, not a foreign, engineer as the technical director of her factory. At the end of the novel, she pays off Paltusov's debts and rescues his reputation.

Boborykin's portrait of Anna Stanitsyna represents a verbal photographic snapshot of Varvara Morozova. According to Muriel Joffe and Adele Lindenmeyr, Morozova was an educated woman who could hold her own in intellectual circles.[52] Left with three minor sons when her insane husband died in 1883, she became the head of the board of the directors of the Tver Cotton Goods Manufacturing Company, and ran the business alone until 1892, when her son Ivan joined her. Unlike other merchants, Morozova greatly improved the material conditions of her employees and educated them. She also appointed the first Russian engineer in the company's history as technical director.[53]

There are obvious similarities between Mariia Mikhailovna and Anna Serafimovna. Both are unhappily married, both are financially independent, and both have children. The difference lies in their education and sense of responsibility. While Anna Serafimovna is very well-educated, has a profession—she is a director of a cotton factory—Mariia Mikhailovna has enough education only to keep up with a conversation in St. Petersburg's salons. While Anna Serafimovna has found the meaning in her life when she became the head of the factory and her household, taking care of her children, Mariia Mikhailovna failed to listen to her cousin who encouraged her to study in order to educate her son. Instead, disillusioned, she left her son in her cousin's friend's hands.

Conclusion

The Russian Nobel Prize Laureate Ivan Bunin regretted that the 20th century did not take Boborykin seriously: "If you want to learn more about modern trends in merchants' lives, in literature, in the bourgeoisie's and workers' environments, with all their tendencies, in the ladies' dresses, in fashionable claims, or in any trivialities of the 1880s-1890s epoch, read Boborykin. He described everything diligently and his material is of good quality."[54] Boborykin left for his posterity numerous photographic snapshots of his time. In his novels, he recreated diligently the historic reality of the 19th and early 20th centuries. But the Russian public failed to understand Boborykin because it longed either for the symbolists' otherworldliness or the universal truth that Tolstoy and Dostoevsky had explored.

Leo Tolstoy, who highly respected Boborykin, tried to persuade him to abandon his pursuit of social trends and focus instead on the inner worlds of his characters because human beings were imperfect and in dire need of praying. Boborykin is reported to have recounted to someone: "Tolstoy preached forgiveness to everyone and asked me to pray. I told him, 'Lev Nikolaevich, you need to atone for your sins by praying and thinking about the future. Why me? I did not smoke, did not drink, and did not sleep around. I will die calmly and knock on the gate to paradise. Apostle Peter will ask me: 'Who is there?' I will answer, 'It is Boborykin!' He will open the gates in front of me instantly and say in a friendly way: 'Please, you are so welcome Pyotr Dmitrievich!' And you sinned, oh, how much you sinned, Lev Nikolaevich!"[55]

Boborykin did not leave a single indication that he believed in any religion. Neither his memoirs nor his fiction contain any reference to the Church because he was a staunch believer in science and secular education. His views were revolutionary for the time. Inspired by George Eliot's novels and other feminist writings, he immersed himself in the study of Russian women in the 19th century and depicted women's difficulties if they failed to marry well. Exposing St. Petersburg high society's baseness, he described literary sexual orgies and openly wrote about women's and men's rampant infidelities. In raising questions about the subordination of women, Boborykin explored the role that men of different generations played in their lives. In *Victim of the Night* and *Without Husbands*, he contrasted the way educated landowners of the 1840s and the men of the 1860s, forward-looking young minds educated in Europe, attempted to alter women's roles by educating them. In Boborykin's view, the combination of education and a sense of responsibility was the recipe for women's success. And this is not surprising, after all, the positivist spirit in which Boborykin was educated made him a staunch believer in the emancipative and equalizing power of science and secular education.

Notes

1   The Russian term *Kitai-gorod* is untranslatable. It is an historical area adjacent to Red Square behind the GUM Department Store. The term has nothing to do with the western concept of Chinatown. The Russian term "kitai" has an unclear provenance and is related either to the Italian "città" (town) or to a Tartar term "kitai" (fortification).

2   Pyotr Boborykin. *Vospominaniia: Za polveka*, 2 vols, (Moscow: Khudozhestvennaia literatura, 1965), 1:46.

3   Boborykin. *Vospominaniia*, 1: 47.

4   Boborykin. *Vospominaniia*, 1: 48.

5   Boborykin. *Vospominaniia*, 1: 50.

6   Boborykin. *Vospominaniia*, 1: 52.

7   Boborykin. *Vospominaniia*, 1: 128.

8   Boborykin. *Vospominaniia*, 1: 179.

9   Boborykin. *Vospominaniia*, 1: 183.

10   Boborykin. *Vospominaniia*, 1: 185.

11   Boborykin. *Vospominaniia*, 1: 273.

12   Boborykin. *Vospominaniia*, 1: 274.

13   Boborykin. *Vospominaniia*, 1: 410.

14   Boborykin. *Vospominaniia*, 1: 421.

15   Boborykin. *Vospominaniia*, 2: 101-02.

16   Boborykin, *Vospominaniia*, 1: 488.

17   Emmanuil Khan published *Victim of the Night* in his serial journal *World-wide Labor* in 1868.

18   Boborykin, *Vospominaniia*, 1: 456.

19   Boborykin, *Vospominaniia*, 1: 456.

20   Boborykin. *Vospominaniia*, 1: 457.

21   Pyotr Boborykin. *Zhertva vecherniaia*, in idem., *Sochineniia v trekh tomakh*, 3 vols., (Moscow: Khudozhestvennaia literatura, 1993), 1: 33.

22   Boborykin. *Zhertva Vecherniaia*, 1: 46.

23   Boborykin, *Zhertva Vecherniaia*, 1: 126.

24   N. Strakhov. "Vospominaniia," in *Biografia, pisma, i zametki iz zapisnoi knizhki F. M. Dostoevskogo* (St. Petersburg, 1883), 173-74.

25   Boborykin. *Vospominaniia*, 1:196.

26   Boborykin. *Vospominaniia*, 1: 197.

27   E. J. Dillon, *Russian Traits and Terrors* (Boston: B. R. Tucker, 1894), 142.

28   Sergei Witte, *The Memoirs of Count Witte* (New York: Doubleday, 1920), 137.

29   Dillon, *Russian Traits and Terrors*, 147.

30   Dillon, *Russian Traits and Terrors*, 150.

31   Dillon, *Russian Traits and Terrors*, 150.

32   Dillon, *Russian Traits and Terrors*, 151.

33   *Grazhdanin*, April 3, 1889, quoted in Dillon, *Russian Traits and Terrors*, 151.

34   Vladimir Mikhnevitch, *Iazvy Peterburga: opyt istoriko-statisticheskogo issledovaniia nravstvennosti stolichnogo naseleniia* (St. Peterburg, Limbus Press, 2003), 425.

35   Barbara Engel, *Mothers and Daughters: Women of the Intelligentsia in 19th-century Russia*, (Evanston: Northwestern University Press, 2000), 32.

36   See William Wagner, *Marriage, Property and the Law in Late Imperial Russia* (Oxford: Oxford University Press, 1994), 59-100, and Barbara Engel, *Breaking the Ties That Bound: the Politics of Marital Strife in Late Imperial Russia* (Ithaca: Cornell University Press, 2011), 80-100.

37   Pyotr Boborykin, *Sobranie romanov, povestei, i rasskazov.* 12 vols, (St. Petersburg: Izdanie A. F. Marksa, 1897), 2: 15-16.

38   Anna Volkova, *Vospominaniia, dnevnik i stat'i* (Nizhnii Novgorod, 1913), 44-45.

39   Richard Stites, *The Women's Liberation Movement in Russia: Feminism, Nihilism, and Bolshevism, 1860-1930* (Princeton: Princeton University Press, 1978), 8.

40   Jessica Tovrov, "Mother-Child Relationships among the Russian Nobility," in *The Family in Imperial Russia: New Lines of Historical Research*, ed. by David Ransel, (Urbana: University of Illinois Press, 1978), 38.

41   Boborykin, *Zhertva Vecherniaia*, (Moscow: Khudozhestvennaia literatura, 1993), 1:48.

42   Boborykin, *Zhertva Vecherniaia*, 1:48.

43   Engel, *Mothers and Daughters*, 11-12.

44   Tatiana Passek, *Iz dal'nykh let: Vospominaniia*, 2 vols. (Moscow: Gosudarstvennoe izdatel'stvo khudozhestvennoi literatury, 1963), 1:358.

45   Tovrov, "Mother-Child Relationships among the Russian Nobility,"38.

46   Tovrov, "Mother-Child Relationships among the Russian Nobility," 25.

47   Laurie Bernstein, *Sonia's Daughters: Prostitutes and Their Regulation in Imperial Russia* (Berkeley: University of California Press), 190.

48   I. Golosenko, *Rossiia: sotsiologiia prostitutsii* (St. Petersburg: Rossiiskaia Akademiia Hauk, 1997), 14-17.

49   Pavel Buryshkin, *Moskva kupecheskaia* (Moscow: Sovremennik, 1991), 40.

50   Buryshkin, *Moskva Kupecheskaia*, 40.

51   Pyotr Boborykin, *Kitai-gorod* in *Sochineniia v trekh tomakh*, 2: 63.

52   Muriel Joffe and Adele Lindenmeyer, "Daughters, Wives, and

Partners: Women of the Moscow Merchant Elite," in *Merchant Moscow: Images of Russia's Vanished Bourgeoisie*, eds. James West and Iurii Petrov (Princeton: Princeton University Press, 1998), 98.

53   Joffe and Lindenmeyer, "Daughters, Wives, and Partners: Women of the Moscow Merchant Elite," 103.

54   Alexander Bakhrakh, "Bunin v khalate," in *Bunin v khalate i drugie portrety po pamiati, po zapisiam*, (Moscow: Vagrius, 2005), 81.

55   Bakhrakh, "Bunin v khalate," 82.

2

Евразийские корни фонологической теории: Бодуэн де Куртенэ в Казани

Борис Гаспаров

Хорошо известно, что понятие фонемы и связанное с ним различение фонологии и фонетики как двух разных лингвистических дисциплин, имеющих дело, соответственно, с функционально значимыми признаками звуков языка и их материальными (акустическими и артикуляторными) свойствами, было разработано в Казани в начале 1880-х годов. Это

Казанский университет, 1840-ые годы.

"Иван Александрович" Бодуэн де Куртенэ (Jean Baudouin de Courtenay), 1845-1929.

достижение явилось результатом коллективной работы группы молодых лингвистов Казанского университета, бесспорным главой которой был "Иван Александрович" Бодуэн де Куртенэ (Jean Baudouin de Courtenay), в то время профессор общего и индоевропейского языкознания в Казани. Обособление фонологии как самостоятельной области лингвистики, предметом которой являются чистые функции в отвлечении от материальных свойств звуков, послужило первым теоретическим прорывом к пониманию языка как структуры. Идея о том, что эмпирическим фактам, наблюдаемым в речи, соответствует на ноуменальном уровне система идеальных ценностей, основанная на отношениях между отдельными элементами, была сформулирована в качестве фундаментального принципа лингвистики четверть века спустя Фердинандом де Соссюром. Соссюр был знаком с работами Бодуэна; еще позднее, в 1920-30-е годы, фонология получила систематическую разработку в качестве важнейшего компонента структурной модели языка в работах Н.С. Трубецкого и Р.О. Якобсона, видевших в Бодуэне своего непосредственного предшественника и учителя. Таким образом, работы "Казанской школы" в области теории фонемы по праву считаются одним из главных источников, на которых покоятся теоретические основания современной лингвистики.[1]

Идея фонемы была сформулирована в годы пребывания Бодуэна в Казани (1875-1883). Мне кажется, однако, что значение Казани как среды, в которой совершилось это важнейшее событие в истории современной лингвистики, не оценено в достаточной степени. В работах, посвященных Бодуэну и его идеям, Казань обычно фигурирует лишь в качестве внешнего — хотя, конечно, вполне благоприятного — "обстоятельства места". Надо сказать, что Бодуэн попал в Казань в 1875 году почти случайно;[2] уже через восемь лет последовал переезд в Дерпт, затем в Краков, Петербург, Варшаву; на протяжении своих почти полувековых "годов странствий" после Казани Бодуэн продолжал преподавательскую и научную деятельность, в орбиту которой входили все новые поколения учеников.[3] Однако если взглянуть на более широкий контекст, в котором протекала работа Бодуэна в Казани, на те явления интеллектуальной и социальной жизни, с которыми его деятельность прямо или косвенно пересекалась, становится более заметной та роль, которую казанская среда сыграла в становлении идеи фонемы. Более того, я убежден, что и сама идея, будучи помещена в данный контекст, обнаруживает в себе некоторые черты, без этого остающиеся незамеченными. То, что для последующих поколений лингвистов выглядело чисто теоретической концепцией, имеющей универсальное значение, при своем зарождении было тесно связано с духовным климатом, идеологическими веяниями, этническими проблемами, характеризовавшими Российскую империю в целом, и Казань и окружающие земли в частности, во второй половине XIX века.

Для Бодуэна и его учеников различие между фонемой и звуком определялось прежде всего тем, что они принадлежали к двум разным аспектам языковой деятельности — физическому и психологическому. Звук как чисто материальное образование, производимое работой органов речи, противополагался психологическому представлению о звуке в сознании говорящих; дуализму звуковой стороны языка соответствовало разграничение двух дисциплин — "антропофонетики" и "психофонетики", предметом которых должен был стать физический и психологический аспект звука, соответственно.[4] Эта апелляция к психологии не была принята структурной лингвистикой XX века, для которой ноуменальный план языка существовал в виде объективного, внеличностного логического порядка, а не в виде психологического представления. Последователи Бодуэна видели в его "психологизме" дань ментальности минувшего века, от которой идея фонемы должна быть освобождена, с тем чтобы достигнуть чистого теоретического воплощения;[5] в их глазах, Бодуэн, гениально предвосхитив некоторые черты *лингвистической теории XX века*, не был в состоянии довести свою мысль до логического завершения в силу того, что она оставалась в плену "психологизма". Между тем, если отложить в сторону склонность структурализма видеть в идеях манифестацию универсального ноуменального порядка (о которой мы в свою очередь теперь можем говорить как о продукте "минувшего века") и взглянуть теперь на вещи в исторической перспективе, можно увидеть, что именно "психологизм" Бодуэна, то есть отношение к языку с точки зрения того, как он переживается говорящими, позволил ему выйти из рамок *лингвистических понятий своего времени*. Обстоятельства, в которых мысль Бодуэна кристаллизовалась в годы его пребывания в Казани, позволяют лучше понять этот аспект его теории, увидеть те конкретные пути, которые вели в возникновению понятия фонемы.

Господствующим направлением в лингвистике второй половины XIX века было представление о языке как объективной (в позитивистском смысле) материальной сущности. Язык рассматривался как собрание материальных единиц — слов и грамматических форм, функционирование и развитие которых подчиняется строгим законам, столь же неукоснительным и независимым от индивидуальной человеческой воли, как законы природы. В этой перспективе, психологическому аспекту отводилась вторичная роль, в качестве "человеческого фактора", интерферирующего с объективными законами языкового развития. Описание языка было полностью изолировано от той реальной среды, в которой он употребляется говорящими. Господствующее направление в лингвистике вообще игнорировало описание живых современных языков, считая своей единственной задачей реконструкцию праязыка и формулирование "объективных" исторических законов, согласно кото-

рым каждый язык развивался из праязыкового корня к своему
позднейшему состоянию.

Убежденный сторонник принципа *личной свободы*, сама
жизнь которого, с ее драматическими переменами мест и об-
стоятельств, как бы утверждала независимость *личности* от
"объективных" условий, — Бодуэн постоянно подчеркивал
в своих высказываниях о языке уникальность языкового опыта каждой личности.[6] Эта личная позиция отразилась и в его
лингвистических воззрениях, которые с самого начала, еще до
приезда в Казань, во многом расходились с господствующими
в то время понятиями.

Во-первых, Бодуэн считал главным предметом лингвистики *современные* языки в их живом употреблении. По его
словам, "основательное изучение новых языков, которые про-
должают жить и поэтому доступны всестороннему наблюдению, значительно более поучительно ..., чем изучение языка,
переставшего существовать и доступного лишь через письменность".[7] Ниже мы увидим, какое значение имело в творческом
мире Бодуэна это недоверие к "письменности", оторванной от
звучащей речи, и какой резонанс этот интеллектуальный мо-
тив получал в казанской среде.

Во-вторых, Бодуэн подчеркивал *смешанный* характер всех
языков; он категорически утверждал: "... нет и быть не может
ни одного чистого, не смешанного языкового целого. Смешение есть начало всякой жизни как физической, так и психи-
ческой".[8] Очевидна связь этой позиции с личным жизненным
опытом. Однако в контексте идей Бодуэна такой подход имел
и более широкое значение. Он был связан с тем, что Бодуэн
смотрел на внешние формы языка, употребляемые говорящими, как на проявления их внутренней духовной жизни.
Отклонения от формальной "чистоты", всевозможные "погрешности" в употреблении языка, возникающие в смешанной
языковой среде, — все то, что академической лингвистикой
того времени рассматривалось только как нарушения объективного языкового порядка, — привлекали Бодуэна в качестве
диагностических моментов, дающих исследователю возможность прорваться сквозь внешнюю оболочку языковых форм и
заглянуть в языковое сознание говорящих.

Докторская диссертация Бодуэна была посвящена лингвистическому и этнографическому описанию резьян — миниатюрной южнославянской народности (3-5 тыс.) на северо-востоке Италии, говорящей на диалекте, близком сербохорватскому языку, но относительно обособленной в языковом и этническом отношении. Центральное место в его исследовании занимает описание одной характерной фонетической черты резьянского говора — гармонии гласных: черты типичной для тюркских и финно-угорских языков, но уникальной для славянского и вообще индоевропейского языкового мира. Более того, в резьянском говоре гармония гласных сочетается с типично славянским сильным и подвижным ударением — тогда как для финно-угорских и тюркских языков характерно слабо выраженное ударение, чаще всего фиксированное на первом слоге. Согласно Бодуэну, эта черта резьянского говора соответствует смешанному славяно-тюркскому этническому происхождению его носителей, о котором свидетельствует их внешность, самосознание и обычаи. Бодуэн упоминает "неславянские физиономии" резьян в качестве свидетельства присутствия в них "туранского элемента".[9] Это обстоятельство придавало особенную пикантность тому факту, что сами резьяне считали себя выходцами из России, мигрировавшими на Балканы в далеком прошлом. Все эти наблюдения приводят Бодуэна к выводу: "Резьянские говоры, сообразно племенному происхождению их носителей, являются славянскими говорами, подвергшимися сильному туранскому влиянию".[10]

Таково было первое соприкосновение Бодуэна с "евразийской" (славяно-туранской) этнической, психологической и языковой амальгамой, в которой история и современное состояние, реальное поведение и самосознание, заимствованные языковые черты и их новое функциональное освоение переплетались друг с другом. Хотя в это время он еще не пришел к формулированию идеи о дуализме физического и психологического аспекта в языке, изучение резьян явно послужило к этому подготовкой. Именно в этот момент Бодуэн получил назначение в Казанский университет.

По прибытии в Казань Бодуэн организовал лингвистический кружок, собиравшийся еженедельно у него на квартире.[11] Наиболее важными для нас фигурами в этом собрании являлись Н.В. Крушевский (Nikolaj Kruszewski), написавший диссертацию под руководством Бодуэна и ставший затем его младшим коллегой по университету, В.А. Богородицкий, впоследствии широко известный специалист в области экспериментальной фонетики, славянского и тюркского языкознания, и В.В. Радлов — знаток восточных языков, впоследствии прославленный ориентолог, служивший в то время инспектором татарских и башкирских школ Казанского учебного округа.

Каждый член кружка вносил свой вклад в общее дело. Лингвистический профессионализм Бодуэна, его широкие теоретические и практические знания в области индоевропейской и славянской лингвистики сыграли решающую роль в научном развитии его учеников. Философские интересы и познания Крушевского оказались очень полезными для выработки понятийного аппарата новой лингвистической школы; ему, в частности, принадлежала важная роль в формировании таких ключевых терминов, как фонетическая "альтернация" и "фонема".[12] Богородицкий проявлял особую склонность к детальному описанию акустических и артикуляторных свойств звуков живого языка — область интресов, которая привлекала также Бодуэна. Оба с огромным вниманием следили за всеми техническими новинками в области экспериментальной фонетики. Когда в Казани демонстрировалась акустическая "говорящая машина" Йозефа Фабера, синтезировавшая звуки различных языков путем механической имитации работы органов речи, Богородицкий и Бодуэн составили подробные описания ее работы, высказав при этом сожаление, что такое замечательное изобретение используется в коммерческих развлекательных целях, будучи "потеряно для подлинной науки".[13] Наконец, уникальные познания Радлова в области неиндоевропейских языков также отвечали интересам Бодуэна. Именно по инициативе последнего в Казанском университете было возобновлено преподавание татарского языка — впервые после перевода казанской ориентологии в Петербург в 1854 г.[14] Для этой цели в университет был приглашен Радлов, под руководством которого Бодуэн занялся изучением тюркских языков. Ко всему этому надо добавить, что все члены кружка, за исключением самого Бодуэна, имели богатый опыт в качестве преподавателей, инспекторов, составителей учебников и пособий по русскому языку в школах для нерусских детей (татар, башкир, чувашей и др.). Сочетание теоретических интересов в области лингвистики и общей методологии науки, изощренных фонетических экспериментов и практических проблем преподавания неродного языка, все это на фоне многонационального и многоязычного окружения, создавало уникальную социальную и иеллектуальную амальгаму, послужившую питательной средой для новой лингвистической теории.

На протяжении всей своей деятельности Бодуэн проявлял острый интерес к проблеме соотношения между звуками речи и их отражением на письме. Дуализм устного — письменного был для него тесно связан с дуализмом физического — психического в языке; то, каким образом произносимые звуки отображаются на письме, могло служить свидетельством, хотя бы косвенным, того, как эти звуки отображены в сознании говорящих. Обсуждение соотношения между звуками и буквами занимает огромное место в его лекционных курсах и многих статьях. Бодуэну вторили его ученики — Богородицкий и Крушевский. Последний, в частности, замечал, что поскольку относительно древних языков нам известны лишь буквы, но не звуки, которые им соответствовали в речи, это в значительной степени обесценивает "археологическое направление в лингвистике" по сравнению с изучением современных языков.[15] Органической частью этого подхода являлся интерес Бодуэна и его учеников к экспериментальной фонетике как дисциплине, целью которой является как можно более точное описание звуков языка как таковых, в отвлечении от каких-либо нормативных или теоретических презумпций, — звуков, как они произносятся говорящими в различных конкретных ситуациях.

Осознание неизбежного разрыва между произношением и письмом вело к формулированию различных общих принципов, лежащих в основе разных систем письма, и вытекающих из этого различных типов соотношений между звуком и буквой, имеющих место в разных языках. В частности, Бодуэн указал на то, что в русском языке существует асимметрия между гласными и согласными в отношении передачи их различительных признаков на письме; в сфере консонантизма существует тенденция обозначать два различных согласных (например, парные твердый и мягкий согласные: *л* и *л'*) одной буквой, тогда как в сфере вокализма господствует обратное соотношение — один гласный обозначается в разных случаях двумя разными буквами (например, гласный *а* после твердого и мягкого согласного передается соответственно буквами *а* и *я*).[16]

Эта теоретическая проблема приобретала осязаемые черты в казанской ситуации. Идея о том, что в разных языках могут по-разному соотноситься фонетические и графические различия, выступала с особой наглядностью в условиях тесного сосуществования русского и татарского (а также других тюркских и финно-угорских) языков. Существует явное различие в отношении той роли, которую выполняют гласные и согласные в оформлении слова в русском и тюркских языках: в первом характер гласного определяется качеством предшествующего согласного, тогда как во вторых характер гласного определяется соотношением с другими гласными в слове (по принципу гармонии). Для говорящего по-русски, различие между *ы* и *и* зависит от предшествующего твердого или мягкого согласного; для говорящего по-татарски, аналогичное различие обусловливается характером других гласных в том же слове. Это различие создает разные психологические ожидания у говорящих, ведущие к неправильному восприятию того, что они слышат в чужом языке. Дети с родным татарским языком, изучающие в школе русский язык, "не слышат" различий между гласными в слове, которые говорящему по-русски кажутся физически очевидными, поскольку их восприятие звуков настроено в соответствии с механизмами, принятыми в их родном языке; они не обращают внимания на характер предшествующего согласного, пытаясь вместо этого определить характер безударных гласных в слове в соответствии с характером гласного под ударением, то есть привести менее ясно слышимые звуки в "гармонию" с наиболее отчетливо произносимым ударным гласным. Эти помехи в восприятии реально звучащей речи, вызываемые различием "психофонетической" настроенности, находят отражение в характерных ошибках, допускаемыми татарскими учениками в школьных диктовках: слово *глухой* уче-

ники передавали как *глохой* или *глухуй,* слово *ворота* — как *воро-
то* или *варата.*[17] Богородицкий с энтузиазмом указывал на эту
область как "непочатый еще угол для исследователя: русская
речь татар и других инородцев; русская речь в устах немца,
перса, армянина и пр.; в устах поляка, чеха и т.д. Все это ждет
исследований".[18]

Проблемы соотношения между произношением и его пе-
редачей на письме представляли интерес не только для описа-
тельной и теоретической фонетики; они приобретали перво-
степенную важность в работе русско-татарских школ, в которых
обучались дети крещеных татар. Идея подобных школ, в которых преподавание опиралось бы на родной язык учеников, как
наилучшего средства приобщения инородцев к православию
и русской культуре, была задумана и на протяжении десятилетий с огромной убежденностью проводилась в жизнь Н.И.
Ильминским. Вопрос об отражении звуков речи на письме
послужил тем связующим звеном, в котором разработанная
Ильминским система патронирующего просвещения нерусских народов неожиданно соприкоснулась с идеями Бодуэна о
связи языка и сознания и тех последствиях, которые осознание
этой связи должно иметь для теоретической лингвистики.

Николай Иванович
Ильминский (1822-1891)

Николай Иванович Ильминский лучше известен историкам, изучающим национальную политику Российской империи, чем лингвистам. Знаток восточных языков (он был профессором ориентологии Казанского университета) и церковнославянской письменности, человек, пользовавшийся покровительством таких могущественных фигур имперского мира, как Д.А. Толстой и К.П. Победоносцев, он отказался от "высокой" академической и бюрократической карьеры, посвятив свою жизнь делу просвещения инородцев, — просвещения в духе православия и русских духовных ценностей, но на основе их родного языка и культуры. Избранный в Российскую академию, Ильминский отклонил звание академика, потому что оно потребовало бы его переезда в Петербург, а значит, оставления Учительской семинарии и Школы для крещено-татарских детей в Казани, в работе которых он видел свою миссию.

Ильминский создал широко разветвленную сеть просветительных учреждений для крещеных "инородцев". Ее вершиной служила созданная в 1868 г. Переводческая комиссия, осуществлявшая переводческую работу (в первую очередь текстов Священного Писания) и руководившая подготовкой двуязычных учебников и пособий. Эта работа проводилась на основе сотрудничества между русскими специалистами, знакомыми с различными тюркскими, финно-угорскими, монгольскими, палеоазиатскими языками, и носителями этих языков, получившими хотя бы элементарное русское образование; Ильминский был неутомим в разыске людей, способных принять участие в переводческом деле.[19] Следующий уровень составляла открытая в 1872 году Семинария, в которой представители разных народностей, уже имеющие начальное образование, приобретали известные познания в русском и церковнославянском языке, достаточные для того, чтобы стать священниками и учителями в своей родной среде. На протяжении десятилетий Ильминский вел борьбу с церковной администрацией, настаивая на том, что священниками среди новокрещенных народностей должны назначаться выходцы из их среды, разделяющие со своими прихожанами родной язык и культурную основу, даже если их компетентность в обращении с литургическими текстами оставалась ограниченной, — а не русские священники, хорошо знающие службу, но неспособные общаться с приходом. И наконец, основанием системы служила сеть начальных школ, в которых дети приобщались на элементарном уровне к религиозному образованию и русскому языку, — и то и другое на основе их родного языка. Образцом для них служила казанская Школа для крещено-татарских детей, созданная в 1865 году, первоначально на личные средства двух профессоров-ориентологов — Ильминского и Е.А. Малова (профессора Казанской духовной академии), но вскоре получившая поддержку со стороны частных лиц и правительства. Казанская школа сделалась центром, от которого по всей восточной части империи расходился все более широкий круг школ для крещеных детей самых различных народностей — от Волги до Камчатки, от казахских степей до земли самоедов. После смерти Ильминского в 1891 году, его последователи и почитатели сравнивали его со Стефаном Пермским — русским святым четырнадцатого века, создавшим письменность на языке пермяков, с тем чтобы проповедовать Евангелие на их родном языке. Некоторые выражения из некролога Ильминскому, написанного Победоносцевым, явно отсылали к знаменитому "плачу пермских людей" из жития Стефана Пермского Епифания Премудрого: "Но имя этого человека — родное и знакомое повсюду в восточной половине России и в далекой Сибири — там тысячи простых русских людей и инородцев оплакивают его кончину, тысячи богобоязненных сердец умиленных поминают его в молитвах, как великого просветителя и человеколюбца".[20]

Теневые аспекты деятельности Ильминского хорошо известны.[21] При всей искренной озабоченности делом народного просвещения и духовным благосостоянием крещенных инородцев (отношение его к некрещенным было в лучшем случае индифферентным, а то и прямо враждебным), Ильминский видел в своей деятельности средство привести своих подопечных в лоно русской духовности, спасая их таким образом и от "мрака" нехристианской веры (безразлично, мусульманства или язычества), и от потенциального растлевающего влияния Запада, — средство более действенное, чем грубое руссификаторство эпохи Александра III. Позиция Ильминского была, в сущности, сходна с миссионерской стратегией иезуитов, которая тоже, как известно, нередко вступала в конфликт с более прямолинейно настроенной центральной католической иерархией. В этой статье, однако, предметом нашего внимания будут не политические аспекты деятельности Ильминского, но ее филологическая сторона — те представления о природе языка, которые он стремился поставить на службу своим миссионерским целям.

Идея Ильминского о том, что найти путь к умам и сердцам прозелитов, сделав их обращение в православие действительным, а не чисто формальным, можно лишь при условии, если они получат возможность приобщаться к новой вере на своем родном языке, диктовалась острым осознанием связи между духовным миром людей и родным языком, которым они пользуются в повседневной жизни. По словам Ильминского, "богослужение и поучение на языке родном производят на инородческих прихожан действие пробуждающее и оживляющее. Родные звуки, даже сами по себе, бьют прямо в созвучные стороны сердца".[22]

Мысль о связи сежду "звуками" родного языка и тем откликом, который они вызывают в душе говорящего, при всем различии в стиле выражения, живо напоминает мысль Бодуэна о дуализме физического (звукового) и психического аспектов в языке. Со своей собственной точки зрения, в качестве языковеда, Бодуэн, подобно Ильминскому, остро чувствует различие между "живым" знанием языка и "мертвым" заучиванием языковых форм, не оставляющим никакого духовного отклика; примером последнего для него служат рутинные "так называемые грамматики" и их преподавание в школах:

Ученики должны зазубривать бессмысленные определения и положения, чуждые всякой связи с живым материалом и, стало быть, психически мертвые.[23]

Конечно, идеологический фон, стоящий за представлением о "живом" и "мертвом" знании у Ильминского и Бодуэна, драматически различен. Ильминский видит в живительном действии на души звуков родного языка залог духовного "пробуждения" инородцев; т.е. приобщения их к православию;

свое пасхальное письмо к Победоносцеву, в котором он делится этой мыслью, он заканчивает патетическим восклицанием: "Христос воскресе! Да воскреснет Бог и расточатся врази Его — враги веры и отечества". Бодуэн же видит в схоластической приверженности к "букве" препятствие на пути к свободе мысли и правам личности и народов:

> Кто имел несчастие пройти курс заурядной школьной грамматики ... со смешением письма и языка, букв и звуков, ... физиологии с психологией, ... тот только с трудом отучится, а может быть и никогда не отучится, смешивать человека с паспортом, национальность с алфавитом, национальность с вероисповеданием, национальность с государственностью, происхождение человека с его гражданскими правими, различие пола с различием прав интеллектуальных, политических и экономических ...[24]

Трудно представить себе что-либо более различное, чем убежденность Бодуэна в равенстве всех народов, защита им свободы личности от посягательств государства, официальной религии и патриархальных традиций, с одной стороны, и тяжеловесно консервативный, елейно-патронирующий дух межнациональной имперской "соборности" (разумеется, под духовным руководством русского народа), лежащий в основе воззрений Ильминского, с другой. И однако, в их воззрениях на природу языка и методы его изучения и преподавания обнаруживается удивительно много общих черт. Оба были убежденными сторонниками образования на родном языке. Высказывания Бодуэна по этому поводу полностью соответствуют взглядам Ильминского, отличаясь от последнего лишь характерным подчеркиванием личного "права":

> ... язык родной ... должен быть признан языком преподавания. ... Для педагогики не существует никакого общеобязательного государственного, церковного или "классического" языка. ... Каждый ребенок имеет право требовать от учителя осознательненья его собственного

языка, этого неисчерпаемого материала для самых широких и глубоких наблюдений.[25]

Подобно Бодуэну, Ильминский отдавал решительное предпочтение современным языкам, употребительным в живой речи, перед архаическими книжными языками. Оба, в частности, высказывались в этой связи против классического образования в гимназиях. Опять-таки, идеологическая основа этой позиции была у них резко различной, даже противоположной. Бодуэном двигала антипатия ко всяческим языковым и идеологическим окаменелостям. Ильминский руководствовался идеей "соборной" иерархичности; он видел духовную жизнь нации как органический континуум, простирающийся от эзотерического знания (такого как церковнославянская письменность или классическая словесность), которое должно оставаться предметом попечения немногих, до народного просвещения, в котором это высшее знание должно претворяться в простые истины, гармонически соответствующие условиям и потребностями "живой жизни". Первый негодовал: "Общеобразовательная роль так называемых 'классических языков' есть не что иное, как унаследованный от прошлого пережиток и, с современной точки зрения, навеянный внушением предрассудок".[26] Второй проповедовал: "Зачем нам язык Платона и Гомера, когда мы нуждаемся в языке Евангелия и Богослужебных книг? Если бы удалось мальчишкам в самом деле проникнуться красотами аттической речи, то они будут га́довать простотой (буйством) христианского изложения. ... Я не говорю об академии, там пусть наука будет научная".[27] Однако из этих, столь различных по своей модальности рассуждений делается тождественный вывод: предметом изучения и преподавания должен стать живой, повседневно употребляемый язык.

Мне кажется, что это сходство не является ни случайным, ни парадоксальным. В его основе лежит неудовлетвореннсть позитивистским разрывом между материей и духом, между объективно данными формами и тем, как они отображаются в духовном мире личности. И Бодуэн, и Ильминский, каждый с своей точки зрения, глубоко чувствовали двойственную природу языка: тот духовный, психологический мир, который стоит за его "звуками" и незримо в них соприсутствует. В этом отношении, и просветительская деятельность Ильминского, и теоретические поиски Бодуэна решительно расходились с позитивистским воззрением на язык как простую совокупность материальных форм, господствовавшим и в академической науке, и в деле преподавания языков, и в государственно-бюрократической руссификаторской политике.

Я не располагаю свидетельствами о прямых контактах между Ильминским и Бодуэном в годы пребывания последнего в Казани. Хотя Ильминский оставил университет в 1872 г., кажется маловероятным, чтобы они совсем не знали друг друга. Однако во всех известных мне исторических и биографических источниках, относящихся к обоим деятелям, их имена никогда не появляются вместе. Ильминский так же мало мог привлечь тех из младших современников, кто впоследствии писал о Бодуэне (например, Якобсона, Шкловского, Фасмера, Щербы, Богородицкого в советский период его деятельности), как Бодуэн — тех, кто писал об Ильминском (например, Победоносцева). Мне кажется, однако, что связь между этими двумя казанскими деятелями имела под собой прочную основу, не зависевшую от личных отношений между ними. Такой основой являлась общность как многих людей, принадлежавших к кругу Ильминского и Бодуэна, так и тех *лингвистических и методических задач*, которые ставились и решались в обоих этих кругах. Мысли Ильминского о том, как и для чего, какими средствами и в какой степени следует обучать ребенка его родному и чужому языку, получали распространение и реализацию среди учителей и филологов, занятых различными формами преподавания национальных языков и русского языка в национальных школах, — в их числе Радлова, Богородицкого, Н.Ф. Катанова, участвовавших в то же время в *лингвистическом кружке* Бодуэна. Эти идеи воплощались в учебниках, хрестоматиях, переводах, фонетических транскрипциях, работа над которыми побуждала к постановке и решению множества конкретных задач в области фонетики и теории письма. Сферы деятельности Ильминского и Бодуэна составляли как бы непрерывный континуум, в котором задачи преподавания русского языка нерусским детям, проблемы правописания и транскрипции, описание фонетики различных языков в ее отношении к письму, и наконец, общая теория звукового строя языка переплетались, выступая как органическое продолжение друг друга.

Система Ильминского вызвала потребность в создании учебных материалов, в которых элементарные тексты по-русски сопровождались бы переводами и двуязычными словниками. Это в свою очередь потребовало решения проблемы — какую систему письма использовать для материалов на родном языке учеников? Следует ли для переводов на татарский язык использовать арабское письмо, принятое в литературном татарском языке и преподаваемое в медресе? Именно такова была первоначальная идея Ильминского и его окружения, полагавших, что использование арабского письма сделает процесс обучения более привлекательным для татарских детей. Они имели возможность убедиться, к каким катастрофическим последствиям ведет навязывавшаяся петербургской бюрократией система обучения, опиравшаяся на учебники, в которых материал национального языка коверкался почти до неузнаваемости в силу примитивной передачи его кириллическими буквами, рабски следующей правилам русской орфографии. Например, казанские деятели неоднократно указывали на непригодность Краткого учебника для татарских школ В. Казаса (Симферополь, 1877). Катанов отмечал, что принятая в этом учебнике транслитерация уничтожает эффект гармонии гласных в татарских словах;[28] Богородицкий жаловался на те трудности, с которыми он столкнулся, пытаясь воспользоваться этой книгой, прежде всего, опять-таки, в силу искаженной передачи татарского вокализма (*кёрсиз* вместо *кёрсӳз*).[29]

Первые учебные материалы, созданные в Казани, опирались на арабское письмо, что вызвало резкое неодобрение центральной администрации. В частности, учебник и книга для чтения, составленные Радловым,[30] подверглись уничтожающей критике в Журнале Министерства народного просвещения (январь 1874). Рецензент, В. Смирнов, обвинил Радлова в том, что его книги способствуют более распространению татарского языка, нежели русского; он настаивал на том, что в подобного рода учебниках следует стремиться как можно шире употреблять русский язык, а если и пользоваться переводами на татарский, то делать их как можно более близкими к синтаксическому строю русской речи и к русской орфографии. Отвечая рецензенту в следующем выпуске журнала, Радлов ссылался на то, что в своей работе он "следовал советам известного ориентолога Н.И. Ильминского". Возражения Радлова против того типа кириллической транслитерации, который предлагался рецензентом, были те же, что и со стороны других членов казанского филологического и педагогического круга, а именно, что в этом случае утрачивается гармония гласных — центральная черта татарской фонетики.

Однако со временем Ильминский, по его собственным словам, "разлюбил" арабское письмо. Он пришел к выводу, что на деле оно оставалось малопонятным для его учеников, — в силу как плохого соответствия арабского письма фонетическому строю тюркских языков, так и того, что архаизированный татарский литературный язык, для передачи которого традиционно служило арабское письмо, был далек от того, на котором дети действительно говорили. Вследствие этого, Ильминский принял решение опираться при обучении на современный татарский разговорный язык; поскольку этот язык не получил формальной кодификации в татарской письменной традиции, открывалась возможность снабдить его такой формой письма, которая лучше, чем арабская письменность, отвечала бы свойствам его фонетики. Высказывания Ильминского по воспросу о живом языке и передаче его на письме поражают своим сходством с позицией Бодуэна:

> ...непосредственное знакомство с крещеными татарами, киргизами и частью туркменами охладило мою прежнюю ревность к книжному татарскому языку и воспитало во мне решительное уважение к живой народной речи как единственному памятнику данного языка. Народный язык я стал считать особенно важным и необходимым в деле миссионерском и учебном. Арабско-татарский алфавит я разлюбил, особенно тогда, когда ... увидел его несоответствие киргизской фонетике и вообще неспособность к выражению звуковых особенностей разных тюркских наречий.[31]

Теперь Ильминский пришел к убеждению, что кириллический алфавит лучше подходит к передаче звуков тюркских языков. Однако для того чтобы адекватно соответствовать тюркской фонетике, употребление кириллических букв не должно следовать правилам русской орфографии. Татарское слово должно передаваться кириллицей таким образом, чтобы это соответствовало его собственной природе, даже если с точки зрения русских написаний такая передача будет выглядеть странной. По мысли Ильминского, такая терпимость и гибкость вообще характерна для православной культурной традиции, в отличие от "догматизма" ислама и католицизма: первая преследовала свои миссионерские цели, давая новообращенным народам их собственную письменность (в этом отношении пример Кирилла и Мефодия был затем продолжен Стефаном Пермским); вторые же настаивали на сохранении единой системы письма, невзирая на то, как мало она подходила к звукам тех языков, к которым она применялась.

Германцы для выражения своих собственных звуков употребляют сочетания по две, по три и более согласных букв; орфография венгерцев, которых язык, как финский, резко отличается по звукам от латинского языка, просто можно сказать — бестолкова, потому именно, что католичество не дозволило им в дополнение к латинскому алфавиту принять особых букв для выражения специально-маджарских звуков. ... Православная церковь допускает значительную свободу в отношении внешностей, лишь бы сохранялись дух и истина веры; напротив в рабстве духовном держит своих исповедников деспотическое латинство.[32]

Разумеется, эта идея Ильминского преследовала отнюдь не только филологические цели. Предлагая татарским детям способ, писать на их родном языке, гораздо более легкий, чем арабское письмо, школы Ильминского подрывали национальное религиозное образование, открывая путь русскому влиянию. (Надо сказать, что и в татарском национальном движении в это время возникает идея модернизации литературного языка и перевода его на более удобную систему письма — конечно, не на кириллической, а на латинской основе, — с целью облегчить задачу национального просвещения; эта идея получила реализацию лишь после революции, в 1920-е годы). Вместе с тем, однако, школы Ильминского противостояли грубой и прямолинейной руссификации, проводившейся имперской бюрократией, — попыткам утвердить русский язык и православие чисто административными мерами, не принимая во внимание "психологию" обращаемых, то есть их языковую и культурную почву. Любопытно, что такая позиция была не совсем несовместима с позицией Бодуэна — этого врага всяческих форм национального угнетения, который позднее, в 1913 году, даже попал в тюрьму на короткое время за резкие высказывания по вопросу о равенстве наций. Дело в том, что вместе с тем Бодуэн был врагом всяческих барьеров между народами; в его глазах, контакты между людьми с разным родным языком, разной религией, культурой, этническим просхождением были естественным способом существования и развития каждого языка и культуры. Горячие высказывания Бодуэна о недопустимости смешения "языка с письмом" и "национальности с вероисповеданием", в сущности, не противоречили идее православного миссионерства среди нехристианских народов и реформы их письменности, отвечающей целям миссионерского просвещения.

Принципиальное новшество в использовании кириллического алфавита, введенное Ильминским, состояло в сохранении гармонии гласных при передаче татарских слов русскими буквами. Прежняя, "руссифицированная" транскрипция использовала буквы я, ю, ё, которые в русском алфавите указывают палатализацию предшествующего согласного, а не особое "умлаутное" качество гласного. Ильминский предложил вместо этого употреблять буквы ä, ÿ, ö, отражающие альтернацию гласных по правилу гармонии, а не качество предыдущего согласного звука. Если перевести реформу транскрипции, осуществленную Ильминским, в термины теории письма Бодуэна, можно сказать, что это новшество нейтрализовало передачу различий между согласными и выявило различия между гласными, отразив тем самым разницу функций, принадлежащих этим группам звуков в русском и тюркских языках.

В своей работе Ильминский и его молодые коллеги настаивали, по его выражению, "на необходимости приспособления к инородческими звукам".[33] С этой целью они вслушивались в речь школьников, отмечали типичные ошибки, которые они делали на письме, подбирали сходные по звучанию слова и наблюдали, каким образом дети опознают различие между ними. Например, Ильминский рассказывает, как он ввел новый знак *ы̆у*, после того как обнаружил, что в речи учеников имеется особый звук, который они отличают от простого *у*:

> В первом издании букваря я писал *су* — вода, *аулъ* — деревня, *аю* — медведь. Теперь мы пишем *сы̆у, ауы̆л, айы̆у*. Это сочетание *ы̆у*, род двугласной, внушено мне крещено-татарскими мальчиками, которые по чутью употребляли его в своих письмах.[34]

Мы видели, что такой повышенный интерес к фонетическим деталям живой речи, основанный на понимании того, что письмо не есть первичная реальность языка, но лишь вторичное ее отображение, полностью разделялся Бодуэном и его учениками. Непосредственную связь между этим направлением в работе учительской Семинарии и кафедры языковедения университета являли собой труды Богородицкого в области экспериментальной фонетики русского и татарского языков и их отношения к письму.

Теперь нам нетрудно конкретно проследить те конкретные звенья, которые соединяли в единый континуум зарождавшуюся на рубеже 1880-х годов в Казани теорию фонемы с деятельностью Школы для крещено-татарских детей и лингвистического кружка Казанского университета.

Ключевым понятием, соединившим практические наблюдения над звучащей речью с целью адекватной ее передачи на письме с теоретическим вопросом о природе звуковых единиц языка, явилось понятие фонетического чередования, или альтернации. Фонетическая альтернация — это такое изменение звукового состава корня слова, которое осознается как различие на фоне общего сходства; она возникает в словах, тесно соотнесенных в сознании говорящего — например, в разных морфологических формах одного и того же слова, или родственных словах: вода—воде или вода—водяной (альтернация *д/д'*), бегу—бежишь (альтернация *г/ж*). Определение этого феномена, выделение различных типов альтернаций и описание их характера в разных языках — преимущественно славянских и тюркских — занимает огромное место в работах самого Бодуэна и его учеников. Этой проблеме была посвящена одна из центральных работ Крушевского, систематически рассмотревшего различные чередования гласных и согласных в индоевропейских языках в рамках новой теоретической концепции;[35] непосредственно под влиянием Крушевского, Радлов написал аналогичное исследование применительно к тюркским языкам, центральное место в котором, естественно, заняли чередования, связанные с гармонией гласных.[36] Сам Бодуэн, как мы уже видели, ревниво относился к своему приоритету в этой области; впоследствии он специально посвятил проблеме альтернации свой самый обширный теоретический труд.[37]

Понятие альтернации позволяет выявить два принципиально различных типа звуковых чередований, происходящих в речи. В одном случае, произошедшее изменение звука сознается говорящим, в другом — появляется в его речи автоматически, как следствие воздействия соседних звуков. Альтернация первого типа переживается говорящим как преднамеренное языковое действие; альтернация второго типа, хотя и изменяет реальное произношение, не изменяет звуковой "образ" в сознании говорящего и остается им незамеченной (если, конечно, его внимание не привлечено специально к этом явлению — как это происходит, например, с фонетистом при экспериментальных наблюдениях над звуками речи).

В различных языках материально сходные изменения звуков могут получить разный альтернационный статус, в зависимости от того, как эти изменения переживаются в сознании говорящего. Так, имеется взаимная зависимость между палатализацией согласного и "умлаутным" характером следующего за ним гласного: мягкий согласный вызывает передвижку гласного вперед, и напротив, умлаутный гласный оказывает палатализующее воздействие на предшествующий согласный. Причина этой связи чисто физическая, обусловленная координацией работы органов речи в пределах одного слога. Однако в славянских и тюркских языках этот физический процесс получает различное осмысление в сознании говорящих. В слогах типа ма-мя, мо-мё говорящий по-русски осознает изменение согласного, тогда как изменение гласного происходит автоматически; в аналогичных случаях говорящий по-татарски сознает изменение гласного, не замечая того действия, которое оно произвело на предшествующий согласный. У русско-говорящих — даже лингвистов, не привыкших вслушиваться в оттенки реального произношения, возникает иллюзия, что гласный в этот случае остается "тот же", а меняется лишь согласный; соответственно, у говорящих по-татарски возникает иллюзия, что меняется только гласный, при сохранении "того же" согласного. Как показали работы казанских фонетистов, оба представления не соответствуют акустической реальности: и в русском, и в татарском языке имеет место (хотя и в различной степени) ассимиляционное изменение как гласного, так и согласного.[38] Однако сходство физических процессов не отменяет, а напроив подчеркивает различие в том, как эти процессы отражаются в языковом сознании.

В практической сфере преподавания языка это различие проявлялось в тех ошибках, которые ученики делали в произношении и написании слов чужого языка, в силу того что их восприятие определялось системой представлений, выработанных в родном языке; это в свою очередь делало необходимым выработать такую транскрипцию и систему письма, которая была бы адекватной звуковому строю каждого языка. Мы уже видели, какие усилия предпринимали в этом направлении Ильминский, Богородицкий, Радлов и др. В теоретической сфере — это различие позволило поставить вопрос о соотношении физического и психического аспекта в звуках языка, то есть о двойной — материальной и идеальной — природе языковых явлений. Кульминацией усилий в этом направлении явилось определение понятия фонемы.

Из многих вариантов определения фонемы, предлагавшихся самим Бодуэном в различных работах, Крушевским, Богородицким, С.И. Буличем,[39] мне кажется наиболее выразительным с точки зрения общего философского смысла нового понятия определение, данное Бодуэном в 1899 г. в статье для Польской энциклопедии ("Fonema, fonemat"):

> Ф о н е м а ...: психически живая фонетическая единица. Пока мы имеем дело с преходящим говорением и слушанием, нам достаточно термина з в у к, обозначающего простейшую фонационную, или поизносительную, единицу ... Но если мы встанем на почву действительного языка, существующего в своей непрерывности только психически, только как мир представлений, нам уже не будет достаточно понятия з в у к а, и мы будем искать другого термина, могущего обозначить психический эквивалент звука. Именно таким термином и является термин ф о н е м а.[40]

В этом определении, несмотря на некоторую его импровизационную "рыхлость" (характерную вообще для стиля Бодуэна), привлекает острота ощущения мира сознания как "живой" основы языка, стоящей за "преходящими" позитивными фактами — "говорением и слушанием".

Бодуэн проницательно сознавал бесплодность мышления и деятельности, принимающей во внимание внешние формы вне отнесенности их к "живым" внутренним сущностям, что было типично для идеологии позитивизма вообще, и для современной ему лингвистики в частности. В этом отношении его мысль органически вписывалась в круг идей и дел, составлявших содержание интеллектуальной жизни в Казани и несших на себе несомненный отпечаток той среды, в которой и для которой эта деятельность совершалась. Смешение и столкновение языков, этносов, культур, религий способствовало осознанию "преходящего" характера всех внешних форм, развивало способность отличать, говоря словами Бодуэна, звук от буквы, человека от паспорта, физический феномен "говорения" от его истоков в сознании. В условиях этой среды высвечивалось то общее, что было в интеллектуальной позиции таких на поверхности различных фигур, как Бодуэн и Ильминский, — признание неразрывной взаимной связи между внутренними духовными сущностями и их внешним проявлением.

В основе такой позиции у Ильминского лежит православная духовная традиция, с ее нежеланием слишком жестко следовать кодифицированному "закону" и форме; в том новом философском и идеологическом воплощении, которое эта традиция получила в русской мысли XIX столетия, от Киреевского и К.С. Аксакова до Достоевского и Владимира Соловьева, ее центральной темой стало преодоление характерного для "запада" обособления идеального и материального, мысли и действия, субъективного и объективного, индивидуального и коллективного. Позиция Бодуэна — это позиция раннего предвестника модернизма, идеи которого предвосхищают и подготавливают интеллектуальный прорыв начала XX века. Казань оказывается той средой, где эти два течения, столь несходные по своему происхождению и идеологической модальности, сливаются в единую амальгаму конкретных идей, устремлений, человеческих контактов. Именно здесь, в "глухой" провинции, в "глухие" 1880-е годы (как все это стало выглядеть впоследствии, ретроспективно, с точки зрения сначала авангарда, а затем советской идеологии), складывается та уникальная духовная инфраструктура, которая ляжет в основу русского Серебряного века, с его слиянием эстетического и интеллектуального модернизма с традициями русской религиозной философии и этики.

Таковы были духовные основания "психологизма" Бодуэна. Он впервые увидел язык в двойной перспективе: как собрание поддающихся эмпирическому наблюдению материальных форм и как их идеальный отпечаток в сознании говорящих. Дуализм в подходе к языку, то есть расщепление предмета исследования на идеальный "язык" и эмпирическую "речь", является, как известно, одной из основополагающих аксиом структурной лингвистики, и Бодуэну принадлежит заслуга едва ли не самого раннего формулирования этого принципа. Однако дуализм Бодуэна возникает из психологической экстраполяции наблюдаемого в речи материала, а не логико-реляционной модели, как у его последователей в XX веке. Это различие, как мне представляется, имеет принципиальное историческое значение — если видеть в истории нечто большее, чем подготовку "единственно научного", восторжествовавшего впоследствии метода.

Апелляция к психологическому миру личности означает, что между психологическим языковым миром и его физическими проявлениями существует необходимая взаимная связь и зависимость. Мысли человека так же летучи и преходящи, как "говорение"; и то и другое может быть описано только друг через друга, в постоянном соотнесении друг с другом. Вот почему в трудах Бодуэна и его учеников такое большое место занимает вслушивание в детали звучащей речи, интерес ко всяческим "смешанным" феноменам, ко всем "неправильностям" и отклонениям от предустановленного; поэтому также их лингвистические труды естественно сопрягаются с методикой и практикой преподавания языков. Летучесть, смешанность, импровизированность, даже прямые "погрешности" живой речи ценны в силу того, что в этих ее качествах проявляется соотнесенность ее с сознанием. Бодуэн категорически утверждал: "... у языка нет пространственности и беспрерывности ... Язык существует только в индивидуальных мозгах, только в душах, только в психике индивидов или особей, составляющих данное языковое общество".[41] Этим его позиция существенно отличается от классического структурализма второй-третьей четверти XX века, видевшего во внутреннем аспекте языка идеальный логический порядок, а во внешних проявлениях — его вторичную, по необходимости несовершенную реализацию. В этом отношении структурная модель парадоксальным образом продолжила то категорическое разделение внешнего и внутреннего, которое было характерно для позитивизма, — с той лишь разницей, что акцент был сделан на внутренней логической, а не внешней материальной форме. Принципиально смешанный характер языка, личностная, индивидуальная природа языкового знания, — все эти аспекты остались так же чужды структурной лингвистике, как и современной Бодуэну академической науке. Может оказаться, что выработанные в Казани более столетия тому назад представления о природе языка и мышления заключают в себе живой потенциал, идущий дальше структурной модели языка и способный вписаться в современный мир идей, — подобно целому ряду других явлений русской филологической и философской мысли конца XIX — начала XX века.

В заключение мне хочется упомянуть два любопытных эпизода из жизни 1920-30-х гг., которые можно рассматривать как своего рода "послесловие" рассказанной здесь истории. Первый связан с возникновением "евразийской" философии истории, начальным импульсом к которому послужила книга Европа и человечество (София, 1929) Н.С. Трубецкого — будущего создателя структурной фонологии. Не вдаваясь в подробности этого эпизода в истории русской мысли и истории лингвистики, скажу лишь, что для Трубецкого фонология в качестве новой антипозитивистской науки о звуках языка была неразрывно связана с тем, что он считал характерной чертой "евразийской" ментальности: способностью подняться над внешними фактами, охватывая любой предмет в широком обобщении, обнаруживающем его скрытую сущность; в этом отношении теория фонемы в глазах Трубецкого так же противостояла традиционной эмпирической фонетике, как евразийский тип мышления — духу "западного" позитивизма.[42] Связь идей Трубецкого с фонологией Казанской школы хорошо известна и сознавалась им самим. Теперь, после того как мы рассмотрели "евразийский" субстрат казанской фонологии, можно утверждать, что ассоциация между евразийством и теорией фонемы была не просто фактом личного самосознания Трубецкого, но имела под собой историческую почву. В этой перспективе, история становления концепции фонемы оказывается тесно сопряженной с "евразийской" социальной проблематикой, идеологией и историософией.

Другой "постскриптум" относится к реформе орфографии татарского и других тюркских языков, последовавшей в советское время. Перевод с арабского письма на латинское, осуществленный в середине 1920-х гг., оказался недолговечным; уже в начале следующего десятилетия последовала новая перемена тюркской письменности на основе модифицированного кириллического алфавита. Таков был исторический парадокс, приведший к осуществлению идей Ильминского. В мою задачу не входит обсуждение того значения и тех последствий, которые имела эта реформа в контексте советской идеологии и национальной политики. Мне хотелось лишь привлечь внимание к той множественности отголосков, которые мир идей

1880-х годов находит в XX столетии, и к той поистине причудливой трансформации интенций, контекстов, внешней судьбы, которые стали уделом духовного наследия имперской России второй половины XIX века.

Notes

1   Edward Stankiewicz, ed., *A Baudouin de Courtenay Anthology: The Beginnings of Structural Linguistics* (Bloomington, IN, 1972).

2   По получении магистерской степени в Кракове, Бодуэн был направлен Российской Академией на Балканы для собирания материалов для докторской диссертации. После окончания диссертации он получил приглашение в Краков — свой родной универкситет. Однако условия академической стипендии были таковы, что ему было необходимо продолжить работу еще в течение одного года. Краковская вакансия была упущена, и год спустя Бодуэн принял предложение Казанского университета.

3   В частности, "Московская" и "Ленинградская" фонетическая школы, на протяжении большей части этого столетия вовлеченные в полемику друг с другом, обе восходят к по-разному интерпретированному наследию Бодуэна.

4   См., например, четкую формулировку в докладе "Об одной из сторон постепенного человечения языка в области произношения, в связи с антропологией (читано на заседании 19-го марта 1904 г.": "... в языковедении мы должны по-настоящему заменить понятие 'звука' понятием его психического эквивалента, понятием его постоянно существующего представления, которое называем ф о н е м о ю. 'Звуки' же языка ... составляют достояние антропологии", Цит. по кн.: И.А. Бодуэн де Куртенэ, *Избранные труды по общему языкознанию* (отв. ред. С. Г. Барчударов, М., Изд. АНСССР, 1963), т. 2, с. 118-19.

5   С полной категоричностью эту мысль высказал Л.В. Щерба в некрологе Бодуэну: "Психологизм Бодуэна легко вынуть из его лингвистических теорий, и все в них останется на месте. Заслуги Бодуэна не в психологизме, а в гениальном анализе языковых явлений". *Известия Отделения русского языка и словесности*, т. 3, кн. 1 (1939), с. 315.

6   Витольд Дорошевский справедливо указывает на то, что эта черта личности Бодуэна имеет первостепенное значение для понимания его идей: "... можно попытаться найти ту центральную 'точку приложения сил', на которую в конечном итоге опирались разносторонние устремления Бодуэна де Куртенэ как ученого и как человека. Этой центральной точкой опоры для Бодуэна был постулат незави-

симости индивида от среды, полной, ничем не ограниченной свободы личности". В. Дорошевский, "О И.А. Бодуэне де Куртенэ", И.А. Бодуэн де Куртенэ, *Избранные труды...*, т. 1, с. 29.

7   "Обозрение славянского языкового мира", *Избранные труды....*, т. 1, с. 137.

8   "О смешанном характере всех языков", *Избранные труды ....*, т. 1, с. 363.

9   И.А. Бодуэн де Куртенэ, "Резья и резьяне", *Славянский сборник* , т. III (1876), секция 1, с. 330.

10   И.А. Бодуэн де Куртенэ, *Опыт фонетики резьянских говоров* (Варшава-СПб.), 1875, с. 120.

11   О составе кружка и тематике его занятий подробно рассказал впоследствии сам Бодуэн ("*Лингвистические заметки и афоризмы*". — *Избранные труды ...*, т. 2, с. 49-50), а также Богородицкий: "Казанский период деятельности И.А. Бодуэна-де-Куртенэ", *Prace filologiczne*, т. 15 (1931) , тетр. 2.

12   По словам самого Бодуэна, именно Крушевский предложил употреблять термин "фонема" в том новом значении, в котором он сделался центральным понятием новой теории. См., например, его работу *Versuch einer Theorie phonetischer Alternationen* (рус. перев.: "Опыт теории фонетических альтернаций". — *Избраные труды ...*, т. 1, с. 279, сн. 2). В очерке Бодуэна о Крушевском, написанном после смерти последнего, звучит нота ревности по поводу приоритетеа "... Крушевский изложил эту 'теорию' более философски, содержательнее и точнее, чем это сделал я, но трудно также отрицать, что он только придал иную, более удачную форму тому, что узнал от другого". ("Николай Крушевский, его жизнь и научные труды", *Избранные труды ...*, т. 1, с. 166).

13   И.А. Бодуэн де Куртенэ, "Краткие исторические сведения, касающиеся говорящей машины Фабера"; В.А. Богородицкий, "Несколько слов по поводу говорящей машины Фабера" — в кн.: *Протокол двадцать второго заседания секции физико-математических наук Общества естествоиспытателей при Императорском Казанском университете, 11 декабря 1882 года* (Казань, 1883), с. 16-20 и 21-32.

14   М.В. Черепанов, *Отражение принципов Казанской лингвистической школы в исследованиях Н.В. Крушевского* (Саратов, 1969), с. 1). См. о закрытии казанского востоковедения петербургской академичесой администрацией: Б.М. Данциг, *Ближний Восток в русской науке и литературе (Дооктябрьский период)* (М., 1973), с. 360-66.

15   Н. Крушевский, "К вопросу о гуне. Исследования в области старославянского вокализма", *Русский филологический вестник*, т. 5 (Варшава, 1881), с. 3.

16   "Некоторые отделы сравнительной грамматики славянских языков (отрывки из лекций)", *Русский филологический вестник*, т. 5 (Варшава, 1881), с. 300-02.

17   В.А. Богородицкий, *Изучение малограмотных написаний* (Воронеж, 1881) (отд. оттиск из журн. *Филологические записки*); позднее включено в книгу Богородицкого *Очерки по языковедению и русскому языку. Пособие при изучении науки о языке* (Казань, 1901), гл. 9.

18   В.А. Богородицкий, *Неправильности русской речи у чуваш (Диалектологические заметки, II)* (Казань, 1909).

19   Так, он писал Победоносцеву (16 февр. 1886) о нуждах Переводческой комиссии: "В отчете Камчатского Преосвященного упоминается один образованный гольд ... (его имени и прозвища в отчете не обозначено). В Охотске и других тамошних местностях должны быть грамотные тунгусы. Из корейцев в отчете поименован Тимофей Сыоны Цхе. Вот эти и им подобные инородцы: кореец, гольд и тунгус, да еще прибавить бы к ним толкового и грамотного гиляка, и следует прислать в Казань для упомянутой цели". *Письма Н.И. Ильминского к Обер-прокурору Святейшего Синода Константину Петровичу Победоносцеву* (Казань, 1895), с. 183.

20   К.П. Победоносцев, "Н.И. Ильминский", *Русский вестник* (февр. 1892); отд. изд. (СПб., 1892).

21   См. всестороннее освещение деятельности Ильминского: Robert P. Geraci, *Window on the East: National and Imperial Identities in Late Tsarist Russia* (Ithaca: Cornell University Press, 2001).

22   Письмо к Победоносцеву 11 апр. 1883, *Письма Н.И. Ильминского* ..., с. 39.

23   И.А. Бодуэн де Куртенэ, *Введение в языковедение* (литогр. курс лекций) (СПб., 1908), с. 8.

24   "Значение языка как предмета изучения" (1906), *Избранные труды* ..., т. 2, с. 133.

25   Ibid., с. 134 и 137.

26   Ibid., с. 135.

27   Письмо к Победоносцеву 25 июля 1889, *Письма Н.И. Ильминского* ..., с. 308.

28   Н.Ф. Катанов, *Отчет о поездке 1898-го года в Уфимскую губернию* (Казань, 1909).

29   В.А. Богородицкий, *О крымско-татарском наречии (Диалектологические заметки, 5)* (Казань, 1903), с. 1.

30   В. Радлов, *Грамматика русского языка, составленная для татар Восточной России*, ч. 1 (Казань, 1873); В. Радлов, *Первая книга для чтения* (Казань, 1874).

31   "О применении русского алфавита к инородческим языкам",

в кн.: Н.И. Ильминский, *Избранные места из педагогических сочинений* (Казань, 1892), с. 5-6.

32   Ibid., с. 19.

33   Письмо к Победоносцеву 16 апр. 1883, *Письма Н.И. Ильминского ...*, с. 49.

34   "О применении русского алфавита ...", с. 8.

35   N. Kruszewski, *Ueber die Lautabwechslung* (Казань, 1881).

36   V. Radlow, "Die Lautalternation und ihre Bedeutung für die Sprachentwicklung, belegt durch Beispiele aus den Türksprachen," *Abhandlungen des fünften internationalen Orientalisten-Congress gehalten in Berlin im September 1881* (Berlin, 1882). Приношу глубокую благодарность профессору Казанского университета С.М. Михайловой, любезно предоставившей мне текст этой работы.

37   J. Baudouin de Courtenay, *Versuch einer Theorie phonetischer Alternationen. Ein Kapitel aus der Psychophonetik* (Strassburg, 1895).

38   См. серию работ В.А. Богородицкого, в которых рассматриваются различные комбинаторные изменения соседних звуков в слогах русского языка: "Об изучении русской речи", *Русский филологический вестник*, т. 6 (Варшава, 1881), с. 274-82; *Введение в изучение русского вокализма* (Варшава, 1882) (отд. оттиск из РФВ); *Наблюдения посредством мышечного чувства над произношением звуков русского языка* (Казань, 1906); *Заметки по экспериментальной фонетике, 5: Наблюдения над произношением с помощью губного прибора Розанелли* (Казань, 1907). (В заглавии ошибочно — "Розапелли"). Впоследствии ученик Богородицкого Г. Шараф экспериментально доказал, соответственно, присутствие комбинаторной патализации согласных в слогах татарского языка: Г. Шараф, "Палятограммы звуков татарского языка сравнительно с русскими", *Вестник Научного общества татароведения* (Казань, 1927), 7, с. 65-102.

39   Буличу — в то время одному из членов кружка Бодуэна в Казани, впоследствии ректору Дерптского / Юрьевского университета (проводившему его руссификацию), принадлежала, в частности, статья "Фонема" в *Энциклопедическом словаре* Брокгауза — Эфрона.

40   Русский перевод цит. по изд.: *Избранные труды ...*, т. 1, с. 351.

41   "Язык и языки", *Избранные труды ...*, т. 2, с. 71.

42   См. об этом мою статью "The Ideological Principles of Prague School Phonology," in *Language, Poetry and Poetics. The Generation of the 1890s: Jakobson, Trubetzkoy, Majakovskij*, ed., Krystyna Pomorska et al. (Berlin-New York: Mouton de Gruyter 1987), 49-78.

3

Soviet Football, 1917-1941

by Robert Edelman

The history of Soviet football between the wars can be divided into two uneven parts. From 1917 to 1935, the game struggled on the local and national levels to find workable organizational forms. At the same time, political and cultural elites were less than comfortable with the sport's irrationality, emotionality and unpredictability, not to mention its more than occasional violence. In 1936, the game entered an entirely new phase. Responding to football's growing popularity, the state finally permitted the creation of a professional league, and the game took off. By the outbreak of the war as many as ten million fans, nearly all working-class males, were attending matches each year in sizable stadia around the far-flung nation.

Yet, Soviet football was, as it has been everywhere, about embracing a modernity that has been overwhelmingly urban. As such, interwar soccer in the USSR is almost entirely a Moscow story, specifically a story of the swiftly expanding Soviet proletariat. League honors between 1936 and 1940 were shared by the Moscow soccer teams of the two leading sport clubs of the era, Spartak and Dinamo. These two institutions had branches in many cities and practiced a wide range of sports. Yet, only football, particularly Moscow football, reached the level of a mass culture phenomenon. The Spartak-Dinamo rivalry became the centerpiece of the Soviet game.

Spartak represented workers in the service trades while Dinamo was sponsored and supported by the police. Other Moscow teams like Torpedo, Lokomotiv and the army team (TsDKA) had their own constituencies, and the institutions sponsoring these teams had competing interests. Fans in the capital freely chose sides (no one could force them to do this) and, in the process, defined their swiftly changing political, cultural and social identities through the game.

I

Between the revolution of October, 1917 and the outbreak of civil war in April 1918, the Bolsheviks moved cautiously to implement the promises on which they had based their political victory: land, peace and bread. They had said nothing about football. When Russia left the world war and was soon thereafter invaded by multiple armies, there were more pressing matters. The assumption of power had been a relatively bloodless process, but the struggle to maintain that power was an altogether different matter. Like so much else, sport and physical culture were adapted to the needs of a desperate moment. The harsh conditions of the world war had eroded the health of the peasants and workers who had been drafted into the tsarist army. The commanders of the new Red Army confronted the same problem. In May 1918, courses and schools of physical education were created to improve the fitness of recruits under a new institution known as *Vseobshchee voennoe obuchenie* or *Vsevobuch* for short.[1] Physical fitness was seen as essential to success on the battlefield. Similarly, the pre-war Olympic movement was studded with generals and admirals who held the same view of the relationship of sport to war. Yet, in the quest for fitter soldiers, not all sports were created equal. Both Vsevobuch and the first Olympians favored events like track and field, swimming, wrestling, fencing and equestrianism - all of which had direct military applications. Soccer with its rowdy players and fans appeared ill-suited to the training and disciplining of soldiers.

The Civil War was accompanied by massive hunger, disease, disorder and urban depopulation. The ludic pleasures of so spontaneous a game as football fit poorly into the needs of a new regime in peril. The previously existing clubs and other institutions that had supported football were left alone. In Moscow, the old league continued to operate. The biggest change was human. Massive numbers of the propertied men who had played for and run the Empire's sports clubs had left.[2] The foreign colony evaporated, cutting Russia's ties to the motherland of football, Great Britain. New, less privileged social groups, who had been excluded before the revolution, now found the entrances to the playing fields open.

The Civil War finally came to an end in 1921, and soccer, no longer a marginal activity, adapted well to the dramatically changed conditions. After the trials of war, revolution and civil conflict, the new regime was confronted with the enormous challenge of recovery. At the pivotal Tenth Party Congress in March, 1921, Lenin announced the so-called New Economic Policy or NEP. It embarked on a "strategic retreat" from state control of the economy in favor of a limited restoration of the market. In effect, the young state accepted the limits of its power and asked less of the population.[3] The NEP succeeded in bringing back a measure of prosperity, but "the values and behaviors that accompanied this prosperity (dancing, fancy dress, expensive restaurants) were at odds with how Bolshevik moralists imagined communism."[4]

If the NEP was a time of uncertainty and discomfort, it was also an era of great possibility. In the absence of clear blueprints for most of the details of a post-revolutionary society, debates raged across a wide range of human activities. Sports were part of these arguments, entwined in what turned out to be a multi-directional tussle for the support of the state and the favor of the new Soviet audiences.[5] In making these choices, the Bolsheviks had little use for either of the two predominant models of sport practiced under capitalism. The elitist world of amateur sport and the Olympic movement had excluded workers and women. On the other hand, the practices of professional sport had commodified games and the bodies of those who played them. In these debates, football was something of an afterthought.[6] Yet, the sport fit well with the newly liberated worlds of popular culture that burst forth in a society where vast numbers of ordinary Soviet women and men could now make their own choices about entertainment, leisure and recreation.

The change was quick and dramatic. All sorts of commodities, both luxurious and staple, quickly returned to newly opened stores and fashion-conscious boutiques.[7] Revived foreign trade and international tourism brought the USSR back into contact with the dynamic global cultural flows of the early twenties.[8] A new class of wealthy entrepreneurs called NEPmen emerged, and by 1926, there were as many as 100,000 people who fit this description in Moscow alone.[9]

Not knowing how long the "retreat" would last, this overnight "bourgeoisie" spent its gains lavishly and ostentatiously, creating a decadent world of fancy restaurants, night clubs, casinos and cafes which were the scenes of drinking, gambling, dancing, drug taking and widely varietal sex.[10] The post-war "Jazz Age" with its flappers and fast times found an Eastern outpost in Soviet cities.[11] Young male and female proletarians, even party members, came to join the action, tangoing and foxtrotting well into the night at workers clubs and private parties. The pre-war movie industry revived. Alongside the new politically didactic and formally radical films favored by both the Soviet avant-garde and international audiences, another group of Soviet directors sought to make movies that were comprehensible to ordinary folk. Like sports, the movies were a particularly modern form of leisure especially attractive to the young.[12] Both were central and visible parts of the newly global world of highly commercial and increasingly massive popular culture in which Soviet audiences could now take part.

This new cornucopia of pleasures, some brought back from tsarist days, others imported from the vibrant post-war West, were expensive and readily available only to the elite elements of NEP society. Workers, returning to the cities after the travails of the Civil War, found a variety of profit-oriented businesses operating according to the dictates of what was still a limited labor market.[13] The very proletarians who had supported and fought for the revolution could not take part in the new "good life." Nevertheless, the fluidity of the NEP created a broad range of options for young men, workers included. Sport, by its very nature, was an activity of the young, and football was the game most attractive to the audience of laboring boys and young men.[14]

While the game had become a healthy activity for those youths who played it, it also provided an affordable entertainment for the few women and many men who came to watch games in ever growing numbers and who were increasingly willing to pay for the privilege. Government support for sports clubs and their teams was still minimal. In the calmer context of early NEP the state finally sought to put in place a structure for all of Soviet sport. In the process, new kinds of sponsoring arrangements had to be developed. The pre-revolutionary city leagues and clubs were broken up. New entities were created, taking over the previously existing infrastructure. The changes were part of a larger process which witnessed the creation of a Supreme Council for Physical Culture which was part of the Ministry of Health. Clubs were to be organized on what was called a "territorial-production" basis. To limit the professionalism that had already emerged, teams were not allowed to draw members from all over the city. Instead, all the players on a team were to come from a single district or factory.[15]

The party held that sport should not be a business with tickets selling for sizable amounts, nor did the leadership wish to see athletes bought and sold. Yet, so appealing an entertainment was football that it eventually became part of the world of commercialized spectacles during the 1920's. In the 1923 season, the structure of the official Moscow city championship changed. Leagues were reorganized in other cities as well, but national championships did not take place annually. When they did, they were contested between city selects rather than clubs.[16] The city championships were small affairs rarely more than ten games, but this did not mean the players remained idle. Over the course of a spring to fall season, even larger numbers of friendlies were contested. These events were clearly about the making of money. Neither the state nor many factories were yet in the business of lavishly sponsoring sports teams. As Nikolai Starostin, the founder of Spartak, made clear in his later memoirs, ticket sales were the sole source of his team's income. Barnstorming became standard practice for the big sides from the capital, allowing the Moscow clubs to fill their coffers while giving provincial fans a chance to see what then passed for big-time football.[17] Eventually tours became an important revenue stream for the best teams.[18] While they had formally rejected the professional-entertainment model for sport, Soviet authorities were not able to avoid the market dynamics surrounding human activities that attracted sizable audiences. Even when the NEP ended and the market for entertainments changed, the practice of money-making "comradely" matches continued until the very end of Soviet power. Still, NEP football was never fully professionalized. The majority of players held jobs. Mikhail Sushkov, a star from this era, described the character of soccer during the twenties:

> Football [was] an abundant soil for all kinds of machina-
> tions...You can construct an underground *totalizator*...
> for betting on...teams...It is business and the excitement
> around the game is much like what happened in the West.
> You could finance a team, free its players from work, put
> them on the field and have a big advantage over your op-
> ponents. This was against the wishes of the authorities. [It
> was] an underground football black market.[19]

Given the need to generate funds on their own, teams under-stood that they had to play well, and in order to play well, they needed to attract good players. Stars had been part of the pre-rev-olutionary soccer scene, and the twenties were no different. Rules concerning player transfers were vague, and clubs competed for the services of the talented.

Before the creation of Spartak, Nikolai Starostin's team was known as Krasnaia Presnia, named for the working-class neigh-borhood in which it was based. It was, of course, not the only sig-nificant team in Moscow soccer. Rivalries have always been crucial to the success of any spectator sport, and during the 1923 season, Krasnaia Presnia was confronted with a new foe that eventually be-came its most hated and feared opponent, on and off the field. The Dinamo Voluntary Sport Society was founded on April 18, 1923. Ignoring the so-called territorial-production principle of organiza-tion, the new body was neither a neighborhood club nor a factory team. Rather, it was founded and supported by both the regular and secret police. Unlike Krasnaia Presnia, Dinamo was to be a na-tional organization, designed to raise the physical fitness of the na-tion's guardians of order.[20]

Soon after Dinamo's founding in the capital, branches were opened in several provincial cities. Sections were formed in a number of sports, with particular attention given, not surprisingly, to rifle and pistol shooting. Dinamo's emphasis on sports with military and police applications did not mean the new nation's most popular game was ignored. One of the new group's first steps was the formation of a "demonstration" soccer team in Moscow.[21] By the end of the decade, Dinamo would become the Soviet Union's best endowed sport club, and support from the state budget was more substantial than that received by any other sports group.[22]

The growth of the game and the kind of money and privilege it could generate made the sport one form of a popular culture that discomfited numerous members of the government. For these figures, football, when watched rather than played, seemed dangerous. It brought together several thousand members of less than fully cultured social groups in an irrational and uncontrollable spectacle that aroused emotions and often ended in violence.[23] For the guardians of order, there seemed to be no shortage of pathology in the soccer world. Players, especially stars, were in a position to seek greater privileges, higher compensation and better traveling conditions. City selects and even the newly formed national team were not above making such demands just before taking the field. Krasnaia Presnia stayed in the luxurious Hotel Evropeiskaia when they played in Leningrad. Player movement became common, and money-making exhibitions proliferated.[24] The creation of stars proved to be another important part of marketing a team. Young boys admired their manly footballing heroes as they constructed their own identities as urban working-class youths in a time of fluidity and uncertainty.

One element of this hero-making process involved placing players on the Moscow selects and the national team. Foreign trips took precedence over local city championships which went on even if a team's best players were out of the country.[25] Yet, international competitions were limited during the 1920's by the new state's diplomatic isolation. The Soviets were not members of FIFA. Games against foreign teams, especially at the level of national sides, could not take place without the international federation's sanction which was never forthcoming. The Soviet-supported Communist Red Sport International, which competed intensely with a similar group organized by Social Democrats based in Lausanne, could provide competition only against workers sports clubs, just a few of which could give top Russian sides a game. Competition with other national teams was restricted to the less isolated but still revolutionary Turks and the formally amateur Swedes, both of which had the advantage of being members of FIFA.[26]

International matches in Moscow, along with significant intercity games, drew large crowds, providing publicity for players who could then attract fans to regular league games and "friendlies." Accounts of this period describe the highly politicized process of choosing such squads. Here, the early Soviet experience was not that different from any other nation. In trying to have their players named to national teams, the institutions supporting clubs sought to enhance their prestige and extend their visibility and attractiveness to the football audience. Even at this early stage of Soviet history, the creation of heroes was part of the game, and the state was not alone in this process. Players on various select teams became celebrities, enjoying the fruits of their fame, and the chance for fans to see such "international" stars, in turn, enhanced the attractiveness and popularity of their clubs.

By 1925, the NEP had created a new stability. During the latter part of the twenties, there were even more films, soccer games, jazz concerts, casinos, fine fashions, posh restaurants and general jollity. By late 1927, however, the surface calm of "high NEP" began to unravel. The peasantry, allowed to respond to the opportunities of the market, had prospered to the point many urban dwellers viewed them as the moral and political equivalent of NEPmen. When grain procurement did not meet expected levels, food, once so abundant, became harder to find in the cities. There was a steady erosion of living standards which led to further calls for an end to NEP.[27] During this period, elite Soviet soccer had also been a site of much discomfort. In April 1926, the Moscow City Soviet of Physical Culture sought to reorganize the game with the aim of controlling the continuing manifestations of professionalism. Regional sports groupings were now to be broken up and replaced by clubs supported by a trade union or factory. Only the teams of the police and army were exempt from the new order. These reforms, however, had no impact on the growth of football's popularity. Meetings of the best teams attracted ever bigger crowds, making the game

Fig 1. Inside Dinamo Stadium, 1930s.
Fotoagentstvo Sportekspress.

an even larger part of the world of high NEP popular culture. Important matches among the top Moscow clubs routinely attracted 10,000 who paid sixty kopecks to sit; forty-five to stand. Games involving either the Moscow selects or the Soviet national team cost a ruble or seventy-five kopecks and attracted even larger crowds.[28]

By 1928 the sport had become a bigger business than ever. If the number of money-making exhibition games is any indication, it appears the top teams' sports entrepreneurship actually outlived the market conditions of the NEP.[29] The opening of Dinamo Stadium greatly expanded soccer's possibilities. Built in 1928 for the first Soviet Olympic style sport festival, called the Spartakiad, the new arena initially had 35,000 seats and room for another 20,000 standees. It put the USSR, despite its isolation, at the forefront of a world-wide expansion of spectator sport which included a wave of stadium building. Dinamo became the national arena, the chief site for any match of importance. Over time, as many as ninety thousand would cram into every one of its nooks and crannies.

The 1926 attempt to rein in football's excesses had clearly failed. More or less on its own, a spectator sport industry had emerged which undermined the ways the state sought to make use of physical culture. In 1925, the party had embraced elite competitive sport, but in doing so it did not want to create thousands of fans who merely watched high-performance athletes. Rather, the regime wished to inspire the sports audiences to exercise, becoming fitter soldiers and better workers. Elite sport during NEP did not, however, further this process, and attacks on big-time soccer began to appear in the press in 1927. An article published that year was entitled "Do We Need Professional Football?"[30]

In April 1929 the sixteenth Party Congress decreed the abandonment of the market in favor of a centralized, planned economy that was supposed to industrialize the Soviet Union swiftly. NEP-men who had benefited so abundantly from the market now had to find other avenues for their energies. The ambitious, often unrealistic goals of the First Five-Year Plan ended the conspicuous consumption of NEP. Living standards declined in the cities. At the same time, the social differentiation of the twenties gave way to an intense egalitarianism that included a leveling of wages and a variety of affirmative action policies designed to enhance the social mobility of workers. The first Five-year plan also witnessed a "cultural revolution" from above which put an end to the variety of NEP.[31] In a wide range of fields those with talents and knowledge acquired in the pre-revolutionary period were discredited and attacked. While football was touched by these changes, the effect was neither immediate nor entirely clear. The 1928-1930 seasons were conducted similarly to those that had preceded them. Player movement continued unabated. Crowds grew. More weekday games were scheduled causing large numbers of fans to skip work. Friendlies became even more numerous; the trips further afield.[32] In August, 1929, the capital's evening newspaper, *Vechernaya Moskva*, complained about the practice, "The basic goal of the majority of football journeys is to make money. They earn their money, divide it up and go home."[33] A ten day trip by the army team, earned each player 300 rubles. The same newspaper reported, "They play cards, get drunk and spend time with prostitutes."[34]

With the end of NEP, Dinamo came to dominate the Moscow league. As the role of the secret police expanded with Stalin's ascendancy and as its activities received greater budgetary resources, the sports teams of the police shared in the wealth. Dinamo now was able to attract a galaxy of stars. As the police presence became more and more onerous in its impact on the lives of ordinary citizens, resentments began to form among the civilian population. Matches between Dinamo and the team (now called Pishchevik) that would become Spartak became the highlights of each season, drawing 12,000 in 1928 and 20,000 in 1929.[35] One newspaper noted that "games between these two teams are distinguished by their rough play."[36] Having said this, one must be careful not to read

Fig 2. Football and industry were closely linked: Donets in the 1930s. Fotoagentstvo Sportekspress.

too much into this early stage of what would become the greatest rivalry in Soviet sport. The memoirs of players from both teams suggest that at this time the relationship between the two clubs was not as politicized as it would eventually become.

The spring of 1930 saw the establishment of a new, more powerful All-Union Council of Physical Culture. The new organization was especially concerned with limiting the excesses that had crept into the practices of soccer. In 1931, it introduced a new rule that required all players on factory or trade union teams to be actual employees at their factories or members of its trade union.[37] The measure would prove devastating to factory teams which saw their best players dispersed to different clubs. Consistent with the greater advantages given to the structures of force, Dinamo and the army club (TsDKA) were exempt from these limitations, increasing their competitive advantage at the top of the Moscow league.

Ironically, though workers may have watched football, the game lacked proper proletarian credentials in the eyes of those social levelers who were now on the offensive. Soccer practically disappeared from the pages of the nation's newspapers, and sport, in general, played a secondary role in this first frantic phase of "the socialist offensive." Soccer was a high-performance sport played by an elite few and watched by a passive many (even though "the many" were primarily male and working class). The game was thought to undermine the egalitarian goals of this first period of Soviet industrialization. Soon, however, it became clear to Stalin and many others in the party that the tasks set for the nation were so unrealistic and difficult that there were indeed some "fortresses" even Bolsheviks could not storm. In 1932, a second Five-year Plan was announced with more modest and realizable aims. The regime backed away from the abyss. What had been a time for work and work alone, now was followed by a period of greater, if still not extensive, leisure.

Early in November of 1934, Nikolai Starostin , whose career was winding down, was asked by Aleksandr Kosarev, head of the party's youth wing, to take charge of a new national sport club that was to be funded by an organization that served service workers and those in the retail trade. The new sport society was to have members in cities across the USSR and field teams in a broad range of sports, but, from the first, the Moscow football club was the organization's crown jewel. Kosarev also charged Nikolai with coming up with a name that could convey the spirit of the membership and its leaders. After an all-night session, agreement was finally reached on "Spartak", named for Spartacus, the gladiator and rebel slave of Ancient Rome. On April 19, 1935 Spartak's charter was ratified by the state sport committee, and the most powerful civilian sports club in Soviet history opened its doors. Soon thereafter, the last season of Moscow league football began. Very quickly, the new kid on the block provided a serious challenge to Dinamo.

Nikolai Starostin's talents, skills and contacts were surely essential to the founding of Spartak. Moving from the entrepreneurship of NEP to the networking of the Stalinist command economy with its personal-patronage networks required the kinds of contacts Starostin had been able to acquire through his captaincy of the USSR's national team. Having a web of connections, characterized by favor-giving and back-scratching, was the way things got done during the thirties (and later). "Complex social networks based on notions of friendship, mutual loyalty and reciprocal obligation. These were the networks of *blat* and patronage - usually considered, if they are considered at all, in a context of the second economy"[38] One Russian historian described this system as "a reaction of ordinary people to the structural constraints of the socialist system of distribution - a series of practices which enabled the Soviet system to function and which made it tolerable, but also subverted it."[39]

One way for Starostin to advance his cause was to contribute to Soviet prestige at the international level. Soviet clubs had been trampling foreign worker teams for more than a decade, while such lesser powers as Turkey and Sweden had been dominated on the international level. By 1934, both the sporting public and the party leadership were immensely curious about the capacity of Soviet teams to compete against the best foreign professionals, despite the official ban on professional sport. Upon his return from a sports delegation to Paris in 1934, Starostin met with Kosarev to discuss a forthcoming tour of Czechoslovakia by the Moscow selects. Beyond the usual meetings with worker teams, Kosarev raised the possibility of playing against professionals and asked Nikolai if they could win. Nikolai's cryptic reply was that while he could not guarantee success, it was possible to hope for it.[40] Others in the world of Soviet football were not so sanguine.

The Nazi triumph in Germany during 1933 had discredited the earlier Soviet policy which had derided others on the left as no better than the fascists. The Popular Front, uniting all progressive forces required broad engagement with the outside world.[41] As a result, the Moscow selects stepped into a minefield of fears and hopes.[42] The Czechoslovaks had been chosen not simply because of their geographical proximity. That summer they had gone to the final of the second World Cup in Italy, losing to the hosts 1-2. The leading Prague teams, Sparta and Slavia, were among the strongest in Central Europe. Yet, neither team was playing well at the moment. The Czechs instead offered a game with the current league leader, Zidenice of Brno which had just defeated Sparta 4-0.[43] After touring and defeating several worker teams by massive scores, the Moscow selects prepared for the match with trepidation and nervousness. Yet, they would triumph the next day by a score of 3 to 2.[44]

What then to make of this victory? Was the opponent a true test? Had shortcomings in their game been masked by the win? On November 22, 1934, the participants in the tour met at the offices of the sport committee. A variety of suggestions for improvement were raised. Most present supported the call for more such matches, especially on Soviet soil. Beyond these concrete evaluations, the tone of the meeting is worth noting. There was no sense of any bitterness or intense rivalry between the professionals of Spartak and Dinamo who had composed the Moscow selects. Despite serious disagreements on a wide range of matters, the participants called one another by first names. No visible external political agendas were invoked.[45] In the spring of 1935 the stars of both teams again combined in select squads. A team of Czechoslovak all-stars returned the visit, playing various clubs in several Soviet cities. With the intensification of the purge process one year later enormous differences would develop between Spartak and Dinamo, but there was yet one more act of cooperation that would set the stage for fundamental change in the world of Soviet football.

II

Unwittingly, the well-known French businessman Bernard Levy touched off the most profound change in Soviet football history. That moment came in May, 1936 with the creation of a professional football league modeled after similar leagues in capitalist countries. Knowing both Spartak and Dinamo were planning January tours against French worker teams, Levy invited a Soviet side to play his powerful Racing Club de France in Paris on New Year's Day 1936.[46] By doing so, he inflamed an ongoing debate inside Soviet soccer circles which led to the league's formation. A combined team of Dinamo and Spartak players performed spectacularly against Racing but lost 2-1, largely as a result of employing the outmoded five-man forward line instead of the newer "W" formation. On their return to Moscow, Nikolai Starostin and his sporting allies used this partial triumph to argue successfully for the reorganization of the Soviet game along the lines of the professionalism practiced in capitalist countries.

By replacing the chaotic local and national competitions with a clear and consistent All-Union structure, the newly re-organized sport committee provided the regime with a powerful tool for nation-building while giving Soviet fans what proved to be an im-

Fig. 3. Anatoly Akimov makes a save for Moscow selects against Racing Club de France, Paris, January 1, 1936. *Sto let Rossiiskomu futbolu.*

mensely popular mass culture entertainment. In a few years, ten million spectators, nearly all of them working class males, were taking in games each year by sides euphemistically called "demonstration teams." Dinamo Stadium was filled regularly, and big arenas (by the day's standards) went up in other cities. All this attention significantly raised the political stakes involved in the game, and success on the field became even more important to the various institutions supporting teams in the new league.[47] In 1935, Stalin had made his famous declaration, "Life has become better comrades. Life has become more joyous."[48] If 1936 then brought more soccer and fun, it also witnessed the greatest tragedy to befall the Soviet peoples. The "Great Purges" began with the show trials that same year.[49]

The creation of an elite football league fit well with the course of state policy during the late thirties. Close to the end of the First Five-Year Plan, Stalin had moved sharply away from social leveling and wage equality. He had come to realize that the skills and judgment of so-called specialists with professional training acquired before the revolution were a necessary part of future progress. People with those talents expected to be rewarded appropriately. The pre-revolutionary left's goal of social equality was abandoned in favor of social hierarchy. The leadership now felt it was important that the "better and more joyous" life of the moment be filled with the kind of professional sporting entertainments that had appealed to young working men throughout the world. Football was the modern, urban sport par excellence. It provided a shared discourse for the male members of the highly disparate new Soviet proletariat. With so many young peasants moving to the towns and forsaking more traditional versions of masculinity, football provided a modern form of male bonding - a "manly" game for the "New Soviet Man."

From its inception, the league provoked a huge boom in football's popularity. Attendance grew to massive levels, while the press greatly expanded its coverage of the game.[50] The Moscow leaders, Spartak and Dinamo spearheaded this growth in interest which came to approach the cinema as a form of mass culture. Dinamo had been the strongest football team in the USSR between 1928 and 1936, and the antagonism between Spartak and Dinamo intensified with the establishment of the league. Between 1936 and 1940, the two teams shared first place evenly, establishing the greatest rivalry in Soviet sport, outlasting the USSR itself. In 1936, Dinamo won the spring season, while Spartak took honors in the fall. Dinamo were champions in 1937 and. 1940. Spartak won the league-cup double in 1938 and 1939, establishing themselves as the greatest gate attraction in the Soviet game (an average of 53,000 per home match) with Dinamo not far behind.

Football was now big business. The paying of players to free them from work improved the quality of the Soviet game. Soccer players, not to mention team officials and coaches, were compensated at the much the same level as the new Soviet elite of top writers, academics, ballet dancers, film stars and aviators. A model budget drawn up in the late thirties set players' base salaries at 800 rubles per month, roughly eight times the average wage of an industrial worker. This did not include bonuses for wins in the league and cup. Players on various select teams got additional compensation. Head coaches and top team officials were supposed to get 1,300.[51] This can only be described as lavish, especially given all the other privileges players and coaches could gain, including the booty ac-

Fig. 4. Spartak atop a float in the 1937 Physical Culture Day Parade. The score of the match against the Basques is written on a giant boot. Later Spartak would be accused of planning to assassinate Stalin from the float. *Spartak Moskva: Ofitsial'naia istoriia.*

quired on foreign trips and the use of summer houses near team training bases.

In late June 1937, an all-star team of Basque players, drawn from the powerful Spanish league, came to the Soviet Union to raise money for the embattled Republic during the Spanish Civil War. They were to travel the country and play a series of matches against the best Soviet clubs. The Basques were professionals of the highest rank, far more talented than any other foreigners yet seen on Soviet soil. Fans flocked to these matches in record numbers, and the tour served to expand the game's popularity throughout the USSR. Spartak would be the only Soviet club to defeat the mighty Basques. Dinamo lost to them twice. From that moment, Spartak's popularity exploded. This did not mean that Dinamo had little or no support, but by the end of the decade they had been overtaken in the fans' affections by their great rivals. There are many Moscow men who claim to have been at the match against the Basques. They date their love of Spartak from this defining moment, but was this the sole reason for the team's popularity?

Huge numbers of people were coming to their games. Those

who watched football were not immune to the universal phenomenon of choosing a particular team to support. Even at the height of
Stalinism, no one could impose that choice on them. In choosing to
root for Spartak, Moscow fans came to call it "the people's team",
but just who were "the people", and why did they choose Spartak?
Who did comprise Spartak's fan base, and what were the political
meanings of their choices? Aside from their impressive attendance
totals and remarks in the press about their great popularity, there is
little, if any, remaining contemporary evidence concerning the real
reasons for Spartak's enormous support. Indeed, it is unlikely any
such contemporary evidence was ever produced. This was a topic
millions of citizens knew about but did not write about. Only since
the collapse of the USSR have we gotten published accounts which
articulate what everyone, even outsiders, knew. In a 1999 article
published in the monthly, *Sportexpress Zhurnal*, Iurii Oleshchuk, a retired jurist, described rooting for Spartak as a pre-teen in the thirties:

> In our huge apartment house there were mainly *kommunalki*
> [communal apartments]. We were all working class, and in
> the courtyard [*dvor*], the kids all proclaimed they were chil-
> dren of a single class. Our rooting interests were basically
> one half for Spartak and the rest for all the other clubs com-
> bined. In school it was the same. In Pioneer camp, the same...
> Why? Today I understand most clearly that Spartak was the
> home team [*rodnaia komanda*] of ordinary people. Why? The
> name had meaning for us. Then all the kids and even the
> grown-ups knew the name of the leader of the slave revolt
> in ancient Rome...It was studied closely in our schools - a
> story of the struggle of the exploited against the exploiters..
> How could the names of the other teams - Dinamo, TsDKA,
> Lokomotiv or Torpedo compare?

Clearly, for Oleshchuk exploitation had not disappeared with
the revolution, and his resentments found their way to the football
field. Invoking a revolutionary discourse, he was using Bolshevik
language to highlight the betrayal of the revolution's principles.
    Spartak's financial sponsorship by *Promkooperatsiia*, an insti-
tution representing service workers, had a similar resonance. Al-

though the organization was financially strong, for Oleshchuk it represented the ordinary people - barbers, waiters, tailors, sales clerks and food workers who labored under its wing. Even industrial workers, who were formally outside Promkooperatsiia's institutional control and had their own factory teams, identified with Spartak. Among the team's supporters, only one club inspired real hatred - Dinamo. "The relationship of Spartak's fans to Dinamo", wrote Oleshchuk, "was highly antagonistic. Dinamo represented the authorities - the police, the organs of state security - the hated privileged elites. They ate better. They dressed better, and they certainly didn't live in *kommunalki*." Matches between Spartak and Dinamo were, in Oleshchuk's words, "wars on the field and in the stands. There were lots of fights among the fans. Really huge battles were prevented by separating the supporters. Spartak's fans sat in the East tribune [of Dinamo stadium] where the seats were cheaper, while Dinamo's supporters occupied the aristocratic Northern and semi-aristocratic Southern stands."[52]

Such views were not universally shared. Alexander Vainshtein, who co-authored Nikolai Starostin's 1989 memoirs, expressed doubts about social explanations of team support:

> The idea that Spartak is the 'people's team' is a myth. Spartak wasn't the people's team. They were the most popular team. You can't say in terms of categories of fans that ordinary people rooted for Spartak and only KGB people rooted for Dinamo or that army generals rooted for TsDKA. Spartak was the most popular team for many reasons - first that it was not part of the structures of force.[53]

Vainshtein also argued that Spartak had its own support at the highest institutional levels, especially in the party. In that sense, he said, calling them the "people's team" made no sense since the people did not run the team. Of course, virtually nowhere in the world of elite sport do ordinary people run any team. The local soviet did not decide who should play goalie, nor did they set ticket prices or choose the colors of the uniforms.

Attending a match of any Soviet team was not an exercise in order and organization. Getting to an important game on especially crowded transport did not enhance the serenity or obedience of spectators. Mounted police shoved the entering crowds into the stadium. Once inside, the chance of actually finding one's assigned seat often proved impossible. Overcrowding for big games was the rule, and gate-crashers, usually young boys, numbered in the thousands.[54] Begging older men to take them into the stadium was another technique. This approach did not involve possessing an actual ticket. Usually the men told the ticket-takers that the kid was their son. If, however, the boy had tried the trick with someone else a few minutes earlier and had been turned away, the police would ask his new benefactor if he knew his son had another father.[55]

Order was rare in the stands as well as at the gates, especially for games not played at Dinamo, where security was strongest. This wild scene took place at a Spartak-TsDKA match on October 30, 1936 at the army's smaller, far more primitive ground:

> At half-time, spectators who had been behind the barriers began a general attack on the field. Thousands of people poured out like an avalanche and surrounded the playing surface like a tight wall which went right up to the sidelines, surrounded the goals and covered the corners turning the rectangle into an oval.[56]

Fig. 5. Fans crowd the field and destroy a goalpost: TsDKA vs. Spartak, 1936. *Spartak Moskva: Ofitsialnaia istoriia.*

In the second half, the surging fans destroyed one of the goal posts. In the midst of this chaos, Spartak triumphed 3-1 to claim its first league championship.[57] When the same two teams met in May 1937, there was more chaos. School kids who were allowed in free pushed, shoved, screamed and whistled as they pressed through the gates of Young Pioneer Stadium. When the match ended, they stormed the field.[58]

In the broadest sense, these anti-authoritarian attitudes and their accompanying rowdyism raise questions about public acceptance of the regime. Recent scholarship has demonstrated considerable dissent, disorganization and grumbling in Stalin's Russia. This work has revealed a broad social and cultural division between what many Soviet citizens described as a righteous and exploited "us" and a privileged and self-aggrandizing "them."[59] Significant numbers of ordinary men and women made critical comments in a variety of forms and places. Although there were surely millions of true believers, it could not be said the USSR under Stalin was a land of universal contentment. The first two five-year plans had brought much misery, and the later thirties were still a time of scarcity and uncertainty, heightening the regime's fear of the masses.[60] Indeed, much of this complaining was closely monitored by the secret police. Therefore, it is interesting to note that the stadium was one of the few places in the Soviet Union a person could utter the words "kill the cops" and rarely if ever suffer serious consequences.

A gathering of two or three people on the street could easily provoke police attention in Stalin's time, but thousands crammed into the stands was another matter. The police may not have liked it, but they had little choice but to permit sports events, especially football games, at which large numbers of people were crowded together under circumstances that raised their emotions.[61] Two large billboards, one with the latest results - the other with the league standings, were erected near Dinamo Stadium. Even when there was no match, crowds of men gathered near these signs to talk of football and other things. Police spies were surely part of these gatherings, but for thousands of Moscow men the pleasurable male bonding of a shared passion created a community that was simultaneously temporary and ongoing.[62]

For decades, Western scholars argued the workers' inability to change the Soviet system, despite their multiple dissatisfactions, was the result of the regime's use of repression to atomize possible opposition.[63] The authorities, therefore, found football problematic precisely because it brought people together to watch a highly unpredictable spectacle that created both social relations and discourses which undercut the impact of atomization. Having said this, it must be remembered sport's influence was limited. While it brought people together, it did not do so on a constant basis. Historically the stadium has been neither a public nor a private space, but what Clifford Geertz, in the ur-text of sport studies, has called a "focused gathering". For Geertz, as well as Erving Goffmann, both the Balinese cock fight and, by extension, a soccer game are neither crowds nor organized groups but rather something liminal or "in between."[64] The social relations created while going to the stadium, in the stands and on the way home are complex but ephemeral. You can have a long conversation with your neighbors in the stands but never see them again. After the game, as Eduardo Galeano has written, the excited and unified "we" may return to the otherwise atomized "I."[65] Although fans discuss events among themselves and read about them in the press, they possess nothing that can be called "power" until they are once again gathered together. The episodic character of these moments makes them different from so-called ordinary life and creates the "space" for what would otherwise be inadmissable, even dangerous acts and utterances. The practices of spectator sport create "enclaves of autonomy" where "mass audiences" can evade "the goals of those who seek to control them."[66] Even in the highly repressive conditions of the purges, Moscow men used football in just this way.

This does not mean that Soviet soccer games were truly carnivalesque. Rowdyism was the exception, and seating arrangements with the privileged occupying more desirable locations undermined the possibilities for cultural inversion. Nor can it be said the Soviet stadium was the Circus Maximus. Football in the USSR was not a safety valve consciously created by the state. If it had been, the authorities would not have spent so much time complaining, publicly and privately, about the fans' bad behavior, nor would they have so heavily ascribed didactic aims to sport. Clearly, the evidence of tension between subordinate and dominant groups

Fig. 6 The famous 1936 match on Red Square on Physical Culture Day. *Futbol skvoz gody.*

during the thirties is substantial, but it does not directly answer the question of whether the new Soviet labor force was an "us" or a "them." Indeed, the very distinction may be too sharply drawn.

Before the war, Dinamo athletes dominated the multi-sport Spartakiads which made the "civilized" sports on the Olympic program available to working men and women in the best tradition of "rational recreation."[67] Dinamo athletes were enthusiastic participants in the famous Physical Culture Day Parades held each summer on Red Square. By contrast, Spartak took a more spontaneous approach to leisure and sporting spectacles, emphasizing games rather than parades. The events it stressed in its own practice were less didactic. The primary rituals for Spartak fans were such male celebrations as the pre-game metro or tram ride, the pushing and shoving to get to their seats, plus chanting, cheering, booing, drinking and cursing - not to mention the occasional riot - practices more profane than sacred.[68] Press accounts extended the distinctions to encompass the two teams' playing styles. The famed children's writer Lev Kassil noted in *Izvestia* that Spartak played with more "feeling", whereas Dinamo took a "consistent and planned" approach.[69] These differences also tracked with the sponsorship of the two groups. Dinamo, supported by the secret police, was inextricably part of the state sector. Its athletes were to embody the virtues the regime sought to inculcate through sport - discipline, order, health, respect for authority and social improvement.[70] Dinamo was part of an organization subject to military discipline, and the bodies it presented were supposed to give the impression of discipline.[71] By contrast, Spartak was sponsored by the service sector, which made it more a part of the public.[72] In the context of the purges, the police had come to be hated and feared. Support for Spartak was a safe way of keeping distance from what were the most troubling of events.

Spartak's popularity was greatly enhanced by their victory over the Basques in 1937. The next two seasons they would take the double and establish themselves as the top Soviet side. Yet, this dominance discomfited the powerful supporters of Dinamo. Even before the 1937 season ended both football and political circles began a heated discussion about what form the next league schedule should take. In its first two years, this had been a small competition, of first seven and then nine teams. Yet, if soccer was to be a marker of modernity, it made political sense to expand the league throughout the USSR as part of the project of nation-building. A cascade of proposals came from soccer people, the press and the party. Some political leaders favored including 26 or even 32 teams in the top flight, giving each republic at least one team in the first division. While laudable in its sensitivity to the concerns of national minorities, the lack of good teams on the periphery threatened the quality of the competition and raised the possibilities for political meddling. Football professionals, led by Nikolai Starostin, instead preferred what they called the "sporting principle", which favored the inclusion of the best teams based on performance, regardless of their location.[73]

After the double in 1938, Spartak took the 1939 league title by a comfortable margin over a surging Dinamo Tblisi team, led by the brilliant Boris Paichadze.[74] Dinamo Tblisi would also figure in the central event of Spartak's season. By the fall of 1938, the terror, orchestrated at Stalin's orders by the insane Nikolai Yezhov, had gone completely out of control. With so many top leaders and useful functionaries arrested and executed in the party's orgy of self-destruction, the state's economic and political efficiency was suffering severely. The army officer corps had been virtually wiped out. Hoards of innocents had disappeared, creating immense demographic problems. Given that war in Europe seemed imminent, it was essential to rebuild the country's defenses. Yezhov had to go.

The new head of the NKVD was the Georgian, Lavrentii Beria who had held the same position in the Trans-Caucasian Republic.[75] This change proved good for the nation. At Stalin's behest, Beria presided over a massive decrease in the terror. What had been hundreds of thousands of executions in the previous three years now fell to a "mere" two thousand. While overall arrests were diminished, Beria moved quickly to eliminate Yezhov's purported allies. One of them, Aleksandr Kosarev, had been Spartak's political sponsor. He was arrested in November 1938 and executed soon thereafter. It did not help Spartak that Beria was a passionate fan of football and a player of some ability in his youth. His position as head of the secret police put him on the presidium of the Dinamo Sport Society, and he took his duties seriously. While Beria's first loyalty was to Dinamo Tblisi, he was deeply concerned about the plunging fortunes of Dinamo Moscow. He became the Soviet equivalent of a meddling capitalist team owner, involving himself in the operations of many of the top Dinamo clubs. Beria rarely missed a game any Dinamo team played in Moscow, and he and others in the secret police were not pleased by Spartak's ascendancy. If success on the field could soften the public's negative view of the police in the time of the purges, then failure at football could weaken acceptance of their authority and lower their prestige.

It is not clear whether personal animosity, ideological education or a simple will to win drove Beria's actions at this time, but his presumed interference in the regular sporting process soon precipitated one of the most bizarre moments in the history of world football. The 1939 cup competition took place in August and September along with the regular league schedule. Spartak advanced to the semi-final on September 8 in Moscow where they took on Beria's heroes, Dinamo Tblisi. This was an extremely powerful side with excellent players who approached the game with great intensity. Known in the press as "the flying Uruguayans", the Georgians

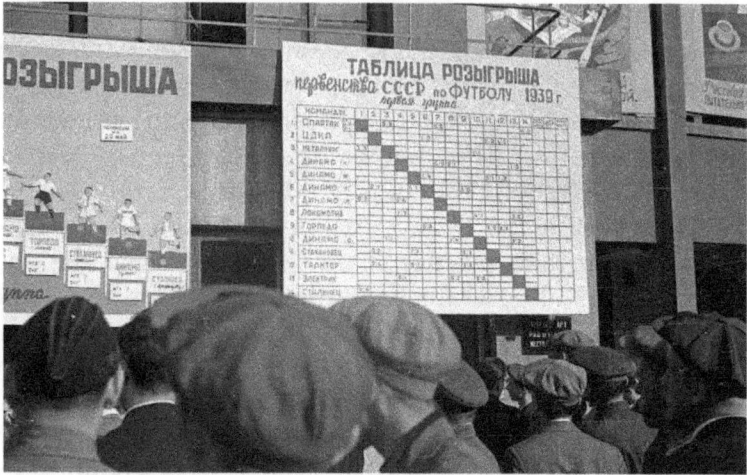

Fig. 7. These two huge signs posted the football league standings and results. Fans gathered around them at all hours to talk soccer. Fotoagentstvo Sportekspress.

took an emotional and technical Latin American approach to the game - distinct from the control and physicality of most Moscow clubs. Especially skilled dribblers and committed individualists, the Georgians vastly preferred attack over defense.

The semi-final, however, proved to be a defensive struggle one that produced a single score. It came in the 64th minute after a scramble in front of the Tblisi goal. Dinamo's Russian goalie, Aleksandr Dorokhov, punched the ball away but directly onto the feet of Spartak's Andrei Protasov whose shot crossed the goal line but failed to make it to the back of the net when the Georgian defender Shota Shavgulidze cleared the ball away. Nevertheless, the referee Ivan Gorelkin awarded the goal. Dinamo lodged a protest which was quickly denied by the football section of the sport committee.[76] Four days later, Spartak defeated Stalinets of Leningrad 3-1 in the final and claimed their second cup in a row. Everyone went home and proceeded with the rest of the season.[77]

But some twelve days after the final, roughly around September 24, Spartak team members and officials began seeing players from Dinamo Tblisi in Moscow. They learned from their Georgian guests that the disputed semi-final was to be re-played on September 30 – three weeks after the final had taken place! The decision to overrule the sport committee had come from the Central Committee itself and had been announced in the Georgian press as early as the sixteenth of September. Given this degree of public knowledge, it is difficult to believe Nikolai Starostin and everyone else associated with Spartak had been unaware of the order to replay the final. Nor is it likely the Central Committee would have informed only one of the participants in the replay. Spartak also had powerful friends who might well have known what was going on.[78] If the club had truly been unaware of the decision, they were left with a mere six days to prepare for one of the biggest matches in their history. Starostin sought to mobilize his political allies, but Kosarev was gone. No direct proof has ever been found to indicate that Beria personally demanded the replay, but one may well ask who else at that level would have cared enough about soccer. The Spartak leader was told the order had come specifically from the powerful party secretary, Andrei Zhdanov. Football's first semi-final to take place after the completion of a final was to occur on September 30.[79]

Going into the rematch Dinamo Tblisi was surely tired from their long train trip back to Moscow, but Spartak was also in poor shape. The younger Starostin brother and most talented family member, Andrei, had broken his hand, and the team's leading scorer Aleksei Sokolov had been disqualified for punching an opponent in the face. In the first half, Spartak was able to take advantage of Tblisi's halfbacks, who involved themselves too eagerly in the offense, allowing Spartak's outside right Georgi Glazkov to score twice. Dinamo's star Paichadze came back with a goal before the half to make it 2-1. Almost immediately after the game resumed, Spartak was awarded a penalty kick, converted by Glazkov for a hat trick. The Georgians attacked furiously, but their best efforts were negated by Anatoly Akimov's brilliance in goal. With four minutes left, however, they finally succeed in scoring off a corner. To add to the tension, Akinov was injured on the play and replaced.[80] The end of the game was played with the crowd of 80,000, nearly all pro-Spartak, in a heaving uproar.

Dinamo protested, claiming the penalty was not deserved. Two days later, their claim was denied, and the cup stayed with Spartak. Their victory was of immense importance to their fans. As the great Soviet sportswriter Lev Filatov noted in 1997:

There was a game played in 1939 that was more important for my younger generation than any that had ever been seen...Never before and never again have I had to root so hard, breathing heavily, my knees trembling ... . For us, what was being decided was not the fate of the cup or the fate of Spartak. What was being decided was the fate of football itself. Would it remain an island of justice or would we wave our hands as we passed the stadium and placed a cross on our bliss?[81]

Along with the triumph over the Basques, the great victory in the forced replay became another chapter of the Spartak saga. They had triumphed over arbitrary power and, thought Filatov, saved the game itself.

If we are to believe Nikolai Starostin, Beria left the stadium in a huff. Beria's team had not defeated Spartak at football, but Stalin's favorite policeman had other, less than sporting tools at his disposal.[82] Soon thereafter he tried, unsuccessfully, to have the Starostin brothers arrested. For all the political freight invested in this one match, however, it is by no means clear Beria's frustration focused on Spartak's victory. The next season, Dinamo Moscow would right its ship, bringing in the brilliant coach Boris Arkadiev and winning the 1940 championship. Spartak finished third, losing 1-5 to their arch rivals before 85,000 in a match some Dinamo players later recalled as the greatest of their careers.[83] Spartak may have led the league in attendance and acquired vast popularity, but this did not mean no one supported Dinamo just as it cannot be said no one among the male working class supported the regime.

To be sure, all workers were not football fans. Yet, it can safely be said that nearly all fans during the 1930's were workers. In creating what can be called "chosen communities" of team supporters, these "lovers of football" were exercising one of the few free choices Soviet citizens could make. To support the civilian Spartak as opposed to the police club Dinamo implied a certain distancing from the party-state. Conversely, rooting for Dinamo suggested greater comfort with the forces of Soviet order. Yet, this was a politics of the everyday in which citizens made what turned out to be highly ambiguous and swiftly evolving choices about their political and cultural identities. Not every Dinamo fan was a Communist, nor can it be said those who supported Spartak were universally non-party. Even at the height of Stalinsim, there was also a different, more diffuse kind of politics, one that had no immediate impact on state policy or on the careers of various highly visible actors. Rather, this was a much more amorphous and multi-directional set of lower-level power relations that ordinary people could use for their own purposes.

While the paucity of solid empirical evidence requires care, it does appear the workers who watched soccer had greater experience of urban life than did the newcomers to the capital. The men who had followed the sport before the revolution and during NEP continued to do so into the late thirties. Many of them had raised families and passed on their love of the game to their sons. Additionally, several Soviet-era students of labor history claimed Moscow workers were becoming older and more skilled, a process that made them more likely to be drawn to the urban activity of sport. In the larger economy of the city, the shift away from female-gendered textiles toward masculinely coded metalworking can also be seen as a sign of an increasingly skilled work force.[84] With the Third Five-Year Plan announced in 1938, an even greater emphasis was placed on heavy industries, creating even more potential members of the football public.[85] The chaos of the First Five-Year Plan had allowed little time for leisure, and the new recruits to the urban labor force were not highly trained. Over the course of the decade, that situation changed. From the league's formation in 1936 up to the war, the capital's workers became more experienced, not only on the factory floor but in the ways of city life.[86]

The regime had sought to use sport to inculcate the rational values of health, punctuality, skill and respect for authority. The state wished to see its "guardians of order" successful on the field and admired by the public. In a 1936 article in the national sports daily, *Krasnyi sport*, the head of the state sport committee I.I. Kharchenko had remarked that Dinamo provided the best model for other sport societies.[87] Yet, mass repression alone never could have achieved support for Dinamo. Chosen communities were just that, the people picked their own heroes. To be sure many football fans from a variety of social strata did choose to root for Dinamo, and just as surely many of them were true believers in the system. At the same time, it would be wrong to see Spartak's fan base as in any way dissident. They were neither anti-Soviet nor pro-capitalist. They had been created with support from an important part of the Communist Party. They did not seek regime change. Spartak fans may have seen the struggle with Dinamo as a case of "us" versus "them", but it turns out the rivalry was really about two different ways of "being Soviet."

Notes

1   Akesel' Vartanian, ed., *Sto let Rossiiskomu futbolu* (Moscow: Rossiiskii futbol'skii soiuz, 1997); 51. (hereafter *Sto let*) Konstantin Esenin, *Moskovskii futbol* (Moscow, 1974), 29; Baruch Hazan *Olympic Sports and Propaganda Games* (New Brunswick: Transaction Books, 1982), 20.

2   Mikhail Romm, *Ia boleiu za Spartak* (Alma-Ata: "Zhazhushy," 1965), 72.

3   Eric Naiman, *Sex in Public: The Incarnation of Early Soviet Ideology* (Princeton: Princeton University Press, 1999), 6; Anne Gorsuch, *Youth in Revolutionary Russia: Enthusiasts, Bohemians, Delinquents* (Bloomington, IN: Indiana University Press, 2000), 24.

4   Gorsuch, 9.

5   Richard Stites, *Russian Popular Culture* (Cambridge, UK: Cambridge University Press, 1992), 37-40.

6   Anatoly Lunacharsky, *Mysli o sporte* (Moscow: Ogonëk, 1930).

7   Gorsuch, 116.

8   Frederick Starr, *Red and Hot: The Fate of Jazz in the Soviet Union* (Oxford: Oxford University Press, 1984), 58.

9   Gorsuch, 116-17; Starr, 58; Stites, 52; Alan Ball, *Russia's Last Capitalists: the Nepmen, 1921-1929* (Berkeley: University of California Press, 1997), 17.

10   Gorsuch, 116-17; Stites, 49; Natalia Lebina, *Povsednevnaia zhizn' sovetskogo goroda: Normy i anomalii* (St. Petersburg: Zhurnal "Neva," 1999), 254.

11   Starr, 60; Stites, 47.

12   Stites, 56, 60, 63; Gorsuch, 65; Lebina, 245-47.

13   Gorsuch, 38-40; A.I. Vdovin and V.Z.Drobizhev, *Rost rabochego klassa SSSR, 1917-1940 gg.* (Moscow: Mysl', 1976); 87, 115.

14   Konstantin Beskov, "Moia zhizn' v futbole," *Futbol*, no. 4, 1991.

15   Lev Gorianaov, *Kolumby Moskovskogo futbola* (Moscow' Moskovskii rabochii, 1965), 94. *Sovetskii sport*, 11/14/50. *Sto let*, 52-53; Esenin, 36.

16   Esenin, 38; Andrei Starostin, *Bol'shoi futbol* (Moscow, 1964), 72.

17   Nikolai Starostin, *Moi futbol'nye gody* (Moscow: Pravda, 1986), 10; idem; *Futbol skvoz' gody* (Moscow: Sovetskaia Rossiia, 1989), 17.

18   *Vechernaia Moskva* (Hereafter VM), 3/27/29.

19   Mikhail Sushkov, *Futbol'nyi teatr* (Moscow, 1974), 107.

20   *Sto let*, 54; Vladimir Verkholashin, *My iz Dinamo* (Moscow: "Fizkultura i sport," 1968), 5.

21   Esenin, 104. *Krasnyi Sport* (hereafter, KS), 5/1/36; Verkholashin, 6.

22   Esenin, 105.

23   *Sto let*, 56.

24   Eduard Nisenboim, ed. *Spartak Moskva: Ofitsial'naia istoriia* (hereafter, SE) (Moscow, 2002), 20-22.

25   Esenin, 36-38. SE, 16.

26   SE, 21. KS, 11/23/24.

27   William Chase, *Workers, Society, and the Soviet State: Labor and Life in Moscow, 1918-1929* (Urbana: University of Illinois Press, 1987), 171.

28   Nisenboim and Rasinskii, *Ot MKS do Spartaka* (Moscow, 2000), 35.

29   Ronald Suny, ed., *The Structure of Soviet History* (Oxford: Oxford University Press, 2003), 220-21.

30   SE, 29.

31   Sheila Fitzpatrick, "The Bolshevik Invention of Class: Marxist Theory and the Making of 'Class Consciousness' in Soviet Society", in Suny, *Structure*, 164-77.

32   VM, 3/2/29, 3/13/29, 10/1/29.

33   VM, 8/6/ 29.

34   VM, 8/9/29.

35   *Fizkul'tura i sport*, 5/12/28, 6/30/28. *Pravda*, 6/19/28.

36   VM, 9/9/29. Sto let, 57.

37   SE, 34. Sushkov, 115.

38   Sheila Fitzpatrick, "Petitions, Patronage and Blat: Reflections on their Importance in the Stalinist System", unpublished conference paper, University of California, Riverside, April 19, 1998, p. 9.

39   On blat see Alena Ledeneva, *Russia's Economy of Favors: Blat Networking and Informal Exchange* (Cambridge, UK, 1998).

40   Andrei Starostin, *Bol'shoi*, 122-23.

41   Barbara J. Keys, *Globalizing Sport: National Rivalry and the International Community in the 1930's* (Cambridge, MA: Harvard University Press, 2006), 159.

42   Of 17 players, 5 were from Spartak; 7 were from Dinamo, 5 from other teams.

43   Mikhail Iakushin, *Vechnaia taina futbol* (Moscow: "Fizkul'tura i sport,", 1986), 30.

44   Sto let, 82. Andrei Starostin, *Povest'o futbole* (Moscow: Sovetskaia Rossiia, 1973), 136; Iakushin, 31.

45   Gosudarstvennyi arkhiv Rossiiskoi Federatsii (hereafter GARF), fond. 7576, opis. 2, delo. 160. ll. 1-51.

46   http://www.sport-express.ru/art.shtml?71816, accessed 9/20/03.

47   See Lewis Siegelbaum, *Stakhanovism and the Politics of Productivity in the USSR, 1935-1941* (Cambridge, UK: Cambridge University Press, 1988).

48   Karen Petrone, *Life Has Become More Joyous, Comrades: Celebrations in the Time of Stalin* (Bloomington, IN: Indian University Press, 2000), 14-15.

49   See Robert Conquest, *The Great Terror: Stalin's Purge of the Thirties* (Harmondsworth: Pelican, 1971); J. Arch Getty, *Origins of the Great Purges: the Soviet Communist Party Reconsidered* (Cambridge, UK: Cambridge University Press, 1985).

50   *Izvestia*, 3/21/40.

51   *Sportekspress*, 3/5/01 and 3/12/01. GARF, f. 7576, o. 13, d. 39, ll. 8-9.

52   Iurii Oleshchuk, "Mistika Spartaka" *Sportekspress zhurnal*, no. 1 1999, 10. All three Oleshchuk quotes are from the same page; see also Andrei Starostin, *Bol'shoi*, 45.

53   Aleksandr Vainshtein, interview with the author, Moscow, 1999. Lev Filatov, "Teatr Andreia Starostina: vospominania kumira", *Fizkul'tura i sport*, no. 5, 1995, 31-32.

54   Oleshchuk, "Fanaty Vremen Bobrova", *Sportekspress zhurnal*, no. 10, 1999, 86.

55   http://www.sport-express.ru/art.shtml?77458, accessed 11/17/03.

56   KS, 11/1/36. Anatolii Akimov, *Zapiski vratar'ia* (Moscow, 1974), 59-62.

57   Vartanian, interview with the author, Moscow, 1999.

58   KS, 5/9/37.

59   See Shiela Fitzpatrick, *Everyday Stalinism*; Lebina; Gabor Rittersporn, *Stalinist Simplifications and Soviet Complications: Social tensions and political conflicts in the USSR, 1933-1953* (Chur-New York: Harwood Academic Publishers, 1991); Elena Osokina, *Our Daily Bread: Socialist Distribution and the Art of Survival in Stalin's Russia, 1927-1941* (Armonk, NY: M. E. Sharpe, 2001); Lynne Viola, *Peasant Rebels under Stalin: Collectivization and the Culture of Peasant Resistance* (Oxford: Oxford University Press, 1996); Michael David-Fox, et al., *The Resistance Debate in Russian and Soviet History* (Bloomington, IN: Slavica), 69-102.

60   Fitzpatrick, *Everyday Stalinism: Ordinary Life in Extraoridary Times: Soviet Russia in the 1930s* (Oxford: Oxford University Press), 42-50.

61   Vartanian, interview, 1999.

62   http://www.sport-express.ru/art/shtml?102517, accessed 4/24/05.

63   Donald Filtzer, *Soviet Workers and Stalinist Industrialization: the*

Formation of Modern Soviet Production Relations, 1929-1941 (New York, M. E., Sharpe, 1986), 1, 8, 255.

64   Clifford Geertz, "Deep Play: The Balinese Cock Fight, in Geertz, ed., *The Interpretation of Cultures: Selected Essays* (New York: Basic Books, 1973), 434.

65   Eduardo Galeano, *Football in Sun and Shadow* (London, 1997), 6.

66   Eric Dunning, *Sport Matters: Sociological Studies of Sport, Violence and Civilization* (London: Routledge, 1999), 3-4.

67   *Fotoal'bom spartakiada* (Moscow, 1929), n.p.

68   On sacred and profane rituals, see Victor Turner, ed., *Celebration: Studies in Festivity and Ritual* (Washington, D.C.: Smithsonian Institution, 1982).

69   http://sport-express.ru/art.shtml?77458, accessed 11/17/03.

70   V. Vinokurov and O. Kucherenko, *Dinamo Moskva* (Moscow, 1973); *Vsesoiuznoe fizkul'turno-sportivnoe ordena Lenina obshchestvo Dinamo* (Moscow, 1956).

71   Christel Lane, *The Rites of Rulers: Ritual in Industrial Society: the Soviet Case* (Cambridge, UK: Cambridge University Press, 1981); Verkholashin.

72   Nikolai Starostin, *Skvoz'*, 29-34.

73   KS, 1/17/38.

74   KS, 6/28/38 and 11/7/39.

75   N.G. Okhotin and A.B. Roginskii, eds., *Kto rukovodil NKVD, 1934-1941* (Moscow: Zvenia, 1999), 107.

76   KS, 9/10/39.

77   Nikolai Starostin, *Skvoz'*, 47.

78   http://www.sport-express.ru/art.shtml?105407, accessed 6/24/05.

79   Simon Martin, *Football and Fascism: The National Game under Mussolini* (Oxford: Berg, 2004); 173-208; John Foot, *Calcio: A History of Italian Football* (London: Fourth Estate, 2006), 33-36; Alex Belos, *Futebol: Soccer, the Brazilian Way of Life* (New York: Bloomsbury, 2002), 141; David Goldblatt, *The Ball is Round: a Global History of Football* (London, Viking: 2006), 627-31.

80   KS, 12/13/39.

81   Filatov, "Romb", 5.

82   "Spartak na pole istorii", NTV, 2002.

83   Esenin, 38.

84   Vdovin and Drobizhev, 183.

85   S.L. Selianskii, *Izmeneniia v sotsial'noi strukture sovetskogo obshchestva, 1938-1970* (Moscow: Mysl', 1973), 8-9.

86   Vdovin and Drobizhev, 112-15; *Istoriia Moskovskikh rabochikh*, 183; Tony Mason, *Association Football and English Society, 1863-1915* (Sussex: Harvester, 1980), 138-67.

87   KS, 7/1/36.

4

Stalin in the Kremlin: One Life-Death Joke from the 1930s

by Boris Briker

The action of the following joke takes place presumably in the second half of the 1930s:

> A peasant visits Moscow. When he sees the Kremlin, he asks a passerby: "What is it? "This is the Kremlin wall." The passerby answers proudly. "And who are these people in uniform?" "They are guards." "And who is inside these walls?" "Stalin." The peasant says: "Now the son of a bitch will never get out of here."[1]

In this joke the peasant confuses the Kremlin, the political center of Moscow, with a place of imprisonment. On one level this is a typical joke about a provincial fool who comes from his village to the center and confuses the center of power or place of worship with its opposition. For example, there are common jokes or stories in which the provincial fool goes to the big city or capital and perceives a palace or a church as a brothel or a public bathroom. According to one scholar of humor, these kind of jokes "represent the center laughing at the periphery, townies laughing at rustics, skilled and white collar workers laughing at the unskilled, and the established laughing at the greenhorns."[2] In our example about the peasant, however, Stalin serves as the satirical target of the joke, not the foolish peasant.

Building upon my previous study of "life-death" jokes of the 1930s, I would like to examine this particular joke within the context of life-death jokes about Stalin and to investigate it against the background of symbols of the cult of Stalin of the 1930s and some popular mythologies of the time.[3]

First, what are life-death jokes? Drawing from theories of humor and jokes by Koestler and Raskin,[4] I apply the combination of incompatible frameworks to the political jokes of the 1930s which I call life-death jokes. The opposition and simultaneous partial equation of opposing contexts, such as life and death, create humor and serve as a structural principal in these jokes: "How is your life?" One man asks another. "Like Lenin's in the Mausoleum." "Why like Lenin's?" "They neither feed us nor bury us." [5]

While the death component in the life-death opposition adds a philosophical dimension to the jokes, it also explains political humor of the 1930s. Ted Cohen gives one of the possible reasons why we make jokes about death: "by laughing at it we want to tame death as an ultimate oppressor."[6] While he uses the word oppressor metaphorically, death in our jokes functions as both an ultimate oppressor in Cohen's terms as well as a real political oppressor, the Soviet State.

One of the most poignant jokes of the time compares non-political universal death (death by fire) with arrest and persecution during Stalinist times:

> It is late at night in 1937. Somebody knocks at the door. The husband says farewell to his family and takes his bag and goes to open the door. While already near the door he hears the voice on the other side: "Don't worry. Everything is great. It is just that our whole house is on fire. Everything is great."[7]

Life-death jokes of the 1930s include all jokes about persecution under Stalin. Moreover, all stages of persecution--such as arrest, interrogation, trial, imprisonment and execution--are included in the death category. Jokes which deal with the overarching fear of persecution in the 1930s also serve as life-death jokes. In the 1930s death and persecution may apply to jokes which do not directly state these themes.

There are two types of jokes which employ a life-death opposition: 1) jokes that feature the lives of common people as the victims of persecution and 2) jokes that subject Stalin and other oppressors to the experiences of persecution.

In the first type of jokes, the reality of life for an ordinary individual overlaps with the reality of death and persecution: "How is life?" "Like in a tram. Some are sitting (in prison). The rest are shaking (from fear)."[8] Stalin may also function in these jokes, but only as an instrument of oppression, not its victim:

> Lenin got up in his Mausoleum and appears before Stalin as an apparition. Lenin asks Stalin about the Five-Year Plan. "How is it going, Iosif?" "Very well, indeed," Stalin says. "What about the people?" Lenin asked. "The people are with me." Stalin answers. "What about your plans for the future, Iosif?" Lenin asks. "We will force another Five-Year Plan." Stalin says. "What about the people?" Lenin asks again. "They will be with me." Stalin says with confidence. "No, this time they will be with me." Lenin's apparition answers.[9]

In the second type of jokes Stalin becomes the victim of persecution. The anonymous authors of these jokes create a context by which the wishful thinking of Stalin's death is expressed. His death is presented in the future tense or in the conditional mood or as an impossible condition:

> An old woman barely manages to get on board a bus. "Thank God," she says. A young Komsomol member turns to her and says: "There is no God, babushka. You should say: Thank Stalin. "You are right, my dear. I am old and not very educated. But tell me, son, God forbid, what if Stalin dies. Whom shall I thank then?" "Then you can say: Thank God."[10]

At a Workers' Meeting, Stalin announces that he is ready to give all of his blood, drop by drop, for the sake of the Communist Party. Then he receives a note: Iosif Vissarionovich, why so slow, drop by drop? Give it all now.[11]

A similar sentiment is expressed by a young boy from an orphanage when some high authority visits:

"Tell us who your father is." "Stalin,"---answers the boy. "Who is your mother?" "Our Soviet Motherland." "Who do you want to be when you grow up?" "I want to be an orphan."[12]

In 1935 when Stalin's mother visited Moscow, one Soviet citizen, an Armenian, even expressed the wish for Stalin's mother to have arranged a pro-choice action: "Such a good beautiful woman. Why could she not have had an abortion?"

The joke under discussion about a peasant who comes to visit the Kremlin belongs to the second group of jokes. Indeed, not providing Stalin with any human features, the anonymous authors of this joke place a purely symbolic Stalin inside the Kremlin walls and then in the end conditionally imprison him. Moreover, it was not a foolish peasant or not only foolish peasants who substitute the Kremlin with a place of imprisonment and destruction. This opposition lies in the symbolic ambiguity of the Kremlin in the language and imagery of the time. This ambiguity is realized in the references to and meanings of the Kremlin in the 1930s as both a center of Stalin's cult and at the same time as a prison or a camp. Hence Stalin becomes both a mythological god and a prisoner. Thus the life-death juxtaposition presented in this joke reflected the ambiguous image of Stalin in the Kremlin, an image which already existed in the popular imagination in the 1930s.

What is the role of the Kremlin in Stalin's cult? The Kremlin served as a political center and metonymical substitution for Soviet power in Moscow since the Soviet government moved to the Kremlin in 1918. However, in the middle of the 1930s, in a new wave of the cult of Stalin, the Kremlin became the home of Stalin as a mythological figure. By 1935 the five-point stars were installed on the Kremlin towers to replace the double-headed eagles of Tsarist times, and in 1937 they were installed again.

On the one hand the "walls of the ancient Kremlin" were connected with Russia's historical past, especially with Ivan the Terrible and his reign, with whom Stalin showed an affinity starting from the mid 1930s. On the other hand, the new stars of the Kremlin tower were directed towards the sky, metaphorically speaking to an eternal future.

This image was depicted graphically in Soviet posters and paintings, as well as poetically in songs and verse. The five-point stars completed the metaphor of the Kremlin as a place bringing happiness to all Soviet people by shedding the rays of its lights all over the country. People sang:

Our happy country is rejoicing.
All of the Kremlin's stars are bright rubies!
And in the big world, in a far-away land
These stars could be seen during the day and in the darkness!

Or:

Keep shining more and more beautifully, oh stars of the Kremlin,
Above our proletarian country,
Above the land of Lenin and Stalin,
Above our beloved Moscow.

Indeed, in these songs the stars of the Kremlin constitute the "constellations of the Kremlin," and they replaced not only double-headed eagles but also real stars in the sky:

And the stars have begun to shine more brightly,
And our pulse is speeding up,
Stalin looks upon us with a smile —
He is just an ordinary Soviet man.[13]

In this last example, though no reference is made to the Kremlin, stars are featured, and Stalin appears in the background of these stars. In this way, the Kremlin was elevated to the level of stars and Stalin was positioned right under the stars.

If we were to formulate a master plot in the texts of the songs featuring Stalin in the Kremlin it would be some sort of communication between the people and Stalin. People sing and dance, fly airplanes, conquer the North Pole, collect crops, build the country. From his perch in the Kremlin above the earth Stalin listens to peoples' songs, looks at them with a smile, waves his hand at them, thinks, extends his reliable hand (сквозь бури и штормы им Сталин протянет надёжную руку свою) and, most importantly, he watches them (мы знаем мы помним чьё мудрое око следит за расцветом Москвы). Once in a while and in the manner of an Olympian god, Stalin descends from the Kremlin (for example, leaving through Borovitskie Gates) to visit Moscow and its people and at the end of the day returns through the central Spassky Gates.

The mythological Stalin communicating with his people against the background of the Kremlin provides a strong visual image for propaganda posters of the late 1930s. In one such a poster with the slogan, "We thank dear Stalin for our happy childhood," children present Stalin with flowers while Stalin appears to embrace them all with his wide chest (Fig.1). The Kremlin here fills the triangular

Fig. 1 (*spasibo rodnomu*): http://ruslife.org.ua/photo/2483533/post17990526/

ДА ЗДРАВСТВУЕТ РАВНОПРАВНАЯ ЖЕНЩИНА СССР,

Fig.2 (*da zdravstvuet*): http://ruslife.org.ua/photo/2483533/post18059408/

gap between Stalin's oversized head and the children, matching the light pink color of the dress worn by one of the children. This pink-ish color of the Kremlin probably realizes the opening lines from the popular song of the time. "Morning paints the walls of the ancient Kremlin with tender color." This bright Kremlin in the colors of dawn fits the bright picture of happy childhood under Stalin. The 1939 poster depicting the sentiment, "Long lives the equality of women in the USSR," features a parade with women leading the procession (Fig. 2). Stalin's gigantic figure on the red silk tapestry pointing at the sky with his finger somewhat parallels the direction

Fig. 3 (*stalinskim dukhom*): http://ruslife.org.ua/photo/2483533/ost17990529/

of the Spassky Tower of the Kremlin in the background. The off white color of the shadow of Stalin's white tunic matches the color of the Kremlin; and in another poster, "With Stalin's Spirit Strong and Powerful is our Army and our Country," the Gulliver-like figure of Stalin towers above troops, tanks, and airplanes (Fig. 3). The red Kremlin here matches the color of the banners, flags, and stars becoming another symbol of military might. The famous 1940

Fig. 4 (*o kazhdom iz nas*): http://ruslife.org.ua/photo/2483533/
ost18059408/

poster summarizes the messages from other posters insofar as it
portrays a peaceful scene of Stalin working in his study at night in
the Kremlin and is entitled "About each of us Stalin cares in the
Kremlin" (Fig. 4). The window frame in Stalin's office provides the
frame for the silhouette of the dark Kremlin with the bright red star
on top.

Fig. 5 (Komar and Melamid): http://www.feldmangallery.com/
pages/exhsolo/exhknm82.html

In 1981-1982 the artists Vitaly Komar and Alexander Melamid
placed the Kremlin in their "View of the Kremlin in a Romantic
Landscape," creating a parody of the image of Stalin in the Kremlin
(Fig. 5). While Stalin is not present in this landscape, his invisible
image appears to fill the space, especially given the context of the
paintings with Stalin from the same series, *Nostalgic Socialist Realism* series. Indeed, according to the comment of art critic Carter Ratcliff, in this landscape which feature the same red curtain and Stalin
behind it "hidden behind a barricade of clichés, Stalin is (only) a
dreaded implication."[14]

If in official Stalinist culture the Kremlin is raised to mythological proportions, in peoples' imagination it evoked completely the
opposite connotation. Indeed, the late 1930s witnessed not only
the elevation of cult of Stalin, but the peak of the Great Terror. The
very shape of the Kremlin with its high walls and towers and military guards suggested not only a palace, but a prison. Similar to
the Kremlin, the Gulag camps are often described by its boundar-

ies and high wooden watchtowers.[15] In the popular imagination in Stalin's time, the Kremlin acquires the meaning of a prison or of a prison camp, something that Joseph Brodsky expressed much later in his poem: "The Kremlin looms like the zone, as they say, in miniature (Кремль маячит, точно зона, говорят, в миниатюре)."[15] The phrase "as they say" gives this poetic line the status of a proverb, something which obviously was fixed in people's memory. Varlam Shalamov goes even further when he discusses the origin of Moscow skyscrapers, the buildings of Stalinist architecture in his short story of 1965, "Lend-Lease." Shalamov's narrator speculates about the mass killings of the prisoners in Kolyma region, committed around 1938:

> With my exhausted, tormented mind I tried to understand: How did there come to be such an enormous grave in this area? (...) But then I realized that I knew only a fragment of that world surrounded by a barbed-wire zone and guard towers that reminded one of the pages of tent-like Moscow architecture. Moscow's taller buildings are guard towers keeping watch over the city's prisoners. That's what those buildings look like. And what served as a model for Moscow architecture—the watchful towers of the Moscow Kremlin or the guard towers of the camps? The guard towers of the camp zone represent the main concept advanced by their time and brilliantly expressed in the symbolism of the architecture.[16]

While architecturally it was the Kremlin which influenced the Stalinist skyscrapers, the perception of the Kremlin as the camp zone especially in the mind of Gulag prisoners paved the way for Shalamov's powerful metaphor. Obviously, Brodsky and Shalamov wrote much later than the 1930s and projected these images on the whole Soviet period. However, there were earlier indications of these parallels.

In popular perception the Kremlin wall, defended by guards who prevent anyone from exiting, could symbolically represent the Soviet state border, as in the following joke:

Why is the Soviet border under lockdown (граница на за-
мке)? So the people of the USSR do not run away.[17]

This joke employs a typical cliché of the time—a lockdown and
the ambiguity of the phrase. After all, a border in lockdown doesn't
allow enemies to penetrate, but it also does not allow anybody to
escape. This second meaning and function of border doubles as the
wall of a prison. In this case the entire Soviet Union becomes such
a prison.

In one of her 1935 *Requiem* pieces, Anna Akhmatova refers
to the historical Kremlin wall as a weeping wall, a site where the
wives of the streltsy wept during the execution of their husbands.'
This wall can serve as a dividing line, separating victims of execution and their loved ones and as such could also be compared to a
prison wall especially given the whole context of the cycle *Requiem*.
Indeed, the lyrical heroine in *Requiem* waits in line for seventeen
months in the 1930s behind prison doors. Various images associated with the prison wall such as jail locks (тюремные затворы)—
or the key's squalls (ключей постылых скрежет) shape this kind
of impenetrable border separating wives and mothers from those
arrested and imprisoned. Moreover, one scholar suggests that the
stars in the line "stars of death stood above us (звёзды смерти
стояли над нами)" in another passage of *Requiem* could imply the
stars of the Kremlin.[18]

In 1940 poem "Stansy" Akhmatova posits the image of the
Kremlin as the site of murder. In this poem she places an Impostor within these walls. In 1940 one could easily make connection
between the impostor among other historical rulers and Stalin in
the Kremlin:

"One cannot live in the Kremlin."
The Reformer was right.
The place is still overrun with microbial swarms — full of
    ancient fury:
Boris's animal fear, the wrath of all the Ivans
And the Impostor's arrogance in place of the people's rights.

"В Кремле не можно жить."
Преображенец прав.
Там древней ярости еще кишат микробы:
Бориса дикий страх, всех Иоаннов злобы
И Самозванца спесь - взамен народных прав.[19]

Let us return to our joke about a peasant observing the Kremlin. It ends with "the son of a bitch will never get out of here." Isn't this line in our joke referring to the impostor from Akhmatova's poem still living in the Kremlin?

Now we see onto what ground our poor peasant stepped when he approached the Kremlin. Everything he names in the joke is loaded with Stalinist mythology: the Kremlin wall, the Kremlin guards, and inside Stalin himself. The pride of the passer-by, a Muscovite who shows the Kremlin to our peasant and completes his tour by alluding to Stalin, as well as the peasants' admiration of the Kremlin--all contribute to the positive image of the Kremlin in this joke. The last phrase, however, turns this idyllic world upside-down. The authors of this joke draw this picture to create a parody of this mythological image not by distorting its elements or its style but by setting this image in an opposing context, that of camp and prison. In this context, walls, guards and Stalin characterize the prisoner's world. Indeed one can imagine some sots art painting in which the ancient Kremlin shining with ruby stars would be surrounded by barbed wire, and Stalin's beautiful white attire would incorporate the elements of prison garb. Now, however, I have stepped into unfamiliar territory.

Notes

1   Evgenii Andreevich, comp. and ed., *Kreml' i narod: politicheskie anekdoty* (Munich: "Golos naroda," 1951), 52.

2   Chrisite Davis, *Jokes and their Relation to Society* (Berlin-New York: Mounton de Gruyter: 1999), 25.

3   Boris Briker, "Anti-Stalinist Humor of the 1930s: Life-Death Jokes" in *Politics of Russian Popular Culture = Przeglad Rusycystyczny* 120: 4 (2007): 33-44.

4   Arthur Koestler, *The Act of Creation, with a New Preface by the Au-*

thor (New York: MacMillan, 1969); Victor Raskin, *Semantic Mechanisms of Humor* (Dordrecht– Boston: D. Reidel, 1985).

5   *Antisovetskie anekdoty: bor'ba narodnoi propagandy s bol'shevistkoi* (Buenos Aires: 1946), 9; Iurii Muzychenko, *Kak pozhivaete? Anekdoty iz sovetskoi zhizni* (Plauen i. Vogtl: Izd. inostrannoi literatury, 1944), 6.

6   Ted Cohen, *Jokes. Philosophical Thoughts on Joking Matters* (Chicago and London: University of Chicago Press, 1999), 45.

7   Dora Shturman and Sergei Tiktin, *Sovetskii soiuz v zerkale politicheskogo anekdota* (Jerusalem: Ekspress, 1987), 301.

8   Andreevich, 21.

9   Eve Garrett Grady, *Seeing Red: Behind the Scenes in Russia Today* (New York: Brewer, Warren & Putnam, 1931), 15-16

10   *Antisovetskie anekdoty*, 53.

11   Ibid., 49.

12   Andreevich, 41.

13   The full text of this popular song of 1937 by V. Lebedev-Kumach is in Stalin. Liudi. Imperiia http://stalinism.ru/Stihi-i-pesni-o-Staline/Pesni-stalinskih-let.html.

14   Carter Ratcliff. *Komar and Melamid* (New York: Abbeville Press), 1989, 131.

15   Ann Appelbaum, *Gulag: A History* (New York: Doubleday, 2003), 187.

16   See a comment on and English translation of this line in Tomas Kempbell, "Trudnosti pereveoda stikhotvoreniia Iosifa Brodskogo 'Predstavlenie' s russkogo na anglijskii" in *Mitin zhurnal*, 1996, N53, 173.

17   Varlam Shalamov, *Kolyma Tales*, tr., John Glad (New York: W. W. Norton), 179-80.

18   *Antisovetskie anekdoty*, 19.

19   Oleg Lekmanov, "'Zvezdy smerti' v 'Rekviem' Anny Akhmatovoi," in *Literatura*, 2002, no. 5, 1.

20   See the text and analysis of different versions of this poem in Sonia L. Ketchian "Axmatova's Civic Poem 'Stansy' and Its Pushkinian Antecedent," in *Slavic and East European Journal*, 37, no. 2 (1993), 194-210.

5

Laughter's Weapon and Pandora's Box:
Boris Efimov in the Khrushchev Era

by Stephen M. Norris

> A man forgets what he wants to forget, but what is real stays
> with him until he dies.
>
> Ilya Ehrenburg, *The Thaw*[1]

This is a story about Soviet propaganda. It involves a cartoonist
named Boris Efimov (born in 1900) and his works drawn from 1918
to 1964. More specifically, it is a story about the continued importance of visualizing the enemy in Soviet culture. This part of the
story also concerns laughter, the healthy feeling a Soviet citizen enjoyed when he or she mocked their enemies.

This is also a story about remembrance, words, and autobiog-
raphies. It involves the very same cartoonist, who became a writer
around 1960. His writings told his story, that of Soviet propaganda,
but also his brother's story. This part of the story concerns death,
family trauma, and second lives, for his brother, Mikhail Kol'tsov,
was shot in 1940 during the purges.

Told episodically and disjointedly, this story is about the relationship between images and words in the Soviet Union after 1953.
It is therefore a story about working and living during the Khrushchev era. It is also a story that illustrates the extraordinary ways
Soviet citizens—even famous ones such as Boris Efimov—had to
play multiple, often paradoxical, roles. Efimov's story reveals these

paradoxes, the tensions between image and word, between propaganda and biography (or history), between living his public life and living his family life.[2] Efimov's Thaw experiences would remain with him, for he continued to produce cartoons and reminiscences right up until his death in 2008.

Laughter as a weapon

In the first 1962 issue of *Voprosy literatury*, the venerable Soviet cartoonist Boris Efimov published the following article, entitled "The Weapons of Laughter [*Oruzhie smekha*]."

> Who among us, the workers in literature and art, after the great forum that affirmed a program for our life in the next decades [the 22nd Party Congress], does not think about how our weapons—fiery words, sharp pens, brushes, and chisels—can take an active part in the education of people in communist consciousness, to help them quickly remove the power of bourgeois ideology, narrow-mindedness, individualism, and careerism?
>
> There is no greater happiness for the artist than the sensation of the authentic connection between his creation and the people's life. Happy is the artist who is capable of expressing the thoughts and expectations of the people not only through pronouncements and declarations, but also in artistic works created in hot pursuit of the events and occurrences in a society's life. This is why the greatest creative satisfaction and even pride is experienced when we—the workers of the satirical genre, a warlike genre--destroy and mercilessly expose all that is hostile to the people's interests.
>
> Of course, any ideological art is a weapon in which the artist fights for something or against something, defends or rejects some kind of principle. But the militant beginning and the fighting spirit is perhaps above all characteristic of the art of satire. The strength of this eternally living, disruptive genre is in the fact that it draws attention to itself, it appeals not only to a person's reason and aesthetic sense, but also to the humor most people feel. A well-aimed, ingenious satirical drawing can be as powerful and persuasive, as in-

telligible and popular, as some detailed, solid article, since it defines events concretely and because the situations in it are facts translated from the language of logical ideas into the language of visual modes.

The entire history of world caricature is filled with the romantic fight of unruly, free laughter and an ineradicable human wit against priests and princes, oppressors and obscurantists. Italian mockery is sharp as a stiletto, French witticisms are elegant, German satire is wicked, although every so often clumsy, the English caricature has a bulldog-like snap, and the well-aimed Russian *lubok* is mischievous--here, there, and everywhere, with differences in their national characteristics, fighting laughter delivered destruction on despotism and obscurantism, on hypocrisy, stupidity, and corruption.

The cradle of the Soviet political caricature was the Leninist *Pravda*. Specifically, through its initiative the satirical drawing took up the same integral and customary element in the newspaper as an editorial or feuilleton. Beginning in the 1920s, the caricature occupied in Soviet publications a place that had never been occupied in the West. Since that time satire was on the foremost front line of art in all the stages in the history of our state. From the great platform of the Soviet press the political caricature spoke with a firm voice and obtained an unprecedented internal and international resonance, and drew each reader nearer to it, entering into his abode, institution, and factory together with a newspaper sheet.

Soviet satire was brought up in the militant school of Bolshevik propaganda and continues the best traditions of revolutionary-democratic thought and the national-patriotic tendencies of Russian realist art.

Laughter is one of the strongest tools against everything that became obsolete yet is still held onto by some important wreck of a person, God knows why, which interferes with the beginning of fresh life. Laughter ... above all is no laughing matter," wrote Herzen. Saltykov-Shchedrin thought that satire is perhaps most effective and achieves its goal only when it vividly expresses the author's idea and he clearly indicates what its sting is directed against. Maksim Gorky declared that the caricature is "a socially significant and most useful art" and referred to the satirical art genre as one that "mercilessly reveals and unmasks everything that is hidden from the masses."

These high principles should now be widely upheld in our fight for the greatness and sincere beauty of mankind and for its harmonious evolution. Not the inoffensive, unassuming joke, but intelligent, caustic, wicked mockery—this is the soul of political satire and one of the most active and strongest means for our ideological fight. The traditions of worldwide satirical art not only did not lose their force, they acquired particular significance today in our aspirations to help formulate the most important moral principles in the people of a communist society.

Art's important mission is clearly indicated in the Program of the KPSS. It has a responsibility to reveal everything that prevents our society from moving forward. Perhaps this means above all through satirical art?

Through what means can works of the satirical genre be most effective? In this sense satire differs little from other art forms and genres in that the level of its skill determines the quality of the product. The artist's task is the tireless improvement of his skill, to search for, invent, and devise new satirical methods and metaphors, new, ingenious caricatures that will speak for themselves This is not easy. The satirical artist must strain his entire imagination in order to avoid repetition and to depict some sort of new caricature that hasn't already appeared many times. Such findings— namely, the bright sparkles of satirical talent and inspiration that accompany each genuine caricaturist--advance the art of political satire, which otherwise could be threatened with the danger of being trampled out.

Vladimir Mayakovsky said once that the first person who revealed that two times two is four was a brilliant mathematician and that everyone who very correctly and conscientiously used this calculation thereafter had made no new revelation.

We have, perhaps, enough caricaturists who persistent-
ly repeat in their work this satirical "two times two equals
four," but as someone correctly noted, art ought to be, unlike arithmetic, more than just algebra. This is why the creative, exacting origins of our satirical images must be sufficiently strong and full-blooded in order to overcome the
uninspired, imitative hack work and instead be the guaran-
tor of new success and progress in Soviet combative, public
satire.

Right now there are still dark intentions among the enemies of peace and socialism, but our forward march will
not be impeded in any way—to negative phenomena, vices,
and concrete bearers of evil, the hatred and contempt of the
Soviet people for everything rotten and harmful will find its
expression in the lashings given by satirical works.

In this epoch of the active building of communism it follows for us to be particularly careful and to improve this
sharp weapon, to ensure that it is impossible for it to be
dulled or to lose its destructive force. Our creations must
be filled with patriotic passion, ideological soundness, and
high artistic skill, a wealth of new forms and methods--with-
out these basic themes, their deep influence on the thoughts
and feelings of the people are unthinkable.[3]

Without having to state it explicitly, Efimov was just the man
for the renewed effort he advocated. After all, he had been perform-
ing the tasks he highlighted from the beginning of the Soviet experiment.

Efimov filled his article with the words of the era. Nikita Khrushchev had ended the 22nd Congress of the Communist Party just a
couple of months earlier. Khrushchev had prepared the congress as
a means to promote his new program that promised communism
would be achieved by 1980. To achieve this aim, Khrushchev asked
Party members to wage war against the enemies they all faced. The
Congress also adopted "The Moral Code of the Builder of Communism," a 12-step program that advocated--among other virtues-
-love for the socialist motherland and a moral purity among members. These steps are what Efimov evoked when he wrote about the

"epoch of the active building of communism" and the necessity of creating satire "with patriotic passion, ideological soundness, and high artistic skill, [and] a wealth of new forms and methods." Soviet propaganda, Efimov was arguing, could help the state reach the dream of communism.[4]

The invocation of the Leninist origins of Soviet satire also reflected the times. Efimov's "Two times two equals four" formula and his reference to the fighting spirit of visual satire that mercilessly mocked the enemy—the weapons of laughter—were his attempt to repackage his Stalin-era attempts to create a communist collective through visual means. In other words, Efimov's 1962 piece asked Soviet readers to continue to indulge in healthy laughter by mocking Soviet enemies, a trait that had long been highlighted as a typically "Soviet" feeling. The words he used evoked the 1962 Soviet Union in which Efimov lived, but the weapon of laughter had served the Soviet state since its foundation.

A special feeling of healthy humor: Boris Efimov and Soviet propaganda

Efimov's life up to 1953 reads as a near-perfect story of the Soviet experiment. Born Boris Fridliand in 1900 Kiev, his family moved to Bialystok shortly after his birth. When war was declared in 1914, the Fridliands moved away from the front: the parents back to Kiev, the eldest son Mikhail to study in Petrograd, and Boris to Kharkov to continue his secondary education. As a teenager, Boris became a self-taught artist. He fell in love with the Russian *lubok*, the Russian satirical cartoon of the early 20th Century, and the satirical cartoons published in the German journal *Simplicissimus*. Through his brother, Boris got his big break. Mikhail participated in a number of Petrograd protests and worked for *Solntse Rossii*. When the State Duma and its Chairman, Mikhail Rodzianko, supported the war aims of the regime and advocated taking the Straits of the Dardanelles, Mikhail asked his brother to draw a cartoon that mocked Rodzianko. It was published in late 1916.

Boris moved back to Kiev in late 1917 and spent the dramatic years of the Civil War based there. Because of the threat of anti-Semitic attacks, Boris changed his last name to Efimov. His brother changed his to Kol'tsov. Efimov's career as a Bolshevik propagan-

Boris Efimov and his older (and later executed) brother, Mikhail Kol'tsov. (From the author's archive).

dist began when he started publishing cartoons for Ukrainian-based publications in 1918. He began working for the Kiev Red Army press service the following year. His satirical posters and caricatures waged the visual Civil War for the Bolsheviks throughout the Ukrainian frontlines, mocking Denikin's forces and Petliura's nationalists. In 1922, Mikhail encouraged his younger brother to move with him to Moscow and to take part in the building of socialism. Boris accepted.[5]

In Moscow, Efimov embarked on one of the most remarkable careers in Soviet history. Soon after his arrival, he was appointed the permanent international affairs caricaturist for *Izvestiia*. He also helped to found the Soviet satirical journal *Krokodil* in 1922. The next year he began work for the new magazine launched by his brother, *Ogonek*. He would work for all three publications until 1991, drawing in his estimate around 35,000 caricatures.

In 1924, Efimov had his first collection of caricatures published by the *Izvestiia* publishing house. In the introduction, Leon Trotsky declared that "Boris Efimov is the most political of our cartoonists. He understands politics, he appreciates it, and penetrates its finer details. ... Efimov's success is remarkable when you consider that he is only at the start of his journey." Trotsky went on to wish Efimov continued success through "honest work and sharp self-criticism."[6]

Success certainly followed. By the 1930s, Efimov's satirical weapons were fired on all fronts. In particular, he warned against the growing threat posed by the Nazis. Efimov had mocked Hitler and his Party as early as 1924; by 1930, they became the primary subject in his satirical arsenal. When the Wehrmacht invaded in 1941, Efimov's cartoons mocking Hitler and his "Berlin gang of robbers" appeared daily. Eventually, both he and his images served as material witnesses at Nuremberg. By that time, because of his well-aimed weapons, Efimov had become a household name in the Soviet Union.

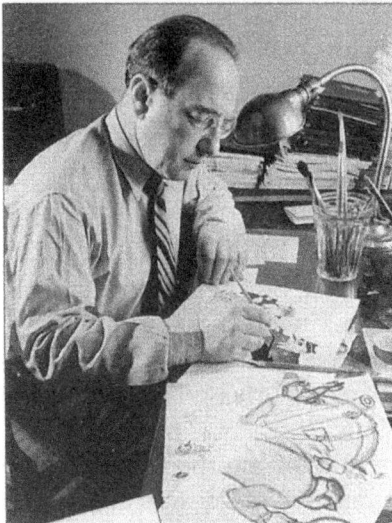

Boris Efimov at work.
(From the author's archive).

Efimov, in other words, literally created Soviet visual propaganda from beginning to end. More than anyone else, he drew what Richard Stites has characterized as the "good-vs.-evil, heaven and hell imagery" that characterized communist visual culture.[7] Efimov's life story also became intimately connected to the life of the Soviet Union itself. Over the course of his remarkable career his images were routinely singled out as the epitome of Soviet propaganda and its aims. Commentators hailed his work as the "satirical weapons" necessary to build communism. Efimov himself declared that "it is impossible to meet a person who is indifferent to a satirical drawing--to a caricature, to a cartoon, to a humorous figure. Whether it is printed in a newspaper or stuck to a stand, a caricature always attracts attention everywhere. It is possible to pay no heed to one note, article, or even photograph, but it is impossible not to notice a caricature."[8] Both the Soviet state and Soviet caricaturists knew that cartoons could mobilize society and in turn be used to create the New Soviet Man.[9] In the officially published analyses about Efimov's cartoons, Soviet writers again and again suggested that the "proper" response to looking at one of Efimov's caricatures was to laugh.[10] Doing so, as the words repeated time and again declared, made you a healthy Soviet citizen.

Two examples will have to suffice. In a 1935 collection of Efimov's work, E. Gnedin declared "The effect Efimov achieves is because of a special feeling of healthy humor, which, in our opinion, forms the distinguishing feature of his creative work. This is the humor of an optimist in the deep, philosophical sense of the word."[11] Efimov, as Gnedin clarified, poked fun at enemies for serious reasons. By exposing the foibles of the Soviet Union's foes through the weapons of irony and satire, Efimov created a sense that socialism would prevail. For Gnedin, Efimov's creative output harnessed satire and humor to the larger goal of building socialism.[12] In the 1952 collection of Efimov's work published by Iskusstvo, M. Ioffe wrote that "Soviet caricature is a strong weapon in our political fight and an efficient means in the ideological training of the masses." "The understanding of these tasks' importance," he concluded, "permeates the creations of our outstanding master of Soviet satire, Boris Efimov. They breathe anger and express contempt for the dark forces of reaction and oppression. They reflect the aspirations and feelings of the entire Soviet people and it is understandable why they are so close to the widest masses."[13]

Efimov's 1962 article that advocated a continuation of the caricature as a satirical weapon aimed at Soviet enemies articulated an old theme. It also provided a justification for Efimov to continue his ongoing life's work, exposing the enemy in visual form, and asking his viewers to join him in mocking them.

Over the course of 40 years, the official language about Efimov's work remained remarkably consistent. His 1962 article is notable only because Efimov himself adopted the language that had been employed so often to describe his work. The visual weapons needed to build communism in the Khrushchev era, Efimov implied, should contain both the spirit of Leninist propaganda and the patriotic culture of the Stalin period.[14] It should contain the "two times two equals four" formula he had developed.

Fighting spirit: An exhibit of Efimov's work

Let's look at some of Efimov's satirical weapons from the era published in *Izvestiia* and *Krokodil* and see how they mocked enemies. Perhaps we can introduce this exhibit with some of the words about Efimov published in the second edition (1950-1958) of the *Great Soviet Encyclopedia*, which declared Efimov to be "a master of political satire" and mentioned that he had not developed his skills in school, but through "working in Bolshevik publications." His talent, the entry declared, could be detected in "his sharp lashes delivered in his satire, which are directed against fascism, against reaction, and against warmongers; he enjoys enormous popularity in the Soviet Union and is widely known abroad."[15]

We could also employ Efimov's characterization of his work:

Cartoonists' images reflect reality, what is going on in the world, and what is going on in our country. Cartoons are a mirror to reality. In my caricatures and political drawings, I portrayed the West. Although the West is a very broad term, if you take it to mean everything outside our country, it seemed to us unfortunately for many years something of an enemy, something contradicting the order and values we had in our country. It is not because people wanted it to be that way, that we should be the opposite of the West. It just happened that way.[16]

"The European Madhouse," Efimov's 1923 cartoon, helped to put the artist on the map (Trotsky particularly liked it). On one edge of the cartoon Benito Mussolini declares "I am Italy." Dressed ridiculously in a Roman tunic and holding a *fasces*, Efimov simultaneously mocks the Italian dictator's political pretensions and his attempts to harness Roman symbols for his fascist system. On Mussolini's left, Efimov lampoons the French Prime Minister, Raymond Poincaré, as an imperialistic aggressor. With an Adrian helmet on his head, the French politician clutches the Versailles treaty and spouts nonsense (he had announced the occupation the Ruhr in January 1923). Next to Poincaré, Lord George Curzon, the British Foreign Minister, lumbers toward oil in the east. Below the British politician lurks Józef Pilsudski, the "First Marshal" of Poland and the victor in the 1919-21 war with the Bolshevik state. Recognizable because of his mustache, the Polish military man is depicted as a latter-day Napoleon, equally small and equally mad as the French Emperor. Other right-wing European leaders--Admiral Miklós Horthy stands behind Mussolini--and former tsarist officers who emigrated and therefore brought their form of "madness" to Europe surround these crazies (Fig. 1).

Сумасшедший дом «Европа».

Fig. 1: "The European Madhouse"

His 1930 "Crusade" continued his identification of enemies by denouncing Pope Pius XI's anti-communist proclamations. The Pope stands atop a cannon labeled "against the USSR." Behind the weapon lurk a British capitalist, a Nazi, and a Japanese imperialist (Fig. 2).

That same year, Efimov drew the following *Izvestiia* cartoon ("Seven Disasters—One Answer") that lined up the Soviet state's enemies who threatened the completion of the 5 Year Plan in 4 years (Fig. 3).

Efimov's 1930s satirical weapons aimed at the Nazis are best exemplified in his 1933 "The Cradle of German Fascism." The spirit of Wall Street helps British capitalists, French politicians, and Ruhr magnates nurse a young Hitler (Fig. 4).

Efimov visually linked fascism to capitalism again in his 1937 cartoon, "From the Heights of Non-Intervention." In it, the Wall Street capitalist lurks by the tree branch that contains British PM Neville Chamberlain and French PM Édouard Daladier. Below the beasts of German and Italian fascism run free (Fig. 5).

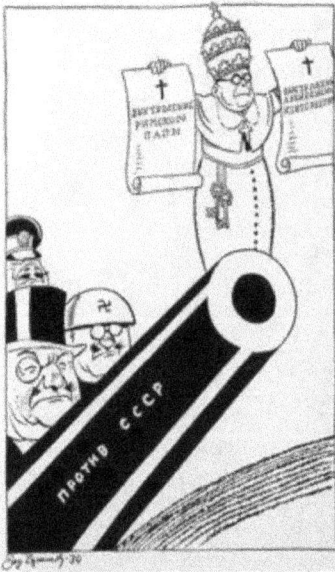

Fig. 2: "Crusade"   Fig. 3: "Seven Disasters—One Answer"

Fig. 4: "The Cradle of German Fascism"

Fig. 5: "From the Heights of Non-Intervention"

Fig. 6: "Berlin Gang of Robbers"

Fig. 7: "Second Front"

His wartime cartoons can be represented by two 1942 caricatures: "Berlin Gang of Robbers," which depicts the Nazi leadership as a group of thugs (Fig. 6), and "Second Front," which rails against Churchill and Eisenhower for failing to help their Soviet allies. Instead, the two leaders sew buttons on uniforms and listen to casualty reports from the Eastern Front (Fig. 7).

After the war, Efimov waged the new cold war by making use of his personal stockpile of satirical weapons. His 1946 "Percussion Concert of Anglo-American Blackmail" reminded viewers of the capitalist world's enmity for the Soviet state (Fig. 8). Churchill banged a bass drum in that image; he reflected Nazi war aims in Efimov's 1947 "A Performance in Fulton" (Fig. 9). Finally, his 1949

Fig. 8: "Percussion Concert of Anglo-American Black-mail"

Fig. 9: "A Performance in Fulton"

Fig. 10: "The American Trombone"

"The American Trombone" morphed Nazis into Americans (Fig. 10).

Efimov returned to these themes in his Khrushchev-era caricatures. One of the primary themes of Efimov's 1950s-60s work concerned the rearmament of West Germany, which was formally announced in 1955 with the formation of the Bundeswehr and West Germany's admission into NATO. His 1958 "Returning Ghosts" featured American President Dwight Eisenhower lifting a grave marked "Wehrmacht" and letting the rotted corpses of Nazis loose. Efimov wrote of American rearmament that "it's the same kind of business" as "the Hitlerite and fascist interventions in Spain, Munich, and Pearl Harbor." This time around, he argued, "American imperialism is dressing up German militarism again" and sending the "Wehrmacht" "against Soviet republics" again. He despaired over "the short memory of the inhabitants of the White House and the Pentagon" (Fig. 11).[17]

Fig. 11: "Returning Ghosts"

Fig. 12: "Familiar Language"   Fig. 13: "Bundeswehr Screen"

In the early to mid-1960s, Efimov portrayed the West German republic and its leaders as unreformed Nazis. Konrad Adenauer could be depicted as Hitler in the 1960 "Familiar Language." The Americans were rearming Nazis, not Germans, in his 1963 "Bundeswehr Screen," while the German "revanchist plan" could be mocked as Nazi-like in his 1964 "Bonn's Sitting Hen" (Fig. 12-13)."

Efimov's other dominant theme in his Khrushchev-era cartoons was the West's continued perfidy. Efimov sounded the warning about Vietnam, Cuba, and Cambodia just as he had warned about Western intervention in the 1920s and 1930s. He also railed against the U-2 incident, mocked President Eisenhower for playing golf after learning of it, and lambasted American leaders for what he called the "adventurism and rashness of the American bosses, who once again are flinging the world to the brink of war."[18] In Vietnam and Cambodia, Efimov would warn, "imperialism is not parting with its predatory schemes" and the Soviet people were once again guarding against it just as the Red Army had guarded the 5-year plan.[19]

The satirist depicted the formation of NATO in 1949 as an "Anti-Soviet cover in a 'defensive' sack" (Fig. 14) and the 1960 U-2 affair as a similar screen ("They Got into Trouble") (Fig. 15).

Fig. 14: "Anti-Soviet cover in a 'defensive' sack"

Fig. 15: "They Got into Trouble"

Fig. 16: "International Games"

Eisenhower—who had sewed buttons instead of opening second front in 1942—now played golf as his minions ravaged the Congo and Cuba and sold Polaris missiles to Nazis in Europe (Fig. 16).

American imperialism threatened Soviet borders and brother socialists. Evoking his mentor Dmitrii Moor's famous "Be on
Guard" poster from 1920 (which featured Trotsky guarding the Soviet borders), Efimov in 1961 noted that "Cuba Is On Guard" (Fig.
17). He also warned against American encroachment in Cambodia (1961's "The Greedy Paws of the 'Free World'") and Vietnam
(1964's "Burned Rear in Saigon") (Fig. 18).

Fig. 17: "Cuba Is On Guard"

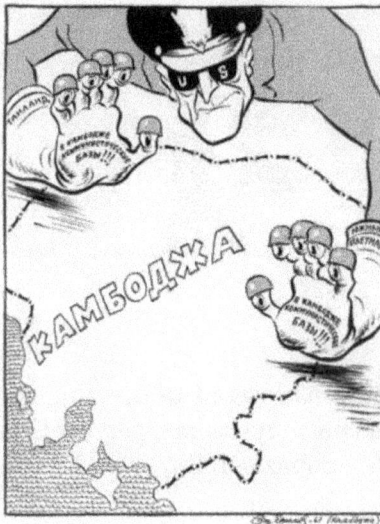

Fig. 18: "The Greedy Paws of the
'Free World'"

Efimov's work was displayed at the infamous December 1962 Manege exhibit. Soviet press reports singled out his cartoons as works drawn by a "great master." These images therefore met the criteria—spelled out by Khrushchev—that art must "reflect the life of the people, inspire people to the building of communism, and instill in man the finest and loftiest sentiments and a profound sense of the beautiful."[20] Khrushchev made it clear at the Manege exhibit that he was "waging war" against the artists who did not follow these aims.[21] Efimov helped Khrushchev in this fight.

Efimov's Thaw-era representations of the enemy evoked themes, symbols, and characterizations he had drawn since 1918. They acted as bearers of a specific form of social memory, namely, the way in which Soviet caricature had always drawn the enemies surrounding the fledgling state (and therefore Efimov's own "two times two is four" formula).[22] By the mid-1960s, Efimov drew images that explicitly reminded viewers of previous cartoons. His 1966 "Mad, Mad, Mad Free World" updated his 1923 "The European Madhouse" and replaced earlier crazies with cowboy Presidents, German revanchists, and KKK Apartheid leaders (the cartoon is also an interesting reference to Stanley Kramer's 1963 film *It's a Mad, Mad, Mad World*, which was screened in the USSR in 1966) (Fig. 19). The same year—the 25th anniversary of Hitler's invasion—

Fig. 19: "Mad, Mad, Mad Free World"

Безумный, безумный, безумный, свободный мир...

Efimov's "Picture About Memory" used a previous cartoon to warn American generals and German revanchists about their ambitions (Fig. 20). He also warned—on the 20th anniversary of Nuremberg—that current enemies of the Soviet state would be judged just as past enemies had (and included his 1946 cartoon "Nuremberg" in his 1966 "Reminder and Warning") (Fig. 21). Finally, his front-page *Izvestiia* cartoon for the 50th Anniversary of the Bolshevik Revolution, "International Review for the Half-Century," visualized the jubilee as a collection of all the enemies the Soviet state had defeated by wielding the weapon of satire. Efimov dated this caricature "1922-1967" (Fig. 22).

Картинка на память.

Слева воспроизводится рисунок, опубликованный в «Известиях» в 1941 году.

Fig. 20: "Picture about Memory"

Напоминание и предупреждение.

Fig. 21: "Reminder and Warning"

Fig. 22: "International Review
for the Half-Century"

Efimov's Thaw-era cartoons therefore suggest that defining the
enemy remained an important function of Soviet visual propaganda.[23] His familiar work served as an anchor in an era where uncertainty abounded. Khrushchev may have declared a war against the
term "enemies of the people," but they still threatened the Soviet
state in Efimov's visual formula.[24] In his 1962 article, Efimov fit his
work into the changing times, evoking Khrushchev's earlier call for
art to be "inseparably linked with the people's life" and to "arouse
the people to a struggle for new victories in the building of communism." The Soviet leader called for artists to "look at things soberly
and take cognizance of the fact that enemies exist, and that they are
trying to utilize the ideological front to weaken the forces of socialism. In such a situation our ideological weapons must be in good
order and must operate unfailingly."[25] Efimov, it's fair to say, had
always kept his satirical weapons sharpened.

Pandora's box: Efimov's life as a writer

The appearance of Efimov's 1962 article, however, also sheds light on his changing views of himself and his role. He began to conceptualize his life in the categories "work, remembrances, and encounters." Most importantly, he began to write, and with his words came a series of revelations.

Before 1961, Efimov had not published words other than the ones he used in his cartoons or short accounts about them. The process of de-Stalinization that in many ways began with Ilya Ehrenburg's 1954 novel *The Thaw* and that exploded after Khrushchev's 1956 Secret Speech provided openings for Efimov to express himself in a different medium.

His 1962 article appeared at a very verbose time in his life. The year before he published two books: *Forty Years: Notes of an Artist-Satirist* and *The Fundamentals of Understanding Caricature.*[26] The former represented the first time Efimov had written an autobiography (see below); the latter was a 70-page treatise on satire as a weapon ("satire ceases to be satire when it ceases to be a weapon," as Efimov phrased it). A year after his article Efimov published *Satire is Not Without Humor*, a short compendium of his images, and *Work, Reminiscences, Encounters*, a longer autobiographical account that builds on his 1961 book.[27] In 1963 he also authored *Stories about Artists-Satirists.*[28] In it, Efimov analyzes the lives and works of Dmitrii Moor, Viktor Deni, Mikhail Cheremnykh, Lev Brodaty, and Konstantin Rotov. All five successfully applied Efimov's formula in their satire and used their images as weapons to combat various enemies of the Soviet state. Efimov knew them all, and his encounters with these well-known artists form the basis of his evaluations of their work. In taking this approach, Efimov writes that he "attempted to outline their creative and human appearances." Their life and work together, Efimov concludes, reveals the special nature of Soviet satire and "the uniqueness of its nature and its forms."[29]

All of these works contained arguments about the special weapon that was Soviet visual satire. Before 1961, other writers and critics had written the words about Efimov and his work. Beginning in 1961, Efimov himself began to put pen to paper and contextualize his images and the special role of Soviet satire.

He also began to write and revise his own biography. Efimov

the writer reaffirmed the historical significance of Efimov the visual satirist. Yet Efimov also revealed a significant part of his life story. His 1963 book *Work, Reminiscences, Encounters* opened with an overview of his life and work through the Great Patriotic War. It is a familiar story to anyone who knew anything about Efimov (which essentially meant anyone who read the book). It is also a story of the Soviet experiment and its visual propaganda. Efimov concluded his first chapter, however, with the following words:

> Against the backdrop of these dramatic events on such a large scale [the Great Patriotic War], of course, the small and unimportant misfortunes and experiences of individual people [*otdel'nye liudi*] played out.
>
> For these individual people, however, it is necessary to say that these misfortunes were not easier, and I was convinced of this when it turned out that the year 1938 managed in eleven months to cause me numerous troubles and misfortunes before it quietly ended, but also extracted from its Pandora's box something that for me was personal: the early December morning, which never will leave my memory, and the phone call that brought me the information about my brother's end.
>
> There was no person closer to me. From the earliest years of childhood, from the first days of my conscious existence, I got used to seeing him next to me--merry, mischievous, inventive. I got used to receiving his patronage, kindness, concern. I got used to trusting his words, to following his advice, to laughing at his jokes, to being happy for his successes, to being enraptured by his talent, energy, and mind.
>
> And then I was suddenly, brutally, and irreparably deprived of him, my only brother, an elder brother-father.
>
> With unceasing pain I thought about his fate, and spent long, wearisome hours going through the motions, along with inexhaustible patience, spending days and weeks in order to wait for a few minute and, as a rule, hold an absolutely empty conversation with an ordinary person who occupied a place in an ordinary office. I wrote all the statements and requests possible, presented petitions, and sent telegrams.

One of these statements led me into a very spacious office, where a polite, small person with a well-trimmed moustache sat. On his smooth, pink face formed a smile, which in other circumstances you might call coquettish. He gave a sufficiently long time to me and, clearly acting his "ordinariness" and politeness, he controlled all of my attempts to learn anything about my brother with a complacent irony.

Smilingly guiding the conversation to general themes and talking a lot about the latest novelties in literature and art, he finally made me understand that my troubles were naive and senseless. And on parting he advised me "to work quietly and to forget quickly about this grave matter.

I thanked him for his consideration and took my leave.

Fifteen years later I was welcomed again into the very same spacious office. The amiable rosy-faced literature expert who advised me "to forget everything quickly" was no longer there. A grey-haired man wearing the gold shoulder-straps of a general entrusted me with a document about the rehabilitation of my brother. Unfortunately it was a posthumous one. We shook hands.

The Communist Party's will and wisdom restored Leninist principles to our life and boldly, severely condemned the violations of socialist legality. Patient and firm hands unraveled the piles of injustice and lawlessness; tore up and destroyed these slanderous cobwebs.

Dry, laconic, juridical terms: "for lack of committing a crime" ... sounded triumphant. They angrily stigmatized falsification and arbitrariness and gave back the good name to the ignoble, slandered Soviet people.

The Party not only restored the honest name [*chestnoe imia*] of my brother, it returned Mikhail Kol'tsov, whom the young generation knew nothing about, to Soviet literature. After an eighteen-year silence, he spoke to readers again through the passionate language in his publications, satiric feuilletons, and travelogues. Published in massive print runs, his works circulated within a very short amount of time. Written many years ago as energetic responses to the

events of the day, they remained alive, interesting, and stir-
ring. The creations of this journalist, feuilletonist, and pam-
phleteer withstood the test of time.

My brother's fate was, like so many others, tragic. A tireless war correspondent, an innate journalist, he was erased
from life and literature. A very active, public antifascist, he
was removed from the ranks of fighters against fascism. He
was absent from the decisive battle with Hitler, which he
sensed and for which he was entirely prepared. He was not
able to see the triumph of a just cause, for which he had
fought his entire life, not able to reach, and to tell about, the
liberation of Budapest and Belgrade, where he, risking his
life, had illegally entered during the prewar years in order
to describe to *Pravda*'s readers what was going on in the
countries chained by Fascist terror.

In *Pravda*, Aleksei Tolstoy and Aleksandr Fadeev called
his *Spanish Diary* the most magnificent, passionate, coura-
geous, and poetic book about the Spanish people's mortal
combat with fascism's beastly, terrible forces. I often think
about the perhaps even more staggering book Kol'tsov
would have written about the great fight of the Soviet people, who destroyed and blew to smithereens these beastly,
terrible forces.[30]

The "Pandora's Box" of "unceasing pain" that Efimov had
opened was a familiar one to many who lived in that era. Efimov's
words represented another "visible return" of a Stalinist victim and
therefore offered more "irrefutable evidence of a parallel history of
great crimes."[31] Like his friend Ilya Ehrenburg (the two had sat next
to each other at Bukharin's trial), Efimov had to live with clenched
teeth in the conspiracy of silence that characterized the Stalin era.[32]
Beginning in 1961, however, Efimov's accounts of his brother took
part in the multiple ways that Soviet citizens began to reappraise
the recent past. Efimov worked hard to have his brother rehabili-
tated. As he recounted in the pages of his autobiography, his brother's "honor" had been upheld by the Party. Kol'tsov's rehabilitation
also meant that truth and justice had prevailed. In short, Efimov's
writing helped to define the concepts of de-Stalinization.[33] The nar-

rative about Stalinist victims encouraged by the Soviet leadership stressed moral rectitude and heroism; victims of repression could therefore see their suffering as part of the new push to achieve communism.[34] Efimov provided this narrative for his brother. His brother's rebirth, however, also forced Efimov to begin to ask questions about his own guilt, questions that tormented him until he died.[35]

Efimov begins the next chapter of his 1963 work with the words: "I could conditionally divide my forty years of work in political satire into two periods: from 1919 to 1938 and from 1940 to 1960. In between these two twenty year periods for me stands the gloomy, unhappy memory of 1939—the unexpected and abrupt break in my work as a political caricaturist."[36] Because his brother had been arrested as an enemy of the people, Efimov was fired from his various jobs. He awaited arrest but continued to draw. In 1940, he managed to publish a few posters and cartoons under the name "V. Borisov." Then came the war, and with it the need for "the weapons of satire," "satirical weapons," and "the weapons of laughter."[37] Efimov was needed again. He started his second life as a cartoonist.

In writing about his experiences,[38] Efimov also began to conceptualize his life in two ways. First, he defined himself as a Soviet artist who helped to build communism by connecting his work with the Soviet public's desire to laugh. He had served the state and its people, as he stressed in his Thaw-era writings, not Stalin. His autobiography therefore fits into the "paradigmatic Russian story: the story of a man forged by history."[39] Second, Efimov began to believe that he had lived a life for his absent brother. Efimov's story about his brother and what he would have done had he lived served as the genesis of Efimov's second life. The triumphs and tragedies Efimov recounts in words about the wartime work he did in pictures becomes the staggering account not written by his dead brother. He also published accounts about his brother in surprising arenas, including a 1969 Tamizdat work that appeared with the London-based Flegon Press.[40]

In his autobiographical writings from the era, Efimov claims that his work is still needed. "The weapons of satire," he concludes in his 1963 work, "are turned against the organizations and provocateurs of the new—cold—war." If the war became hot, he warned, the artist-satirist was ready to use his art to "fight for the people in the struggle for the preservation and consolidation of peace."[41] He would also take part in this struggle on behalf of his brother.

The Thaw in life and work

Efimov's life after 1953 perfectly encapsulates the Khrushchev era. His work and his writings allow us to see not one continuous un-freezing, but thaws and freezes, ice floes and melted snow mixed together. He reaffirmed the style of work that made him famous in the Stalin years and packaged it as a return to the Leninist carica-ture that also waged the new fight against communism's enemies. Efimov's visual and textual responses to the Thaw reveal a con-tradictory yet logical pattern of dealing with de-Stalinization in multiple ways.[42] Efimov the artist reaffirmed the significance of his life's work, waging visual war on Soviet enemies. At the same time, Efimov the artist also became Efimov the writer in the early 1960s. On the page, he wrestled with his brother's death and with it his own complicity in building the Stalinist system that cost his brother his life. And while he continued to draw anti-Western cartoons, Efi-mov published a book about his brother in the West.

Efimov's life and work during the Thaw suggest that the cul-tural codes of the period could be both visual and textual.[43] His work expressed the metaphor of conflict that defined the cultural process of the Thaw. Khrushchev called on the media and on art to serve as an ideological weapon in the continued battle against enemies.[44] No one did this better than Boris Efimov, who employed the sharp weapon of laughter that he had formulated after 1917. Efimov's Thaw, as his 1962 article articulated, provided a chance to reaffirm the significance of his public work and redefine it as part of the renewed attempt to achieve communism. In this sense, primar-ily visual, Efimov's Thaw was an optimistic one.[45]

Efimov's Thaw was also an uncertain one. His quest to restore his brother's honor and to live a second life for Kol'tsov was a deeply personal one. The Thaw started him on another path, one where he began to recount, contextualize, and reflect on his life, his brother's life, and the life of the state he served. Efimov returned to the themes he wrote about in the 1960s again in the late 1990s and early 2000s (he remained remarkably active right up until his death on 1 October 2008, frequently appearing on television and granting interviews to various journalists). In 2005, Efimov would write that the Thaw brought "considerable changes to the country" but also "to me personally." Aleksei Adzhubei, Khrushchev's son-in-law, became the editor of *Izvestiia* and brought with him an honesty and desire to publish new things, including reminiscences about Mikhail Kol'tsov.[46] These changes, ones that led the cartoonist to write about his life and his brother's death, to develop his "second life," also tell us a great deal about the Soviet experiment. By 1960, Efimov had successfully embraced disparate identities and integrated them into a single narrative of the self.[47]

Two months before he died, Efimov declared that his life had been dominated by the force of his brother, his brother's personality, and his brother's spirit. He kept a portrait of his brother on the wall of his room as a reminder of his second life and what had happened to him since 1940. He also declared that he and his fellow satirical artists had helped to create something that people believed in. They had helped to make people laugh.[48]

Near his death, Efimov, in other words, was still living with the ways that the Thaw reshaped his life and with what he found inside the Pandora's Box he had opened.

Stephen M. Norris and Boris Efimov, 16 July 2008. (From the author's archive).

Notes

1   Ilya Ehrenburg, *The Thaw*, trans. Manya Harari (Chicago: Henry Regnery Company, 1955), 198.

2   I thank Kevin M. F. Platt for his helpful suggestions to this article and to this argument.

3   Boris Efimov, "Oruzhie smekha" *Voprosy literatury*, no. 1 (1962): 22.

4   For the context of the Congress, see William Taubman, *Khrushchev: The Man and His Era* (New York: Norton), 507-28.

5   The two therefore took part in what Yuri Slezkine has called "one of the most important, and least noticed, landmarks in the history of Russia, European Jews, and the Modern Age"; namely, the migration of Russian Jews to the center of Soviet power. Yuri Slezkine, *The Jewish Century* (Princeton: Princeton University Press, 2004), 216-17.

6   *Bor. Efimov: karikatury* (Moscow, 1924), vii, viii.

7   Richard Stites, "Heaven and Hell: Soviet Propaganda Constructs the World" in David Goldfrank, ed., *Passion and Perception: Essays on Russian Culture by Richard Stites* (Washington: New Academia Publishing, 2010): 347-65.

8   *Bor. Efimov v "Izvestiiakh". Karikatury za polveka* (Moscow: "Izvestiia," 1969), 223.

9   Caricatures therefore served as an important battlefield for "reshaping the language, culture, and thinking processes of 'the masses' and turning them into politically conscious citizens of the new Soviet state," much like Matthew Leone has argued about the press. Matthew Leone, *Closer to the Masses: Stalinist Culture, Social Revolution, and Soviet Newspapers* (Cambridge, MA: Harvard University Press, 2004), 2. Jeffrey Brooks argues that the Bolshevik monopolization of media served as the primary means to create a public, ritualized political culture: *Thank You, Comrade Stalin! Soviet Public Culture from the Revolution to the Cold War* (Princeton: Princeton University Press, 2000).

10   "A good, healthy humor" could be added to the list of Stalinist values analyzed by David Hoffmann: *Stalinist Values: The Cultural Norms of Soviet Modernity, 1917-1941* (Ithaca: Cornell University Press, 2003).

11   E. Gnedin, "Boris Efimov" in Boris Efimov, *Politicheskie karikatury, 1924-1934* (Moscow: Sovetskii pisatel', 1935), 6.

12   Ibid.

13   M. Ioffe, "Boris Efimovich Efimov" in *Boris Efimov* (Moscow: Iskusstva, 1952), 3.

14   For more on the Bolshevik poster and functions, see Stephen White, *The Bolshevik Poster* (New Haven: Yale University Press, 1988) and Victoria Bonnell, *Iconography of Power: Soviet Political Posters Under Lenin*

and Stalin (Berkeley: University of California Press, 1997). On the turn toward a Russo-centric patriotism under Stalin, see David Brandenberger, *National Bolshevism: Stalinist Mass Culture and the Formation of Modern Russian National Identity, 1931-1956* (Cambridge, MA: Harvard University Press, 2002); and Kevin M. F. Platt and David Brandenberger, eds., *Epic Revisionism: Russian History and Literature as Stalinist Propaganda* (Madison: University of Wisconsin Press, 2006).

15   *Bol'shaia Sovetskaia Entsiklopediia*, Vtoroe izdanie, 15: 566.

16   "Interview with Boris Efimov" for PBS series *Red Files* (1999): http://www.pbs.org/redfiles/prop/deep/interv/p_int_boris_efimov.htm. Efimov did occasionally draw cartoons of domestic situations and problems (many of them are reproduced in his 1963 collection *Satira ne bez iumora*). The vast majority of his cartoons, however, consisted of international issues and therefore of visualizing the enemy.

17   *Bor. Efimov v "Izvestiikah"*, 174.

18   Ibid., 182.

19   Ibid., 192.

20   The words reported the day after Khrushchev's visit to the Manage exhibit in the Soviet press: see *Current Digest of the Soviet Press* 14, No, 48 (1962), 20.

21   See Susan Reid, "In the Name of the People: The Manege Affair Revisited" *Kritika*, 6, no. 4 (Fall 2005): 673-716.

22   Here I am inspired by Alon Confino's call for historians to adapt Aby Warburg's writings on images as bearers of social memory. See Alon Confino, "Collective Memory and Cultural History: Problems of Method," *AHR*, December 1997, 1390-91.

23   The same was true in cinema, where Julian Graffy has detected "Scant signs of a thaw" because "the foreign remains a source of contagion (43)" in numerous films from the era. "Scant Signs of the Thaw" in Stephen Hutchings, ed., *Russia and Its Other(s) on Film: Screening Intercultural Dialogue* (Basingstoke: Palgrave Macmillan, 2008): 27-46.

24   Both Susan Buck-Morss and Miriam Dobson argue that the Khrushchev era witnessed "the start of a fundamental reevaluation of the status of the enemy." See Dobson, *Khrushchev's Cold Summer: Gulag Returnees, Crime, and the Fate of Soviet Reform after Stalin* (Ithaca: Cornell University Press, 2009), 3; also Buck-Morss, *Dreamworld and Catastrophe: The Passing of Mass Utopia in East and West* (Cambridge, MA: MIT Press, 2000). Domestically, as Efimov's work helps to illustrate, the "enemy of the people" concept declined, but internationally, enemies abounded.

25   *Current Digest of the Soviet Press*, 9/35 (9 October 1957).

26   Boris Efimov, *Sorok let: zapiski khudozhnika-satirka* (Moscow: Sovetskii khudozhnik, 1961); idem., Efimov, *Osnovy ponimaniia karikatury* (Moscow: Iz-vo Akademii khudozhestv SSSR, 1961).

27   Boris Efimov, *Satira ne bez iumora* (Moscow: Izdanie Krokodila, 1963); idem., *Rabota, vospominaniia, vstrechi* (Moscow: Sovetskii khudozhnik, 1963).

28   Boris Efimov, *Rasskazy o khudozhnikakh-satirkakh* (Moscow: Sovetskii khudozhnik, 1964).

29   Ibid., 64.

30   Efimov, *Rabota, vospominaniia, vstrechi*, 10-12.

31   Stephen F. Cohen, "Stalin's Victims Return," *The Nation* 15 September 2008: http://www.thenation.com/doc/20080915/cohen.

32   Ehrenburg used this concept in his 1960 memoir, *People, Years, Life* [*Liudi, gody, zhizn'*]. It was only in 1954, during the meetings described above, that Efimov confirmed that his brother had been shot after 14 months of interrogations and not sent to the camps. In the early 1990s, Efimov discovered that his name was also on the arrest warrant sent for Kol'tsov. In the margins of the document, Stalin had written "don't touch" next to Efimov's name.

33   See Dobson, *Khrushchev's Cold Summer*, 81.

34   Ibid., 200-207.

35   Efimov lived his last years at his grandson's dacha outside Moscow. In the room he occupied, he hung a portrait of Kol'tsov across from his favorite chair. When asked about it, he claimed that he wanted to be constantly reminded of his brother's fate. Author's interview with Boris Efimov, 16 July 2008.

36   Efimov, *Rabota, vospominaniia, vstrechi*, 13.

37   Ibid., 13-16.

38   Efimov first began to insert his brother's tale in his life story in his 1961 autobiographical overview of his work, *Sorok let*. In it, he begins by sketching out an overview of his work and historic role of satire in general and Soviet satire in particular. In Chapter Two, Efimov introduces Mikhail as the most significant figure in his life story, including a 1908 photograph of the two of them. The next several chapters recount his early work alongside his brother and famous poster artists such as Deni and Moor and his move to Moscow. On page 203 (chapter 13, the last), Efimov writes about the morning of December 12, 1938, when he learned of his brother's arrest. He does not describe the following year or his brother's rehabilitation in detail—the book ends on the next page.

39   Irina Paperno, *Stories of the Soviet Experience: Memoirs, Diaries, Dreams* (Ithaca: Cornell University Press, 2009), 11

40   Efimov referred to his "second life" in this fashion. Interview with Boris Efimov, 16 July 2008. He would also continue to write about his brother and investigate his fate (he learned that Kol'tsov had not died in a camp in 1942, as he originally was told, but had been shot in Lefortovo

Prison in 1940). See Efimov's *Zhertva kul'ta lichnosti* (London: Flegon Press, 1969) and his *Mikhail Kol'tsov, kakim on byl: sbornik vospominanii* (Moscow: Sov. Pisatel', 1989). The two publications reflect the changing circumstances of investigating Stalinist repressions: the first was published with the famous London samizdat press, the second as a result of Gorbachev's glasnost policies and with them, the return to historical accounts about the Stalin era.

41   Efimov, *Rabota, vospominaniia, vstrechi*, 193.

42   Here I am influenced by Stephen V. Bittner's work *The Many Lives of Khrushchev's Thaw: Experience and Memory in Moscow's Arbat* (Ithaca: Cornell University Press, 2008); and Vladislav Zubok's discussion of the more illberal paths the Thaw took in his *Zhivago's Children: The Last Russian Intelligentsia* (Cambridge, MA: Harvard University Press, 2009).

43   Nancy Condee has argued that the Thaw was mostly a logocentric one, for literature replaced cinema as the most important of the arts and therefore became the primary site of conflict. See her "Cultural Codes of the Thaw" in William Taubman, Sergei Khrushchev, and Abbott Gleason, eds., *Nikita Khrushchev* (New Haven: Yale University Press, 2000), 161.

44   Ibid., 173.

45   Dobson describes the Thaw as "forward-looking, ambitious, and full of hope on the one hand, but disorienting and potentially unsettling on the other" in *Khrushchev's Cold Summer*, 15.

46   Boris Efimov, *Moi vstrechi* (Moscow: Vagrius, 2005), 13-15.

47   I borrow this notion from Martin Sokefeld, "Debating Self, Identity, and Culture in Anthropology," *Current Anthropology*, 40, no. 4 (1999), 422-24. Sokefeld argues that managing difference is an important aspect of the self. Efimov's versions of his life clearly fit into the growing literature on Soviet subjectivity. At the same time, his long life and his constant reinvention of his self defies easy characterization. He spoke (and drew) Bolshevik (as Stephen Kotkin has famously argued), worked on his communist soul (Igal Halfin's and Jochen Hellbeck's works explore this aspect of selfhood in the Soviet system), wore various masks (Sheila Fitzpatrick has written about this subject), internalized trauma and was shaped by fear/repression (Alexander Etkind's work), was shaped by power rather than repressed by it (Eric Naiman and Christina Kaier have recently co-edited a volume dedicated to this), and constructed an illiberal self (Anna Krylova's influential *Kritika* article). He fits all the models and suggests more: he seemed to *know* he was playing a game and had multiple selves. Perhaps this contradiction tells us all we need to know.

48   Interview with Boris Efimov, 16 July 2008.

6

Fiction in the Service of History: A Tale of How *Brief Encounters* Ended Up on the Shelf

by Anna Lawton

Prologue

"What? *Cossaks of Kuban* was banned! And *Eugene Onegin*, and *Loyal Friends!*" Even the members of the Goskino Collegium were astonished at these findings when the Conflict Commission, in 1986, undertook the process of rehabilitating the films that had been kept "on the shelf" for decades.[1] Many in the inner circle wondered about the reasons for condemning those films—and not only those. The films under review turned out to be about two-hundred. They were a mixed bag of different genres and different topics, from art films to mainstream comedies. It was obvious that they could not have been judged by a set of fixed criteria.[2]

The Conflict Commission reviewed films from all periods, but focused primarily on the films produced in the decade 1964-1974, a period of "re-Stalinization" that witnessed a severe wave of artistic repression. A team, headed by Valeri Fomin, was established to conduct an in-depth research of all the cinema archives as soon as they were opened to the public. As a result, the team issued a report which is remarkable for the wealth of information it unveiled. On the other hand, it has been criticized for taking an extreme anti-Soviet position, and presenting censorship as a rigid power structure and the filmmakers as powerless victims.[3]

The criticism is well taken because, in reality, censorship was a complex organism rather than a monolith. Like all other aspects of the cinema industry, it reflected current government policies and, by extension, the cultural atmosphere they engendered.

In the Brezhnev era, the mechanisms of censorship would be best analyzed as an object of social history. Particularly revealing is the relationship between the intelligentsia and the powers that be, a measured Kabuki dance regulated by unwritten rules, which everyone at all levels and from all sides (with few exceptions) was willing to perform in order to attain a goal, serve one's own interests, or simply protect himself/herself. Behind that formal scene, censorship was applied as a network of ambiguous connections.

First and foremost, there was self-censorship. The doctrine of Socialist Realism, established in 1935, was still in force and screenwriters and directors were mindful of the consequences for crossing the line. It was, therefore, common practice to submit a script that was apparently conforming to the rules, only to change the thrust of the story during the filming process. Visual images communicate differently from the written text, and the filmmakers used the power of the camera to create the so-called Aesopian language, suggestive of hidden meanings. At times, they were able to circumvent the system. At times, they were not. A great deal depended on their personal relation with the authorities.

Goskino exercised its patronage and control functions at the ministerial level. There was a chain of command that went from the studios up to the minister's office and beyond, reaching the *sancta sanctorum* of the Central Committee and the Politburo. On the side, there were other watchdogs, such as the KGB (under cover) and the Ministry of Defense for topics touching on war.

But "censorship" was not a term in use. The supervision of film production was entrusted to the "editorial department." Therefore, the various stages, from submission of the script to the release of the film, were rather fluid. Judgment was subjective, and finally rested with whoever had the greater decision-making power. A peremptory telephone call to the head of Goskino, coming from the higher spheres, could reverse a decision instantaneously. And, more often than not, the editors and the administrators aimed at satisfying the popular demand, which reflected the rather prudish and conservative taste of millions of viewers. The "movies for the millions" were a considerable source of revenue for the state treasury.[4]

It was a common practice of the Central Committee members and the Goskino bosses not to leave any track record. They preferred to use oral communication in order to keep the process fluid and unpredictable—and safe for themselves. Another stratagem was to avoid branding a film with an official ban. Official banning was a rare occurrence because it reflected badly on the whole system. Goskino usually released the condemned film with a low classification grade, so that only a few prints were produced and never distributed. Consequently, the film in question would not be officially banned, but simply buried.

An interview with Gleb Panfilov about his film *The Theme* (1979/rel. 1986) is revealing. Asked who blocked the film, Panfilov said:

> No one said 'no,' but no one said 'yes,' so *The Theme* sat around for seven years. Someone will say that of course the film is worthy of attention, that he supports it, but by himself he can't do anything. If only... and on and on." The reason for changing the decision and finally releasing the film is equally perplexing: "Who said 'yes'? Yegor Ligachev [of the Politburo]. At a Conference of Cultural Workers. I wasn't there myself, but I was told about it right away. He said 'we are ready to release *The Theme*. It was shelved—for reasons that are understandable. We don't like the film, but we'll release it.' And that was it. He said he didn't really like it but that he'd release it.[5]

And then, there was the so-called *dachnyi prosmotr* (dacha screening), where members of the Politburo had a film delivered to their dachas for the weekend, prior to its release. There, they would invite an audience of wives, children, grandmothers, domestics, and family friends to have the film judged by "the people." These screenings were a nightmare for the progressive filmmakers, because many films displaying social criticism or formalistic features ended up on the shelf as a result.

Screenwriter Natalia Riazantseva, who wrote the script for Muratova's *Long Farewells* (*Dolgie provody*, 1971), said in an interview:

"In those days, they would take the films to the dachas, and they with the members of their circle watched the films before everybody else. And if the audience started bashing the film, that was the end of it. The film had to be to the taste of the Party ladies... But their taste was absolutely primitive."

Aleksei Guerman, another controversial director of that period, whose films *Trial on the Road* (*Proverka na dorogakh*, 1971) and *My Friend Ivan Lapshin* (*Moi drug Ivan Lapshin*, 1983) were also placed on the shelf, had this to say about the comedic behavior of the "censors":

> All of them [the Politburo members] tried to intervene one way or another, they took the films to their dachas every Saturday... And if they did not agree with a given film, they would call Ermash [head of Goskino] upon their return to Moscow: 'This film is dangerous, forbid it!' At the same time, another Politburo member might call and say, 'It's a good movie, release it!'... Ermash had been the assistant to Kirilenko, a member of the Politburo. Therefore, in a situation like this, he would rush to see Kirilenko, who was very close to Suslov and also very influential as a member of the Politburo. When Kirilenko died, Ermash hired Chernenko's son as his assistant. This guy liked to drink and very rarely showed up at work. But he was a good fellow. Their offices were next to each other, the doors half open. Therefore, everybody knew that there was no point arguing because Ermash would go see Chernenko's son, who in turn would tell everything to papa. This was all very complex indeed. Nevertheless, no matter how flawed, the system worked, and even issued some good movies occasionally.[6]

A "dacha screening"

Boris Borisovich, a prominent film critic and a contributor to *Iskusstvo kino*, as well as popular movie magazines, was invited to one of those showings in 1967, when the film *Brief Encounters* (*Korotkie vstrechi*) by Kira Muratova was under scrutiny. Ivan Ivanovich, special assistant for cultural affairs to the Politburo member who hosted the event, had invited him to make sure the press would review the film with the correct spin. Being himself

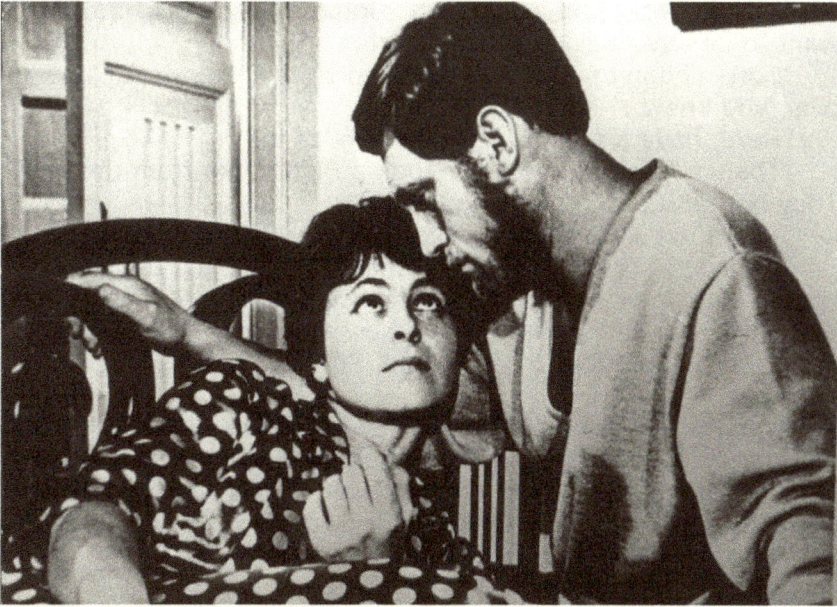

Brief Encounters, 1967. Kira Muratova and Vladimir Vysotsky. Courtesy of *Soviet Screen.*

an educated fellow, Ivan Ivanovich was also curious about the opinion of a "progressive" critic. And, furthermore, the information could come in handy if the security organs ever needed additional material for the critic's file.

Boris Borisovich's juicy vignette of that *prosmotr,* in which he refers to himself in the third person, was found only some twenty years later, after his death, among the papers he never published. It is reported here for the first time.[7]

* * *

Boris Borisovich saw the ZIL limousine parked in front of Ivan Ivanovich's stately apartment building as he turned the corner from the metro station. Ivan Ivanovich was already in the back seat. Boris Borisovich walked faster not to make him wait. It was a clear, cold day. Condensed breath crystals made his beard and mustache sparkle in the sun.

A funny effect, thought Ivan Ivanovich watching him approach. The driver opened the door.

"Hurry, Boris Borisovich. It's already 12 o'clock. We don't want to be late," said Ivan Ivanovich.

"Sorry. I don't feel so well this morning. I overslept. A hangover, you know..."

"Here, have a smoke. It'll take care of it."

"Thanks." Boris Borisovich took a Belomorka from the pack. They both lit up.

"Vasya, let's go. To Sosnovka!" ordered Ivan Ivanovich.

"I know, I know..." the driver answered with the annoyed but resigned tone of someone who knows his job, has performed that task already a hundred times and does not need any fff...urther instructions from no one. So there!

The car left the city behind and entered the highway cutting straight through thick woods dormant under a white lace blanket. It was an easy ride. The car was rolling smoothly on the perfectly plowed road leading to the secluded compound where high Party officials had their dachas.

"Boris Borisovich, you may have heard about this film," started Ivan Ivanovich to test the ground. "There's been some controversy surrounding it from the very beginning. Then, one way or another, it made it all the way through production. But this is the crucial stage: to release it or not to release it."

"Yah, this is the question," mumbled Boris Borisovich under his beard that by now had thawed.

"You know, better than I," continued Ivan Ivanovich, "that many filmmakers, and even some Goskino editors, are concerned with aesthetics rather than content. For the sake of artistic form, they are ready to sacrifice our fundamental values and dangerously deviate from the golden rules of Socialist Realism. Others look at reality through a critical lens and focus on shortcomings rather than exemplary features."

Ivan Ivanovich paused. He realized that his little speech had begun to slip into talking-points mode. But it was too late to change course and he went on.

"We, the Party, have a responsibility before the people. The people look up to us for guidance. And we must fulfill our duty and be vigilant that our screens would display only films that are optimistic, uplifting, featuring a positive hero, celebrating the motherland, the Soviet system, and the struggle toward a common goal, which is to build a better future for all."

Boris Borisovich put out his *papirosa* in the overflowing ashtray and lay back on the cushioned seat. "I'm not a Party member, you know?" he said.

"I know. But every citizen has a duty to work for the common good."

"I agree. I do that by writing according to my conscience."

"Of course, of course... You're an influential voice. The readers like your pieces. I myself am really interested in your opinion on *Brief Encounters.* And also on the director, that young woman, Kira Muratova, half-Russian half-Romanian... Rumors have it that she's a difficult personality, very intractable. What do you know about it?"

"I know what I heard from colleagues, here and in Odessa. This is her first solo film as a director, after she made two previous ones together with her husband.[8] In *Brief Encounters* she also plays the lead role. This film was produced at Odessa Studio, and apparently she had some trouble getting the script approved by Goskino/Ukraine. But her former teacher, Sergei Gerasimov, put his weight behind it. Some objections were raised at every stage throughout production and post-production, and then there were the inevitable clashes of personality. As you said, she's difficult. She has a reputation for being arrogant, uncompromising, self-centered... But then, one can say that of most artists. She is extremely talented."

"She also wrote the script, correct? This makes her an *auteur*, I guess. An attribution that critics like you admire. We don't. It's an individualistic attitude, a way of placing one's own signature on the work and say, that's mine."

"Well, the script is based on a short story by Leonid Zhukhovitsky, and he is listed in the credits. But I don't know how much he actually contributed to the script."[9]

"Ah yes, the short story... *The House in the Steppe*. It came out in 1959, right? A typical product of a time you're so fond of. But, you know, what was acceptable then is no longer acceptable now."

"Like what?"

"Like, for example, the latent eroticism of those 'brief encounters.' Some scenes in the film are too intimate, too sensual."

"And what else?"

"What else... You tell me, after the screening."[10]

The car turned onto a country road and proceeded for a mile in the thicket of the woods. It stopped at a gate in a brick-and-iron palisade guarded by two militiamen. They recognized Ivan

Ivanovich but wanted to see his special pass all the same before letting them in.

The dacha was a two-floor stucco house with a large porch and two columns, in the style of a nineteenth-century country estate mansion.

When Boris Borisovich entered the auditorium he was struck by the look of the room and the quality of the equipment. He expected to find adequate facilities, yes, but this was a veritable theater, with the extravagant décor of a vintage movie hall and a projection booth big enough to accommodate a massive 35mm projector.

The guests had already arrived. They were waiting for the host, browsing and looking at the blown-up photos on the wall featuring the most cherished, and reliable, Soviet movie stars.

Boris Borisovich did not recognize anyone in the hall. There were no colleagues of his, no acquaintances from Goskino, no people from the studios.

"This is not your usual gathering," said Ivan Ivanovich, who noticed his puzzled look. "The guests are family members and close friends. Even house personnel—the cook, the gardener, the chauffeur. Not an intellectual circle, by far. See that lady? She's our host's mother."

Boris Borisovich took mental notes: *short, plump, permed henna-dyed hair, a provincial type.*

"The man she's talking to is her brother. Once he was a prominent Party leader of the Voronezh Oblast, now retired."

Boris Borisovich: *I was right, provincial folks... from the Stalinist cadres.*

"The two boys and the girl romping in the aisle are our host's grandchildren."

Boris Borisovich: *age 8 to 12, spoiled brats.*

"The young couple with the baby, over there. She's our host's daughter."

Boris Borisovich: *a sweet, lovely housewife; the husband, an "apparatchik" on his way up.*

"The older woman who's now taking the baby from her hands is the *nyanya* from our host's hometown. She's been with the family for two generations."

Boris Borisovich: *just like my nyanya—headscarf, 'valenki,' and all... dear Marusya, I still miss you, at my age.*

"The other young people in the group are friends of the couple."

Boris Borisovich: *high-rank 'komsomoltsy,' young profes-sionals, junior faculty of the Party school; that one is strange... humm...*

"Who's the guy in blue jeans with longish hair?" asked Boris Borisovich.

"He's our host's younger son. An embarrassment for the family. His main interest is western music, The Beatles, you know. Were he not my boss' son, I'd say he's a *khuligan.*"

At that moment, the host and his wife entered the room.

Boris Borisovich: *stocky, ruddy cheeks, thick grey hair, push-ing sixty, a pompous ass; the wife, round all over, a pretty face, heavy make-up, a white fur headband that makes her look like an aging 'Snegurochka,' pushing fifty.*

All were seated and the show began.

On the surface the story is simple enough. Valentina is a con-scientious white-collar worker in charge of the regional housing office in Odessa, and a Party executive. Maxim, her lover, is a geologist devoted to an itinerant and adventurous life. He is also a guitar player, which adds to his romantic flair. Their episodic encounters and lengthy separations bring into focus their love and need for each other, but also their basic differences, disap-pointments, and resentments. There is a third character in this love triangle, Nadya, a country girl that Valentina hires as a maid not knowing of her past romance with Maxim. Nadya keeps her secret, having realized that Maxim loves Valentina. In the final scene, Maxim is expected to come home from one of his trips. Nadya sets the dinner table for the couple and leaves the house forever. For Nadya the story ends, for Valentina and Maxim time remains in suspension.

A directorial master stroke, thought Boris Borisovich of this last scene. The camera lingers on the table covered with crystal, silver, and lace, symmetrically framed by two elegantly carved chairs awaiting the lovers. Then, the frame goes black. This final image confirms that the focus of the film is on the space that Val-entina values, pampers, and guards from outside interferences. Her private space, together with the beautiful art nouveau décor, also includes emotions, desires, and expectations. Boris Boriso-vich went on with his thoughts: from Muratova's aesthetic ma-nipulation of space, framing and mise en scene a disturbing pic-ture emerges—the picture of the *embourgeoisement* of the Party cadres, and the search for fulfillment in the individual's private world. This audience will not be able to decode those features, but they may get the message nevertheless. I smell trouble...

The lights went on and the guests were invited to move to the living room for the discussion. Now they were sitting randomly on chairs and sofas, and all eyes were on the host. They waited for him to say a word, to give them a hint of his reaction to the film.

"Dear comrades," he said, "I am here to hear from you and therefore I'll keep my thoughts to myself—although, I'm appalled by the kind of garbage they produce these days. Who wants to start?"

The former boss from the Voronezh Oblast cleared his throat and said, "You're absolutely right. Let's take Valentina. Her character is wrong. She is a medium-level manager, a water and sewage inspector with responsibilities to provide the people with good housing. She should be more enthusiastic about her work. Instead, her attitude on the job, although conscientious, lacks passion. She performs her duty, but she does not relate emotionally to the people, and she is more devoted to her private life than to the Party. She should be reprimanded for that, but there is no such thing in the movie."

"And she gives a bad name to the Soviet woman who serves the motherland with courage and devotion," said the host's mother. "She spends more time at the hairdresser's than at the Party headquarters. This type of *petite bourgeoise*, they want us to believe, represents our society today... She is complacent in her comfortable position as a civil servant, and she longs for the romantic hero who stirs her imagination and her passions. Where did they get this idea? I certainly don't know any such woman in real life."[11]

The host's son-in-law intervened, "Anyway, if our society has mellowed a bit as a result of ten years of 'thaw,' responsible films should condemn it as a shortcoming, and not show it as something inevitable or even appealing."

By now the room was filled with smoke. The host's wife coughed slightly because she was not a smoker, and spoke, "I don't like the fact that Valentina smokes, it's not attractive in a woman. But what I find most objectionable is her attitude toward the family and motherhood. She must be pushing thirty already, still single for no good reason, no desire for children. She's only interested in fooling around with that good-for-nothing. Some scenes of the two together made me blush. Shame on her."

The three grandchildren elbowed each other and started giggling.

"You be quiet! This is not stuff for kids. Had I known..." continued the host's wife with a sigh.

The mother of the baby, replied rather shyly in a small voice, "I think they will get married. They love each other. And he's so handsome..."

"Nonsense!" her husband cut her off. "You should not make this kind of remarks in public. And, besides, you're wrong. Vladimir Vysotsky in that role is not handsome."

"He is, he is..." the other young women objected.[12]

One of the *komsomltsy* took the floor, "Well, comrades, Vysotsky has been a controversial figure for some time now, and it is significant that he was chosen for that role. He adds to the anti-Soviet bias of the whole film. His character is juvenile, irresponsible, a free spirit rejecting without apologies the daily office routine. He is a lover of nature but not a rugged hero. Actually, he is an anti-hero. In spite of his boots, beard, and work clothes, he relies on the comforts of civilization—good camping gear, canned food, a van. It is clear that he is a stranger in the village and feels superior to the country folks."

The guy in blue jeans jumped up and declared, "I love Vysotsky! I have dozens of *samizdat* tapes of his songs. I learned all of them. He's a great artist."

"Shut up, you *negodiai*! Leave the room at once. Out! I won't tolerate this kind of behavior," said the host in a thunderous voice. Then to his wife, "What kind of a son have you raised... What a disgrace."

"I'm sorry, dear," she replied.

A minute of awkward silence, then the boss from the Voronezh Oblast changed the subject. "There is another theme in the film that I find rather disturbing. And this is the treatment of the countryside. Twenty years ago they knew how to make films about village life. Remember those wonderful comedies by Pyr'ev, showing luxuriant wheat fields and happy *kolkhozniki*? Here they show a depleted countryside, and village girls like Nadya pushed into the city for lack of jobs at home, ending up as housemaids to city dwellers. This is depressing, impoverished *kolkhozy* and young people fleeing in droves. This is not the image we want to project of our fertile motherland."[13]

"If I may," said the *nyanya* from the corner where she was sitting with the other domestics. "I really felt sorry for Nadya.

Poor girl. What will become of her? She had to make a living and took that job as a waitress at the roadside diner outside the village, and there she meets the stranger who's handsome and sings so well and takes an interest in her. Well, of course she falls in love... But the next day he's gone. This happened to so many girls. When I was young, I used to cry over the story of "Poor Liza" that our village teacher read to us... And now, I feel like crying again."

"*Nyanya* sees it through a sentimental lens, but she is right," said the host's son-in-law. "All in all, there is nothing uplifting in this film. It shows a gap between the peasants and the urban dwellers, instead of stressing a common purpose. Valentina makes an effort to be nice to the girl, but she is unable to communicate and Nadya remains suspicious and hostile. And Maxim, notwithstanding his professed love for the wild, feels closer to Valentina—the refined woman that he jokingly addresses as *madame*—than to unworldly Nadya."

One of the young female professionals, elegantly dressed and with a smart haircut, offered her opinion, "Actually, I think that Nadya should go to school, get a degree, and find herself a good job. Then she would be able to afford the nice things Valentina has."

"Here we go, here we go," said the host's mother shaking her head. "She likes Valentina's 'nice things'... I'm telling you, this film is insidious, it promotes a bourgeois way of thinking."

Her brother reinforced the criticism, "And it also brings to the fore problems with poor construction work, water supply, housing shortages, corruption among government officials, and disregard for regulations on the part of citizens. All this under the pretext that Valentina tries to fix these problems. So, she's always presented in a good light, while she's actually a negative character."

The chauffeur raised his hand, "Perhaps these things should not be shown in a movie, but I must say that where housing is concerned I've applied for an apartment five years ago and I'm still waiting, living in a *kommunalka* with my wife, three children and my mother-in-law. (Addressing the host) I don't want to be disrespectful, but if you could put in a good word and expedite the process I'll be very grateful."

"Be patient, Vasya. We do the work of the people every day so that you can have your apartment," said the host. "But, tell me, how did you like the movie?"

"To tell you the truth, I could not follow it. It's very confusing. One moment we see that woman, Valentina, and it's today. The next moment it's sometime in the past and the people are different people. It didn't make any sense to me."

"Did you all hear that?" said the host with indignation. "For whom do they make these movies? Not for the people, obviously, who cannot care less about their formalistic tricks."

A well-groomed guy in charge of a cine club cautiously elaborated on the host's comment, "It's true, the *montage* is rather complex. The action has to be reconstructed through flash backs and episodes seen from the point of view of the two women. Therefore, chronology is disrupted, scenes are out of sequence... One must have a certain level of sophistication to understand what's going on—like our audience, for example, who is cultivated. But I agree that to the general viewer it looks like an incomprehensible puzzle."

"And this should not be," intervened the host's mother staring disapprovingly at the cine club manager. "The people have a right to expect from the filmmakers the clarity of the Socialist Realist style. Anything else is an inexcusable indulgence of the intellectual elite."[14]

The session came to a closing. Boris Borisovich looked at his notes, a summary of the main points of criticism he heard:

Valentina's character, played by Kira Muratova, displays negative traits as a Soviet worker and bourgeois tendencies.

Maxim's character, played by Vladimir Vysotsky, underlines the anti-Soviet bias of the film.

Nadya's character, played by Nina Ruslanova. Her first role, good debut. But her character brings to the fore the divide between village and city.

Social problems are emphasized: housing shortage, labor inefficiency, corruption, economic decline of the countryside.

Depressive, dark tone all over.

Sensuality is too open.

Formalistic features, incomprehensible to the masses.

Individualistic personality; K. M. is an *auteur*.

With such a reception, this film will never see the light of the day, thought Boris Borisovich on the way out.

"Well, Boris Borisovich, what do you think? Do you agree with the people's judgment?" asked Ivan Ivanovich.

"I must say that this was a very attentive audience. They

picked up all the issues this film raises. But they viewed them in a negative way, as defects. While I think it's a masterpiece."

"You're not going to write that, are you?"

"I'm not going to write anything before the film comes out."

The host approached Ivan Ivanovich and pulled him aside.

He lowered his voice, "Ivan Ivanovich, I want you to come to my office tomorrow morning first thing with your report. Then, we'll place a phone call to Goskino."

"I hear you," replied Ivan Ivanovich, and left the room.

He caught up with Boris Borisovich who was already outside waiting for the car. It was dark, and the temperature had plunged to twenty below zero. Tiny breath crystals began to appear in Boris Borisovich's beard.

"Boris Borisovich," said Ivan Ivanovich in an official tone, "we count on your discretion. Not a word about this screening. All you heard and saw is off the record."

Epilogue

Brief Encounters was released in a few prints and subsequently recalled. Only one review of the film is known to have appeared at the time, written according to the Goskino line by film critic N. Kovarskii, "Chelovek i vremia," *Iskusstvo kino,* no. 10 (1968): 49-57. Filmmaker Leonid Gurevich allegedly said that he wrote a positive review of *Brief Encounters* for the journal, which was supposed to appear together with Kovarskii's article, but it did not.[15]

Brief Encounters remained on the shelf until 1987. Muratova's other films of that period had a similar turbulent production history and were all embargoed: *Long Farewells* (*Dolgie provody,* 1971), *Getting to Know the Big, Wide World* (*Poznavaia belyi svet,* 1978), *Among the Grey Stones* (*Sredi serykh kamnei,* 1983, transformed beyond recognition by numerous cuts; Muratova asked to remove her name from the credits). Since 1987, all her previous films were released. On the occasion of an evening at the Cinema House to honor her works in 1987, the director told the audience, "I had always known that my films will come out some day. Only I did not believe that I myself would live to see that day."[16]

Muratova has often expressed her bewilderment at the negative reception of her films on the part of the authorities, because in her opinion there was nothing political in them:

They criticized *Long Farewells* a thousand times more than *Brief Encounters*. This cost me eight years of forced inactivity. There was even a resolution of the Ukraine Central Committee against my film. And yet, there's nothing political in it! It's just a family story, an intimate atmosphere. They said 'it's a rotten bourgeois film.' That's it. About *Brief Encounters* they would say: 'Ah, ah! You criticize the local authorities, the municipal administration, you show people who live in poverty, who flee from the kolkhozy,' etc. But then, suddenly, they released it on the sly. Not for long, but released it nevertheless. While *Long Farewells* has been simply forbidden.[17]

Muratova's arduous career may be explained in part by personal relationships. There's a general consensus among both friends and foes that she has a talent for alienating people.

Jane Taubman gives the first chapter of her book *Kira Muratova* the telling title, "Odessa Uncompromising Eccentric." Muratova's friend and screenwriter Natalia Riazantseva described Muratova's personality in an interview:

Generally speaking she did not have any friends, everybody felt that she was superior to them. They felt this very intensely. She is a totally isolated individual, totally different... At the beginning she was well received at the studio [in Odessa]... but this was short-lived. Afterwards she became a public enemy and very few were in good terms with her... [At Lenfilm Studio] she succeeded in creating a nightmarish atmosphere. Frizhetta [Gukasian, editor-in-chief at the studio] would say: 'I don't want to see her anymore, this'll kill me. She'll give me a heart attack.' When Kira started shouting, shouting endlessly, everybody was terrified.[18]

A senior editor at Goskino, Igor Sadchikov, reinforces that impression: "Muratova has a tremendous ego. But a director, evidently, cannot exist without it. A great director is always egotistical to a certain degree. For those people, you only are a thing they need to exploit for their creation... We kept her at the periphery of art... Not all her films were accepted. And those that were, had only a very short run."[19]

Muratova's isolation was compounded by the fact that she was seen as a "foreigner." Guerman, whose parents were members of the intelligentsia, recalls that "it was much easier for me than for Muratova, who was a 'nobody,' without family connections."[20] In her most difficult moments, Muratova enjoyed the support of Sergei Gerasimov, who was a powerful figure in the film industry as head of a production unit at the Gorky Studio, a member of the Secretariat of the Filmmakers Union, and an influential faculty member at VGIK. Although part of the Soviet establishment, Gerasimov was willing to stick out his neck to help young filmmakers.

With the privatization of the film industry Muratova was able to get control of her own production. She made thirteen films in the following years, which won awards at national and international festivals, but none of them went mainstream.

Notes

1   Rolan Bykov, "Plus Sixty," *Moscow News*, no. 29 (1988). Quoted in Ian Christie, "The Cinema," in *Culture and the Media in the USSR Today*, eds., J. Graffy and G. A. Hosking (New York: St. Martin's Press, 1990), 48. On the Conflict Commission see also Anna Lawton, *Before the Fall: Soviet Cinema in the Gorbachev Years* (Washington, DC: New Academia Publishing, 2004), ch. 5.

2   There are at least four lists of those films, each showing a different number: one by Irina Rubanova, vice-president of the Conflict Commission (82 feature films and 30 documentaries, animation and television films); another by K. Galimurza one of the Commission Secretaries (202 films); a third published in *Kinostsenarii*, 4, 1988: 187-91; and a fourth by R. K. Fomina. *Brief Encounters* (*Korotkie vstrechi*, 1967) figures on all the lists. Cited in Martine Godet, *La pellicule et le ciseaux: La censure dans le cinéma soviétique du Dégel à la perestroïka* (Paris: CRNS Editions, 2010), 12. This book is a good survey of post-Stalinist Soviet censorship from a new perspective.

3   The report of the Fomin team is based on materials from the Goskino archives, from former TSGALI (renamed RGALI), Mosfilm and other studios. It was published as a series of articles in the journal *Iskusstvo kino* in 1988 and 1989, with the title "Zapiski iz mertvogo doma." See also, V. Fomin, "Estetika Goskino, ili sotsialisticheskii realizm v deistvii," *Pogruzhenie v triasinu. Anatomiia zastoia*, ed., T. A. Notkina, (Moscow: Progress, 1991), 439-68; V. Fomin, *Polka. Dokumenty. Svidetel'stva. Kom-*

mentarii (Moscow: Progress, 1992); V. Fomin, *Kino i vlast'. Sovetskoe kino: 1965-1985 gody. Dokumenty, svidetel'stva, razmyshleniia* (Moscow: Materik, 1996). See reactions to the Fomin report in Godet, *La pellicule et les ciseaux*, especially the interview with Goskino's senior editor Igor Sadchikov, 257-85.

4   This trend started in the 1920s and became policy under Stalin in the early 1930s, when the head of Soiuzkino, Boris Shumiatsky ordered the film industry to produce "movies for the millions," genre films combining American-style entertainment with domestic subjects and ideology. See Richard Taylor, "A 'Cinema for the Millions': Soviet Socialist Realism and the Problem of Film Comedy," *Journal of Contemporary History*, 18 (1983), 439-61; Taylor, "Boris Shumyatsky and the Soviet Cinema in the 1930s: Ideology as Mass Entertainment," *Historical Journal of Film, Radio, and Television*, 6, no. 1 (1986), 43-64; Denise J. Youngblood, *Movies for the Masses: Popular Cinema and Soviet Society in the 1920s* (Cambridge: Cambridge University Press, 1992). For "movies for the millions" in perestroika times, see also Lawton, *Before the Fall*, 226-34.

5   In Louis Menashe, *Moscow Believes in Tears: Russians and Their Movies* (Washington, DC: New Academia Publishing, 2011), 354.

6   In Godet, *La pellicule et le ciseaux*, 244 (Riazantseva's interview); and *Ibid*, 206 (Guerman's interview) [my translation, A. L.]. See also "Selected readings on censorship and culture under Brezhnev" at the end of this article.

7   These two paragraphs and the narrative that follows are fiction. There is no evidence that *Brief Encounters* was actually shown at a *dachnyi prosmotr*. However, referring to her film *Long Farewells*, Muratova speculated about the reasons for its rejection and mentioned a dacha screening: "There were lots of rumors: it was the obkom, it was the wives of some important people, it had been screened at someone's dacha." Quoted in Jane Taubman, "The Cinema of Kira Muratova," *The Russian Review*, 52, no. 3 (July 1993): 373.

The fictional characters in this narrative do not refer to any real person. However, references to real-life figures, such as Kira Muratova, and circumstances surrounding their works are historically accurate. The objections to *Brief Encounters* raised in the narrative correspond to those found in the scholarly works mentioned in this paper.

About *Brief Encounters* and Kira Muratova in general see "Selected readings on Kira Muratova" at the end of this article.

8   *U krutogo iara* (*By the Ravine*,1961), directors: Alexander Muratov and Kira Muratova. This was a short they made as their diploma work at VGIK. *Nash chestnyi khleb* (*Our Honest Bread*,1965), directors: Alexander Muratov and Kira Muratova.

9   Leonid Zhukhovitskii, *Dom v stepi: rasskazy* (Moscow: Sovetskii pisatel', 1959). This short story inspired the geologist/country girl thread of the film.

10   Goskino strongly objected to scenes of physical intimacy and speech with sexual overtones in *Brief Encounters*, especially in the relationship between the urban man and the country girl, and those scenes had to be cut. See Fomin, *Kino i vlast'*, 19-20.

11   In Muratova's films the protagonists are women, but she has always rejected the term "women's films," or "feminist films," which to her as well as to Soviet women in general had an unpalatable connotation of western political movements. However, part of the value of her films lies in her attention to ordinary women's lives, her insight into women's psychology, and her sharply critical but sympathetic eye in observing their actions, weaknesses and strengths.

12   In the 1960s and 1970s, the poet-bard-actor Vladimir Vysotsky was a thorn in the side of the cultural establishment and a popular idol among young people and intellectuals because of his provocative underground songs on forbidden topics such as sex, violence, official corruption, and crime. Vysotsky died in 1980 and has been openly celebrated as one of the most significant artists of contemporary Russian culture since the time of perestroika. See Lawton, *Before the Fall*, op. cit., Note 189, pp. 298-99; Gerald Stanton Smith, *Songs to Seven Strings: Russian Guitar Poetry and Soviet "Mass Songs"* (Bloomington, IN: Indiana University Press, 1984), 146-99; Richard Stites, *Russian Popular Culture: Entertainment and Society since 1900* (Cambridge: Cambridge University Press, 1992), 158, and Note 18, p. 223.

13   Ivan Pyr'ev directed numerous village musicals which enjoyed Stalin's favor: *Bogataia nevesta* (*The Rich Bride*, 1938); *Traktoristy* (*Tractor Drivers*, 1939); *Svinarka i pastukh* (*The Swineherd and the Shepherd*, 1941) *Cossaks of Kuban* (*Kubanskie kozaki*, 1950). See Grigorii B. Mar'iamov, ed., *Ivan Pyr'ev: v zhizni i na ekrane* (Moscow: Kinotsentr, 1994).

The depiction of poverty in the countryside was a major point of contention with Goskino in the 1960s and 1970s. To retain agricultural manpower in the villages, the government did not issue internal passports to the peasants until the mid-seventies, keeping them bound to the land. When the ban was lifted, the young generation fled to the cities leaving behind the old, but the exodus had already started in the sixties. Muratova was pressed at every stage of production to cut realistic scenes of village life. For the same reason, another outstanding film of those years was not released, *Istoriia Asi Kliachiny kotoraia liubila no ne vyshla zamuzh* (*The Story of Asya Kliachina Who Loved but Did Not Get Married*, 1967), by director Andrei Konchalovsky.

14   Goskino's chief editor Irina Kokoreva wrote in her report: "This indisputably talented work lacks a clear authorial concept. Having fashioned interesting images and situations, the filmmaker fails to evaluate them clearly and from a Party-minded position. As a result, the material can be interpreted in various ways." See Fomin, *Kino i vlast'*, 55; Josephine Woll, *Real Images: Soviet Cinema and the Thaw* (London/New York: I. B. Tauris, 2000), 221.

Taubman writes that after its extremely limited release, "*Brief Encounters* was shown largely in cine clubs, with Muratova present to introduce it and answer questions. Such appearances were then her major means of support," "The Cinema of Kira Muratova," 371.

15   Taubman, "The Cinema of Kira Muratova," 370.

16   Andrei Zorkii, "Beleet parus odinokii," *Sovetskii ekran*, no. 8 (1987), 15 [my translation, A. L.].

17   Godet, *La pellicule et le ciseaux*, 131 [my translation, A. L.]. See also a report of the Lenfilm Studio's Party Committee meeting and resolution about Muratova's film *Getting to Know the Big, Wide World* (*Poznavaia belyi svet*, 1978), in Val S. Golovskoi with J. Rimberg, *Behind the Soviet Screen*, 124-26.

18   Godet, *La pellicule et le ciseaux*, 251-52 [my translation, A. L.].

19   *Ibid*, 73 [my translation, A. L.].

20   *Ibid*, 189 [my translation, A. L.].

Selected readings on Kira Muratova

Zara Abdullaeva, *Kira Muratova: iskusstvo kino* (Moscow: Novoe literaturnoe obozrenie, 2008); Viktor Bozhovich, *Kira Muratova: tvorcheskii portret* (Moscow: Soiuzinformkino, 1988); Martine Godet, *La pellicule et le ciseaux: La censure dans le cinéma soviétique du Dégel à la perestroïka* (Paris: CRNS Editions, 2010); Viktor Gulchenko, "Mezhdu ottepeliami," *Iskusstvo kino*, no. 6 (1991), 57-69; Susan Larsen, "Korotkie Vstrechi/Brief Encounters," in *The Cinema of Russia and the Former Soviet Union*, Birgit Beumers, ed. (London/New York: Wallflower, 2007), 19-127; Anna Lawton, *Before the Fall: Soviet Cinema in the Gorbachev Years* (Washington, DC: New Academia Publishing, 2004), 121-25; Anna Lawton, *Imaging Russia 2000: Film and Facts* (Washington, DC: New Academia Publishing, 2004), 210-15. Natalia Riazantseva, "Za chto?" *Kinostsenarii*, no. 1 (1988), 137-41; Graham Roberts, "The Meaning of Death: Kira Muratova's Cinema of the Absurd," in *Russia on Reels: The Russian Idea in Post-Soviet Cinema*, Birgit Beumers, ed. (London/New York: I. B. Tauris, 1999), 144-60; Jane Taubman, "The Cinema of Kira Muratova," *The Russian Review*, 52, no. 3 (July 1993), 367-81; Jane Taubman, *Kira Muratova* (London; I.B. Tauris, 2005); Josephine Woll,

Real Images: Soviet Cinema and the Thaw (London/New York: I. B. Tauris, 2000), 219-21.

Selected readings on censorship and culture under Brezhnev

Lev Anninskii, *Shestidesiatniki i my: Kinematograf stavshii i ne stavshii istoriei* (Moscow: Soiuz kinematografistov SSSR, 1991); Arlen Blium and Vladimir Volovnikov, eds., *Tsenzura v Sovetskom Soiuze, 1917-1991. Dokumenty* (Moscow: ROSSPEN, 2004); Svetlana Boym, *Common Places. Mythologies and Everyday Life in Russia* (Cambridge, MA: Harvard University Press, 1994); Val S. Golovskoy with John Rimberg, *Behind the Soviet Screen: The Motion Picture Industry in the USSR, 1972-1982* (Ann Arbor, MI: Ardis, 1986); T. M. Goriaeva, ed., *Istoriia sovetskoi politicheskoi tsenzury. Dokumenty i kommentarii* (Moscow: ROSSPEN, 1997); V. Kardin, *Dostoinstvo iskusstva: razdum'ia o teatre i kinematografe nashikh dnei* (Moscow: Iskusstvo, 1967); Anna Lawton, ed., *The Red Screen: Politics, Society, Art in Soviet Cinema* (London: Routledge, 1992); Marcel Martin, *Le cinéma soviétique de Khrouchtchev à Gorbatchev* (Paris: L'Âge d'Homme, 1993); Louis Menashe, *Moscow Believes in Tears: Russians and Their Movies* (Washington, DC: New Academia Publishing, 2010); Dmitry and Vladimir Shlapentokh, *Soviet Cinematography 1918-1991: Ideological Conflict and Social Reality* (New York: A. de Gruyter, 1993); Richard Stites, *Russian Popular Culture: Entertainment and Society since 1900* (Cambridge: Cambridge University Press, 1992); Richard Stites, *Passion and Perception: Essays on Russian Culture*, ed., David Goldfrank (Washington, DC: New Academia Publishing, 2010); Josephine Woll, *Real Images: Soviet Cinema and the Thaw* (London/New York: I. B. Tauris, 2000), especially Ch. 18.; M. R. Zezina, *Sovetskaia khudozhestvennaia intelligentsia i vlast' v 1950-e/1960-e gody* (Moscow: MGU, Istoricheskii fakultet, 1999).

7

Richard Stites, the Soviet West, Media, and Soviet Americanists

by Sergei I. Zhuk

I came to the United States for the first time in October of 1992 as a young and ambitious Americanist from Ukraine. During this trip I was invited by my American colleagues, historians of Colonial British America, to visit a campus of Georgetown University. Before this visit I had already been very skeptical about American historians, experts in Russian and Soviet history. But then after long conversations with two American "Sovietologists" from Georgetown, I realized how wrong I was in my skepticism. These two historians, David Goldfrank and Richard Stites, demonstrated not only their serious knowledge of Russian and Soviet history, but also respect for other people's opinion and tolerance, which was lacking among my senior Ukrainian colleagues.

The second time I met Richard Stites in 1997, when I changed my professional identity by switching my subjects from early American history to Imperial Russian history, and began my American academic career at the Johns Hopkins University as a new graduate student of Russian history. Together with Jeffrey Brooks, my academic mentor, Richard supported all my crazy academic projects. So when I finished my first American project *Russia's Lost Reformation* in 2002,[1] I decided to write a new research project about cultural consumption, images of the West, identity and Soviet youth culture during the Brezhnev era. Supporting my new project, Richard helped me to organize a few panels for AAASS Conventions and suggested me to concentrate on topics which I knew better – on Anglo-American rock music and western films.

In 2008 in Philadelphia, during the AAASS Convention, after a long discussion about my paper on western films and Soviet audiences, Richard asked me about the final title for my new book. I gave him what I had already offered to my editors – *The West in the Closed City: Cultural Consumption, Identity and Ideology in Soviet Ukraine, 1964-1985*. "No, it's too boring," was Richard's verdict, "you need to give a reader a hook, a stimulus, not a mixture of academic fashionable jargon." Richard knew that in my book I used a story of one Soviet industrial city, which was closed by KGB to foreigners because this Ukrainian city became a location for one of the biggest missile factory in the Soviet Union. That is why he offered me a very simple, but catchy title for my book - *Rock and Roll in the Rocket City*.[2]

In my first draft of this book I had almost a hundred pages of the theoretical survey about cultural consumption and identity formation in modern societies. Richard suggested me to cut all this theoretical material from my manuscript. "Remove all this theoretical crap, do not think about your academic reviewer," he used to say, "keep in mind a reader who is interested in your unique stories from the Brezhnev era, do not waste your time on theories, you are a historian, a master of storytelling, you are not boring teacher of cultural studies." This was the last phrase of Richard that I remember from our discussion in 2008. My family – Irina, my wife, and Andrey, my son, - were present during this discussion in Philadelphia. Richard told them about his perception of Russia, its culture and its history. And I remember that my wife and son were fascinated with Richard's understanding of Russian culture. After this conversation, my son, an electrical engineer and computer scientist, who was very critical about "boring" academic books in history, changed his mind and began reading Richard Stites's historical books.

Media and cultural politics of Détente

Richard Stites was the first historian who demonstrated that the 1970s became the critical period in westernization of the entire Soviet society. According to him, this period of détente revealed how the elements of western (capitalist) modernity (through consumption) threatened to replace the socialist modernity not only in imagination but also in reality of the Soviet everyday experience. Paradoxically, by legitimizing consumption of Western cultural products, the official Soviet policy of détente justified an incorporation of various elements of Western modernity (from the new fashions to a commercialization of popular culture) into Soviet ideological practices of the 1970s that increased a disorientation and confusion of both local ideologists and local consumers.

Richard Stites also was a pioneer in the studies of connections between Soviet media and entertainment. He influenced my interest in exploring these connections, especially a role of Soviet media, such as radio, films and television. After reading my chapters about the impact of foreign radio on the Soviet preferences in popular music consumption, he criticized me for an absence in my manuscript of the story of Soviet pioneers of rock music broadcasting. So I looked through my sources again and realized that Richard was right in his criticism. Thanks to Richard, I discovered fascinating stories about Soviet radio and television shows which introduced Soviet audience to the new trends in western popular music.

In 1964, using the western forms of radio broadcasting, Soviet radio introduced a new radio station *Maiak* (A Beacon) with a round-the-clock five-minute news and twenty-five minute entertainment show. This station was the first to introduce Western rock music to the Soviet audiences. In 1967 a radio journalist Viktor Tatarskii came to *Maiak* and created a music show *Vstrechi s pesnei* (Meetings with a Song), which popularized Soviet popular (*estrada*) mass song (Fig. 1). From 1968 to 1975, the Moscow radio station *Maiak* broadcast a special music show by Tatarskii and the journalist Grigorii Libergal with the title: *Zapishite na vashi magnitofony* (Please Make Your Own Tape Recording). Sometimes Tatarskii managed to broadcast his show for one hour each Sunday. Usually, he had only 25 minutes for his show. Tatarskii included the latest western music hits along with his professional commentary. The

Viktor Tatarskii (b. 1939, still active here in 2007), the legendary and highly influential radio journalist during the 1970s.

radio station's administration tried to control him and stop him from playing "loud music." Several times *Maiak* closed his show. After 1976, Tatarskii moved to other Moscow stations and devoted his new shows to jazz music and Soviet *estrada*. Together with the central radio station *Iunost* (the Youth) Viktor Tatarskii and other young radio journalists, such as Ekaterina Tarkhanova, Vladimir Pozner and Igor Fesunenko, organized two new radio shows: *Na vsekh shirotakh* (On All Latitudes) and *Muzykal'nyi globus* (Musical Globe). These shows covered various topics of modern popular music including jazz and rock and roll, and they became the major source of information about western pop music for millions of Soviet rock music fans.[3] American media covered his show, including *Billboard*, February 19, 1972.

Although the recent cultural studies implicitly present a history of westernization of Soviet popular culture, they missed a crucial moment in this westernization – the détente of the 1970s, especially the period from 1972 to 1979. In a contrast to Richard Stites, a majority of recent studies miss and ignore the role of détente in the westernization of Soviet media.[4] During this period Soviet administration bought the official licenses for manufacturing popular music records from the West; the first comic books from the West were reprinted in the USSR, and officially licensed western movies were shown, Soviet TV broadcast the concerts of western popular musicians, Western rock music was incorporated into official Soviet TV shows, such as *International Panorama* and *Vesëlye rebiata* (Funny Guys).

The Soviet music recording company *Melodia* released the first licensed Western music records to satisfy the growing demand among young Soviet consumers for Western music and at the same time, to respond to new ideological requirements of Soviet entertainment. Between 1970 and 1975, *Melodia* already released numerous music compilations that included popular Western rock songs without any official permission from Western recording companies. As a matter of fact the first "bootleg" Soviet release of 1967 included compilation with the Beatles song "Girl" and Rolling Stones – "I Can't Get No Satisfaction." The most popular *Melodia* compilations in the 1970s included "House of the Rising Sun" by the Animals, "Holiday," "I Can't See Nobody," "To Love Somebody" by Bee Gees, "Mary Long" and "Super Trouper" by Deep Purple, "Coz I Lov You" by Slade, "Funny Funny" by Sweet, "Hot Love" and "Bang a Gong (Get It On)" by T. Rex. In the 1970s and early 1980s, *Melodia* also released popular hits by Elton John, Creedence Clearwater Revival, Pink Floyd, Jethro Tull and other rock musicians from the West. Of course, the Beatles and Rolling Stones were represented by twelve *minions* (Soviet version of single music records with four songs), which were released by *Melodia* without any official license from Western recording companies during 1967-1975. In 1976, *Melodia* signed its first official contract with the Dutch recording company OLD ARK to facilitate the release of the album of the Dutch rock band Teach-In. This band Teach In became popular among *Melodia* administrators because it won the Eurovision competition in 1975. Officially, a Teach-In's record was released under a license from CNR b. v. Grammofoonplaten Maatschappij (Leiden, the Netherlands). The *Melodia* record's number was GOST 5289-73 (C60-07403), and its price was 1.90 rubles. I still have this record in my music collection. It was the first original Western music record

that *Melodia* released with an official license. After this, many Western music records reached Soviet consumers through official chan-
nels. These records represented different styles of Western music
– from Billie Holliday's *Greatest Hits in Jazz* to the ex-Beatles' John
Lennon *Imagine* and Paul McCartney and the Wings' rock album,
Band on the Run. These two last albums appeared on the *Melodia*
label many years after their original release in England and without some songs removed by Soviet censors.[5] Popular journals such
as *Krugozor* and *Klub i khudozhestvennaia samodeiatel'nost'* released
various compilations of the Western music on the flex discs which
were included as the music appendices to these journals with songs
by the major stars of Western rock music, from Elton John and Pink
Floyd to Jethro Tull.

The beginning of détente in US-Soviet relations and the relax-
ation of international tensions also resulted in some changes in
youth cultural consumption.[6] Young Western pop music enthusiasts could not only listen to Soviet music records with popular
Western music hits, but also watch their music idols on Soviet television. The Central Soviet TV program always prepared a special
music variety show which was shown on the New Year's night.
During the late 1960s and early 1970s, this show usually included
a long concert with famous Soviet and foreign musicians and actors that were predominantly from socialist countries. This show
was called *Novogodnii Ogonëk* or "The New Year Merry Twinkle"
in English. Various Soviet celebrities, politicians, journalists, artists,
musicians and singers were invited to *Ogonëk* as guests. Some sat
at tables with wine, champagne and snacks, while others played
music, danced or sang. Classical music, traditional folk and Soviet
popular songs dominated this show. Sometimes popular singers
from socialist countries such as Karel Gott from Czechoslovakia or
even Dean Reed from US appeared guests of the *Ogonëk* TV show.[7]
Millions of Soviet fans of Western pop music were pleasantly surprised that after a traditional long and boring *Novogodnii Ogonëk*
show on the early morning of January 1, 1975, the central Soviet TV
station broadcast an unusually long concert of Western pop music
stars. These stars included the most popular names played in the
Soviet discotheques, such as ABBA, Boney M, Dowley Family, Don-
ny Osmond, Silver Convention, Joe Dassen, Amanda Lear, Smokey

and Baccarat. After 1975, each year Soviet TV aired similar shows at least once a year, usually very late at night. Since January 11, 1977, Soviet TV had organized a special show "Melodies and Rhythms of Foreign Estrada," which included the most popular stars of Western rock and disco music. Until perestroika "Melodies and Rhythms" was the only one TV show which gave a unique opportunity to millions Soviet fans see their idols on the Soviet TV screen at least once a year. During the 1970s Soviet TV also organized the broadcasting of variety shows, which included covers of the most popular western hits in Russian by various Soviet vocal instrumental ensembles. The "TV Benefit Performances" of the famous Soviet film stars such as Larisa Golubkina (1975) and Liudmila Gurchenko (1978) and Evgenii Ginzburg's show "Magic Lantern" (1976) offered very good covers of songs from the British rock opera, *Jesus Christ Superstar*, and also from the Beatles and Paul McCartney's albums by various Soviet rock bands (VIA) such as Vesëlye rebiata from Moscow and Poiushchie gitary from Leningrad.[8] Many young television viewers requested for these TV shows to be replayed. Young enthusiasts of rock music requested a replay of the Golubkina's show with a Moscow band Vesiolye rebiata covering McCartney's hit 'Ms. Vanderbuilt" (entitled as "Nasha koroleva khot' kuda") numerous times.

Soviet film industry had been already "westernized" by the 1970s as a result of official emphasis on commercial success. In the USSR during the mid-sixties gross movie ticket sales was at roughly 1 billion rubles annually, of which the state was said to have collected 440 million in "pure profit." Eventually, the notion of commercial success in Soviet film industry led to its internationalization and purchase of more foreign movies, which brought more profits to this industry. For every ruble in its budget, Soviet officials estimated income from foreign film purchases at 5 rubles; in the case of commercial western films it could reach 250. The Soviet Ministry of Culture began to purchase large numbers of films abroad – from 63 in 1955 to 113 in 1958, with plans for over 150 in 1960. In the period 1954 to 1991 the USSR imported 206 films from India, 41 from the USA, and 38 from France. In 1960 each film from the capitalist world drew an average audience of more than 500,000 in Moscow, while Soviet productions averaged 357,000 and socialist bloc pictures, 133,000.[9] As we see, the commercial interests of the Soviet state and the official culture of détente became the most important impetus in westernization of the Soviet popular culture.

According to my own research of Soviet film consumption during the Brezhnev era, just in 1973 alone, the main Soviet authority for the acquisition and distribution of foreign films, *Soveksportfilm*, bought more than 150 feature films from 70 countries (50 of them came from the capitalist western countries). During the period of détente, this number grew. More Western films reached Soviet moviegoers by the end of the 1970s than the previous decade. During the entire Brezhnev era the few Western movies, which were released in the Soviet Union played a more significant role in the "Westernization" of Soviet youth than western popular music or books. In 1966 almost 60% of all movies shown in Ukrainian cities were of foreign origin, 50% of them were films from the "capitalist" West. Ten years after, in 1975, almost 90% of the films were foreign movies, and almost 80% were western ones, in 1981 more than 95% of all movies were of foreign origin, and 90% came from western capitalist countries. More than 90% of all western films came from Western Europe, and fewer than 10% from the USA. According to the personal diaries of Ukrainian middle school students, during the normal school week in the 1970s each of them watched two or three movies per week. During the school breaks they watched usually six to seven films per week, 90% of all these films were films from Western capitalist countries.[10] To some extent, all these findings of mine proved Richard Stites's ideas about a crucial formative role of détente in mass westernization of the Soviet society.

Socialist modernity and identity of a Soviet americanist

Richard also suggested me to begin another research project. After a long conversation with me about my previous academic experience as a Soviet Americanist, who had studied a social history of colonial British America with such an honest and decent Soviet historian as Nikolai Bolkhovitinov, Richard said, "You know it looks like American studies in the USSR became a tool of the real people's diplomacy helping Soviet people to understand America better than official publication in newspaper *Pravda*. You must write your own unique insider story about Soviet studies of US history. You can use your own stories of the Soviet Americanists' community as a micro-model for the study of Soviet Westernized intellectuals, from Khrushchev's thaw to Gorbachev *perestroika*. It will be fascinating book!"

So I devoted my new book project *Peoples' Diplomacy: A History of American/Canadian Studies and National Politics in Russia and Ukraine since Stalin* to the memory of Richard Stites, a great inspirational scholar and visionary, good friend of Russia. My new book will be a tribute to his role in changing intellectual landscape in both American and post-Soviet space. Richard inspired major themes of my new book. He used to say to me, "do not concentrate on the boring historiographical debates, or institutional history, write about people, their personal stories, and explore their academic careers and private life!" Following Richard's advice, I will write about personal histories of the Soviet experts in American studies and their role of the Soviet discovery of America and, paradoxically, the Soviet intellectual self.

From the beginning, the creation and institutionalization of American studies in the Soviet Union in the 1970s was directly connected to a self-perception of socialist modernity and limits of its "openness" among Soviet intellectuals. As Volodymyr Yevtukh, a Ukrainian Americanist and politician, noted in December 1995, "to be a Soviet Americanist, a Soviet expert in US and Canadian history, meant to be a very special, real modern scholar, who was different from a boring and traditionalist scholar, an official Communist expert of the Soviet past and Soviet realities." And he continued, "Everybody understood that despite all our official anti-Americanism in the Soviet Union, for us, Soviet intellectuals, American civilization symbolized a modernity of the entire humankind. According to Communist ideology, the Soviet Union also was a modern, progressive civilization. That is why, we, Soviet scholars, studied the United States not only to criticize Americans, but also to learn from American experience how to be a part of modernity. At the same time to study America for us was an attempt to avoid our Soviet 'closedness' and associate with 'open' western civilization."[11]

More than 90% of former Soviet Americanists, whom I had interviewed since 1990s in both Russia and Ukraine, acknowledged how attractive for them were the images of modernity (*sovremennosti*), ideas of cultural and technological progress, they always associ-

Lev Izrailovich Zubok (1894-1967), one of the first Soviet Americanists, with his wife, and their son Martin, the father of Prof. Vladislav Zubok mentioned and cited in this essay.

ated with the United States and the English language as a signifier of the connections to American modernity, to the "opened" western world. Even the first post-war generation of Soviet intellectuals, "Stalin's last generation" according to Juliane Fürst, or "Zhivago's Children" according to Vladislav Zubok, a generation, whose representatives became the founders of the first Soviet schools of *amerikanistika* in Moscow and Kyiv, grew up under influence of the controversial images of the United States as the Soviet allies in the World War II, as a progressive modern country that developed forbidden but very popular trends and fashions, especially in music and films. All subsequent generations of the Soviet Americanists from the 1960s, the 70s and the 80s were influenced by the similar images, sounds and ideas of the western modernity they associated mainly with the United States.[12]

To some extent, the entire Soviet Americanist's identity was built around this notion of western (American) modernity and its English linguistic expressions. To be *sovremennyi* (modern), "cool" was a major point of an academic career for many Soviet Americanists, especially after Stalin. The different representatives of So-

Aleksei Viktorovich Efimov (1896-1971), another founding father of Soviet *amerikanistika*.

viet Americanists emphasized their desire to be modern, to be progressive, when they selected a field of American studies for their academic career. For many of them, this notion was also connected to certain material privileges – travels abroad, access to Western (especially American) cultural products. To be an Americanist for them was to be "a very special (*osobennyi*) scholar, to be ahead of times, to be an agent of intellectual progress, part of the open world (*chastitsei otkrytogo mira*)."[13]

In building their identity, Soviet Americanists distanced themselves not from American scholars, but from their Soviet colleagues, who represented the more conservative, traditionalist and orthodox fields of scholarship, especially a Communist party (CPSU) history and a recent history of the Soviet Union. They constructed their scholar ideal as the opposite to an image of "*k-p-esesnik*" (a historian of the Communist party, *KPSS* in Russian abbreviation). A representative of the most numerous group of college history professors in the Soviet Union, a Soviet expert in communist party history was an object of ridicule by the representatives of more progressive (and more modern) Soviet field for historical research, which was known as "*vseobshchaia* universal (world) history." Soviet historians who studied US history were part of this westernized modern school of Soviet scholarship. Soviet Americanists always criticized "*k-p-esesniks*" and specialists in contemporary Soviet history as the "Marxist-Stalinist crammers," the conservative memorizers of "Marxist classics," "retrograde defenders of Soviet closedness," and ridiculed them for a lack of cultural (including historical) erudition and for their bad linguistic skills. Paradoxically, a traditional Soviet dichotomy *kul'turnost'* vs. *beskul'turie* from the Stalin era became a major building block for an identity of Soviet Americanists. To be cultured was associated with open-mindedness.[14] The very act of pursuing American studies in the Soviet Union signified of a modern, cultured Soviet intellectual vis-à-vis a boorish and ignorant pedant from the field of CPSU history or recent history of the Soviet Union. A notion of the special role of the Soviet Americanists as agents of modernity affected their attitudes not only toward their colleagues, CPSU historians, but also to other Soviet scholars who were engaged in official propagandist fields of political science and social studies known as *nauchnyi kommunizm*. They sometimes even criticized their colleagues from the US-Canada Institute (ISKAN) because the last ones did their research on the request from the communist ideologists and the KGB, therefore losing their status of agents of modernity and defending "Soviet closeness." Historians from a Bolkhovitinov center (formerly the Sevostianov center) sometimes distanced themselves as "serious academic researchers" from ISKAN experts, calling them "*koniunkturshchiks*," who worked for so-called "*directivnyi*" organs."[15]

Soviet Americanists as modernity agents and "envy of Moscow"

Soviet Americanists employed flexible discursive strategies to convey the desired meaning without violating the constraints of the then politically acceptable language. They used so-called internalist, factological approaches, trying to avoid any theoretical conceptualization. According to some scholars, Soviet academic discourse was "not as a container of a particular ideology or theory, but rather as a mechanism for advancing a certain agenda via disciplinary knowledge." As Slava Gerovitch noted, "Instead of depicting the Cold War solely as a clash of ideologies, it may be more productive to examine the discursive strategies that were employed to shape the image of the opponent and to build up 'our' ideology against 'theirs.'"[16] In this context, Soviet Americanists actively developed various discursive strategies to appropriate the image of the opponent to the needs of the current situation. At the same time they connected the opponent's image to their mental construction of progressive modernity and to their assumed role of the agents of this modernity in both Russia and Ukraine.

Both these mental constructions and assumed roles were affected by the psychological complex of tensions, which had existed between Soviet provincial population and Muscovites since the Stalin era. Historically, the tensions between provincials and Muscovites created a unique and mass psychological phenomenon of mature socialism in the USSR known as "envy of Moscow." This phenomenon was Stalin's legacy, a result of creation of Moscow as a show case of the socialist achievements for the entire Soviet Union. With all limitations in socialist production, distribution and consumption of manufactured goods and cultural products in Soviet provinces, from a provincial point of view, Moscow looked like a "socialist paradise" with the best food stores, best schools, theaters, libraries and museums. Moscow was a symbol of the entire Soviet civilization, a trend-setter for all provinces, but at the same time an object of intense envy for the millions Soviet provincials.[17]

In September of 1999, Sergei N. Burin, a younger colleague of Bolkhovitinov, noted an important development that affected the intellectual history of American studies in Russia and Ukraine: "Envy has always been a fundamental element in constructing the Soviet personality since Stalin's times. Beginning with Yuri Olesha, all Soviet writers noted this. Provincials envied Muscovites because Moscow had the better living conditions. Muscovites envied provincials, if they made successful careers and traveled abroad. In my opinion, envy killed the Soviet Union, when the local intellectual elites from national republics transformed their envy of Moscow into their new national politics. Envy became the most important factor in shaping the entire intellectual history of the Soviet Union, including its academic life and, to some extent, effecting the development of American studies as well."[18]

This envy of Moscow produced a new anti-Moscow folklore that spread all over the Soviet Union. As early as the 1950s, provincials began calling Muscovites *chmo* (acronym from combination of the Russian words *chelovek Moskvy i Moskovskoi oblasti* – a resident of Moscow and Moscow region). According to the retired Soviet military officers, in the 1950s a sudden influx of the physically weak and effeminate young conscripts from Moscow region into the Soviet Army resulted in their senior officers complaining about unpreparedness of these young soldiers from Moscow for the requirements of military service. Eventually, Soviet military officers used acronym *chmo* in their documents to mark the names of the conscripts from Moscow and Moscow region. In the 1960s and the 70s this acronym left Soviet army circles, penetrated Soviet civilian population, and became a popular word used to characterize any weak and effeminate male character. As a result, people forgot about the Soviet army origin of this term.[19] Traditionally, provincial population in the USSR distanced themselves from Muscovites, using various bad words, including *chmo*.

As Richard Stites emphasized in our conversation, in the USSR provincial intellectual elites always tried to join Muscovite elite. If they failed to do so, they eventually also began developing certain anti-Moscow feelings. This phenomenon influenced the attitudes of various provincial Americanists toward their colleagues from Moscow. The major perception of the provincial intellectuals was that ISKAN (since 1967) and other Soviet centers for American studies offered jobs only to the representatives of Moscow elite, to the young members of the ruling families in Moscow etc. For people from the provinces, all young (and sometimes not very young) Americanists from Moscow were "the golden youth," *mal'chiki mazhory* and *chmo*.[20] This "envy of Moscow" became a significant element in formation of the regional version of Soviet intellectual self among the Ukrainian Americanists. Following Richard's suggestions, in my new book project I will study various forms of this phenomenon.

Richard Stites and new Soviet cultural studies

During the Cold War, especially before the 1980s, Soviet society was presented as one-dimensional, monolithic and predictable entity in both sides of ideological division – in the Soviet studies in the West and in a History of the USSR/Communist Party in the Soviet

Union as well. Despite the prevailing different theoretical models of interpretation – a totalitarian/modernization model in the West and Orthodox Marxism-Leninism in the USSR – Soviet studies in both capitalist West and socialist East explained the major developments in the similar way, emphasizing mostly political, economic and ideological moments in a boring stability of the Soviet civilization. During the 1970s and the 1980s, the sudden rise of the "revisionist" school in Western historiography, especially with a publication of the brilliant studies by Sheila Fitzpatrick, Stephen Cohen, Leopold Haimson and other western scholars, revealed the new data from the Soviet/Russian archives and introduced the fresh ideas and theories of a new social and new cultural history. The entire new generation of western scholars such as Richard Stites, Vera Dunham, Laura Engelstein, Sheila Fitzpatrick, Jeffrey Brooks and Denise Youngblood replaced the one-dimensional traditional interpretation of Soviet society with a wealth of variety of different cultural practices, they had discovered in everyday life of Soviet people. All this changed a development of the Soviet studies, and eventually contributed to a tremendous popularity of cultural studies among both western and post-Soviet historians.[21]

The rise of the Western "revisionist" historians coincided and was stimulated by the events of perestroika and the resulting collapse of the Soviet Union in 1991. During this period new archival collections were opened in the Soviet Union and post-Soviet states. Many former Soviet scholars could travel abroad and use funding and resources (both financial and theoretical) from the western research centers. The unique scholarly dialogue and collaboration between the western and former Soviet scholars were established during this time. Many talented Soviet intellectuals with different professional background, such as Serhii Plokhy (trained as a historian of early modern Ukraine), Yuri Slezkine (a linguist and expert in Portuguese), Irina Paperno (trained as an expert in Russian literature and associated with the Tartu school), Dmitry Shlapentokh (a historian of France and Russia), Aleksei Yurchak (a radio engineer and producer of famous Leningrad rock bands), Andrei Znamenskii (a historian of American Indians), Vladislav Zubok (trained as an expert in US politics), and myself (a social historian of Colonial British America) left their post-Soviet countries and joined western academia, teaching now Soviet/Russian/Ukrainian studies in American universities. All this experience contributed to the expanding and changing the field of Soviet studies, which became a real international phenomenon nowadays.[22]

In the early 1990s, Richard Stites was the first historian who wrote a complete and still the most popular history of popular culture and entertainment in Russia/Soviet Union since 1900. He covered major media of popular culture and various cultural forms, including music, films, television, variety shows and popular literature. He had already included a description of various forms of cultural practices, known later as "cultural consumption," or "imaginary West" in his pioneering efforts to analyze popular culture and everyday life of the Soviet society during the Cold War.[23] Both post-Soviet scholars, who began their new academic careers in the West, and young Western scholars, who study a cultural history of the Soviet Union now, were influenced by Richard Stites's ideas, approaches and research themes. For many of them, including myself, his work and life became an inspiration, and a real role model for writing the new cultural history of Soviet and post-Soviet space.[24]

Notes

1   Full title: *Russia's Lost Reformation*: *Peasants, Millennialism, and Radical Sects in Southern Russia and Ukraine, 1830-1917* (Washington: Woodrow Wilson Center/Baltimore: Johns Hopkins University Press, 2004).

2   Sergei I. Zhuk, *Rock and Roll in the Rocket City: The West, Identity, and Ideology in Soviet Dniepropetrovsk, 1960-1985* (Baltimore: Johns Hopkins University Press/Washington, D.C.: Woodrow Wilson Center Press, 2010).

3   See about this in Sergei I. Zhuk, *Rock and Roll in the Rocket City*, 90, 97, 246 (In my book, I misprinted his first name incorrectly as Aleksandr). See also information in Western media about his show: *Billboard*, February 19, 1972, and an internet interview with him: "Viktor Tatarskii: 'Vstreche s pesnei' reitingi ne nuzhny" in http://www.radioportal.ru/5005/viktor-tatarskii (no longer accessible).

4   See Kristin Roth-Ey, *Moscow Prime Time: How the Soviet Union Built the Media Empire That Lost the Cultural Cold War.* (Ithaca: Cornell University Press, 2011), 12. Compare with the first history of Russian comics books in José Alaniz, *Komiks: Comic Art in Russia.* (Jackson, MI: University Press of Mississippi, 2010).

5   Bagirov, *"Bitlz"*: *Liubov' moia* (Minsk: Parus), 160-62.

6   See about a détente from the American point of view in Walter LaFeber, *America, Russia, and the Cold War, 1945-1966*, 8th ed. (of a continuously updated monograph from 1969, covering through 1967, to 2002, covering through 2000) (New York: McGraw Hill, 1997) esp. 282-98.

7   See a story of the "Soviet TV Ogonёk" that was established in April of 1962 in Leonid G. Parfёnov, *Namedni. Nasha era, 1961-1970* (Moscow: KoLibri, 2009), 44; cf. Kristin Roth-Ey, *Moscow Prime Time*.

8   See about this in Sergei I. Zhuk, *Rock and Roll in the Rocket City*, 239, 240. See also Fedor I. Razzakov, *Gibel' sovetskogo TV: Tainy televidenia ot Stalina do Gorbacheva. 1930-1991* (Moscow: EKSMO, 2009), 7-260, especially 76, 96-97, 109-10. He had already written a series of popular books about Soviet cinema, radio, theater and television.

9   Kristin Roth-Ey, *Moscow Prime Time*, 36.

10   Sergei I. Zhuk, *Rock and Roll in the Rocket City*, 125, 126, 166. See also my essays: Sergei I. Zhuk, "The 'Closed' Soviet Society and the West: Consumption of the Western Cultural Products, Youth and Identity in Soviet Ukraine during the 1970s," in *The Crisis of Socialist Modernity: The Soviet Union and Yugoslavia in the 1970s*, eds., Marie-Janine Calic, Sabine Dabringhaus, Dietmar Neutatz and Julia Obertreis (Göttingen: Vandenhoeck & Ruprecht, 2011); 87-117, and Sergei I. Zhuk, "Zapad v sovetskom 'zakrytom' gorode: 'chuzhoe' kino, ideologiia i problemy kul'turnoi identichnosti na Ukraine v brezhnevskuiu epokhu (1864-1982 gody)," *Novoe literaturnoe obozrenie*, 2009, 100 (6): 548-65.

11   I quote here my interview with Professor Volodymyr B. Yevtukh, December 15, 1995, Kyiv. From 1990 to 2011, I interviewed more than one hundred people for my project about a role of the western cultural influences on Soviet people during late socialism. The majority of these people were from big industrial cities in Russia (Moscow and Leningrad/ St.Petersburg) and Ukraine (Kyiv, Dniepropetrovsk, and Odessa). I made transcripts of all my interviews (the most recent ones are on audio tapes). I also took notes from diaries some people made available to me, and xeroxed some of their pages. All interview transcripts and diary notes are in my possession.

12   See in detail about this in Zhuk, *Rock and Roll in the Rocket City*, especially, 126-38.

13   I quote a letter of Nikolai Bolkhovitinov to me, December 12, 1988. According to British scholars, "human self is envisaged as neither the product of an external symbolic system, nor as a fixed entity which the individual can immediately and directly grasp; rather the self is a symbolic project that the individual actively constructs out of the symbolic materials which are available to him or her, materials which the individ-

ual weaves into a coherent account of who he or she is, a narrative of self-identity." See in detail: John B. Thompson, *The Media and Modernity: A Social Theory of the Media* (Stanford: Stanford University Press, 1995), 207, 210.

14   See about this dichotomy in Juliane Fürst, *Late Stalinist Russia: Society between Reinvention and* Reconstruction (London: Routledge, 2006), 12, 23, 202, 236. See about a lack of historical erudition among party's historians in a letter of Nikolai Bolkhovitinov to me, from Moscow to Dniepropetrovsk, December 12, 1988, and in various interviews, especially my interview with Sergei N. Burin, September 5, 1999, Moscow. Burin used to criticize the experts in CPSU history as "stupid nationalistic assholes."

15   See an interview with I. Beliavskaia in "K vykhodu v svet 25-go vypuska: Yubilei I. A. Beliavskoi," *Amerikanskii ezhegodnik, 1995* (Moscow: Nauka, 1996), 8-18, especially p. 16.

16   Slava Gerovitch, "Writing History in the Present Tense: Cold War-era Discursive Strategies of Soviet Historians of Science and Technology," *Universities and Empire: Money and Politics in the Social Sciences during the Cold War*, ed., Christopher Simpson (New York: The New Press, 1998), 217-18.

17   See about this in Zhuk, *Rock and Roll in the Rocket City*, 210-11, 278-79.

18   I quote my interview with Sergei N. Burin, September 5, 1999, Moscow. Burin referred to a famous short novel by the Soviet Russian writer, published in 1927. See its English translation: Yuri Olesha, *Envy*, tr., Marian Schwartz (New York: New York Review Books, 2004).

19   See my interviews with Ivan Mikhailovich K., a retired colonel of the Soviet Army, June 3, 1990, Kyiv, and conversation with Valentin V. Piskarev, a retired colonel of the Soviet Army, March 12, 1991, Moscow. These officers explained the origin of the word *chmo*. Compare with my interview with Kalashnikov.

20   More than 90% of my interviewees from both Russian and Ukrainian provincial universities shared these notions. Different scholars from provincial universities such as A. Sergounin from Nizhnii Novgorod, V. Kalashnikov from Dniepropetrovsk, and A. Belonozhko from Zaporizhie, used the word *chmo* to characterize their Moscow colleagues.

21   See about revisionism in the American Soviet studies in David C. Engerman, *Know Your Enemy: The Rise and Fall of America's Soviet Experts* (New York: Oxford University Press, 2009), 9, 286, 294, 305-08. See about a new popularity of cultural studies and about mutual influences between western and former Soviet scholars in: Laura Engelstein, "Culture, Culture Everywhere: Interpretations of Modern Russia, across the 1991 Divide," *Kritika*, 2, no. 2 (Spring 2001): 363-93. Soviet historians also

were influenced by such a charismatic medievalist as Aron Gurevich who popularized the ideas of the French *Annales* among the Soviet reading audience. See about this in Roger D. Markwick, "Cultural History under Khrushchev and Brezhnev: From Social Psychology to *Mentalités*," *The Russian Review*, 65, no. 2 (April 2006): 283-301. See also Catriona Kelly, Hilary Pilkington, David Shepherd, and Vadim Volkov, "Introduction: Why Cultural Studies," in *Russian Cultural Studies: An Introduction*, eds. Catriona Kelly and David Shepherd (New York: Oxford University Press, 1998), 1-17.

22   See in Laura Engelstein, "Culture, Culture Everywhere," 389ff.

23   Richard Stites, *Russian Popular Culture: Entertainment and Society Since 1900* (New York: Cambridge University Press, 1992), 98-203.

24   See, especially, Vladislav Zubok, *Zhivago's Children: The Last Russian Intelligentsia* (Cambridge, MA: The Belknap Press of Harvard University Press, 2009), Juliane Fürst, *Stalin's Last Generation: Soviet Post-War Youth and the Emergence of Mature Socialism* (New York: Oxford University Press, 2010); Stephen V. Bittner, *The Many Lives of Khrushchev's Thaw: Experience and Memory in Moscow's Arbat* (Ithaca: Cornell University Press, 2008); Stephen Lovell, *Shadow of War: Russia and the USSR, 1941 to the Present* (Oxford: Wiley-Blackwell, 2010); Benjamin Tromly, "An Unlikely National Revival: Soviet Higher Learning and the Ukrainian 'Sixtiers,' 1953–65," *The Russian Review*, 68, no. 4 (October 2009): 607–22; idem, "Soviet Patriotism and its Discontents among Higher Education Students in Khrushchev-Era Russia and Ukraine," *Nationalities Papers*, 37, no. 3 (2009), 299-326; Gleb Tsipursky, "'As a Citizen, I Cannot Ignore These Facts': Whistleblowing in the Khrushchev Era," *Jahrbücher für Geschichte Osteuropas*, 58, no.1 (March 2010): 52-69; idem, "Citizenship, Deviance, and Identity: Soviet Youth Newspapers as Agents of Social Control in the Thaw-Era Leisure Campaign," *Cahiers du monde russe*, 49, no.4 (October-December 2008): 629-49.

8

Cars and the Particularities of "Personal Property" in the Brezhnev Era

by Lewis H. Siegelbaum

Cars have served as convenient devices to explore a wide array of social practices, cultural meanings, and economic strengths and weaknesses in both the developed and developing worlds as well as, to a lesser extent, the erstwhile Second World of state socialism. They are judged to have been "the central vehicle of all twentieth-century modernization," and "the best exemplification of the development of a putative globalization;" "the exact equivalent of the great Gothic cathedrals," and a form of "opium." They have been interpreted as both a "mania" and a utopia.[1] By using the car as a vehicle to explore the ambiguities and contradictions within the Soviet discourse of "personal property," this essay is intended to contribute to the expanding historical literature on consumption and material culture in the late Soviet era It draws on Igor Kopytoff's concept of "the cultural biography of things" to suggest that the automobile, often defined in terms of its inherent qualities, possessed a high degree of cultural malleability, or in Kopytoff's terms was "endowed with culturally specific meanings and classified and reclassified into culturally constituted categories."[2] It argues in effect that while other goods such as refrigerators and vacuum cleaners also took on meanings particular to the social and cultural formations in which they were embedded, cars - partly because of their relative scarcity and partly because of the lengths to which aspirant and real owners would go to obtain and maintain them - had richer biographies.

Khrushchev's discriminating consumerism

We can begin to highlight the biographical specificity of cars by referring to the major shift that Nikita Khrushchev effectuated in the political legitimacy of the Communist path to modernity – essentially reorienting it from steel mills to consumer goods. This was, as Susan Reid has described it, a "high-risk strategy," for it meant trying to create a form of modern civilization distinct from capitalism yet at the same time accepting many of the benchmarks of progress defined by the capitalist West and in particular the United States. Implicitly and even explicitly, in the quest to catch up and overtake the US in terms of standard of living, the standards and consumption levels – the norms to which the Soviet Union was aspiring – were those of the US. Such had been so with steel mills, but in the case of steel mills and other means of production, a semi-sacred body of texts extending back to *Capital* enshrined the benchmarks. The riskiness of abandoning tons of pig iron as an index and adopting discrete articles of personal consumption was made manifest by the American National Exhibition held in Moscow's Sokolniki Park in July 1959. There, beckoning in all its seductiveness was the technologically saturated American dream kitchen, the very kitchen where Khrushchev "debated" with Vice-President Richard Nixon the advantages of their respective countries and the systems each represented.

This American Trojan horse proved not nearly as successful in discrediting the communist project among Soviet citizens as some western commentators have claimed. As Susan Reid notes, this was partly because the dimensions of the American kitchen were far larger and the variety of appliances far greater than what most Soviet citizens considered appropriate to their circumstances. The Americans' "soft-power" initiative also belied the tremendous advances during the Khrushchev era in the provision of family kitchens thanks to the mass housing campaign.[3] Thus, it is conceivable that when a photograph appeared in *Izvestiia* of a Soviet housewife baking pies with her daughter and telling her that "our kitchen is

Table 1: Production of Durable Goods and Destination of Cars, 1950-1965 (in thousands of units)

Year	1950	1955	1960	1965
Televisions	na	495	1726	3655
Refrigerators	na	151	530	1675
Washing Machines	na	87	895	3430
Passenger Cars	65	108	139	201
of which:				
sold to population	23 (36%)	64 (59%)	62 (45%)	64 (32%)
exported	5 (8%)	13 (12%)	30 (22%)	49 (24%)
distributed	36 (56%)	31 (29%)	47 (33%)	88 (44%)

Source: *TsSU SSSR, Narodnoe khoziaistvo SSSR v 1967 g.* (Moscow: Gos. stat. izd-vo, 1968), 200-01; V. M. Iamashev, "Volzhskii avtozavod: prervannyi ryvok za mirovoi modernizatsiei," in A. E. Livshits and P. A. Nakhmanovich (dir.), *Istoriia OAO "Avtovaz": Uroki, problemy, sovremennost'. Materialy I Vserossiiskoi nauchnoi konferentsii, 26-27 noiabria 2003 g.* (Tol'iatti: OAO Avtovaz, TGU, 2003), 234.

just as good as the American one shown at the exhibition in Sokolniki," many *khoziaiki* would have nodded their heads in agreement or at least not dismissed the assertion as outlandish.[4]

Far less often noted, however, was the presence at the same exhibition of a bevy of automobiles – twenty-one Detroit beauties in all. The cars evidently made quite an impression.[5] But the notion that "our cars are just as good as the American ones," while arguably defensible in terms of durability or functionality, was quite beside the point.[6] If, as Table 1 demonstrates, access to domestic appliances was part of the package of gifts that the Khrushchevian state offered to Soviet families, complementing the family apartments that most historians see as emblematic of the era, Khrushchev made it abundantly clear that he did not consider cars part of the bargain. On the contrary, in one of his speeches to the Twentieth Party Congress he actually argued in favor of reducing access to cars for personal use by state and party functionaries. He condemned their assignment and that of drivers to individual officials as wasteful and instead proposed a rental system.[7] That system was launched with much fanfare beginning in 1959. Khrushchev described it to a mass meeting in October of that year as follows:

> We want to set up a different arrangement from capitalist countries for using passenger cars...We will use cars more rationally than the Americans. We will give full development to taxi fleets from which people can obtain cars for necessary trips. Why would a person break his neck over where to keep a car, why take the trouble when there is a better way that answers to the interests of society as a whole and to each citizen?[8]

Why indeed when *Pravda* could report from Kiev on "smart Moskviches and Pobedas ...lined up as if for a parade" just waiting for prospective renters. Sure, many a potential customer found himself waiting in long queues, taking various tests, and being subjected to «further complications."[9] But at least they did not suffer from the burdens of actually owning a car. "Poor Americans," a Soviet vacationer told the writer Muriel Reed during her trip to Sochi a few years later but still while Khrushchev was in power. "They can't seem to live without a car, a refrigerator, or a television." "Wouldn't you like to have a car?" Reed asked him, not bothering to inquire about the other two items. "I don't have to want a car. It's enough for there to be better public transportation."[10] Public transportation was indeed improving and would continue to do so in the future. In fact, as Academician S.G. Strumilin assured readers of *Izvestiia*, eventually the desire to own a car, a dacha, or an individual plot of land would "gradually wither away ...as requirements are met more and more out of public funds. The people themselves," he added, will throw away personal cars and dachas ...like so much excess baggage when modern boarding houses with all the conveniences spring up in the best and most picturesque locations, offering separate rooms, yachts, motor scooters for pleasure rides, and helicopters for excursions, etc., and when excellent cars of all models and colors (just pick one to suit your taste!) are lined up in the public garages, just waiting for passengers.[11]

But evidently many comrades, impatient with the arrival of this bright future, chafed at not having their own cars. To the end, though, Khrushchev resisted. In his memoirs, he insisted that "before we go around purchasing foreign auto factories, we should concentrate on organizing the production of feed for our livestock, pigs, and poultry on an industrial basis..." The thinking to which he adhered while in power was that it made "good economic and political sense to put the interests of millions who want to be well fed above the interests of thousands who will get pleasure out of buying a Fiat."[12] Alas, no sooner had he been forced to retire than the genie was let out of the bottle.

Parsing personal property

The new leadership in the Kremlin – evidently Aleksei Kosygin – initiated contact with the Italians pursuant of a deal, the "biggest deal of the century" in the words of multi-millionaire US diplomat Averell Harriman. Signed in 1966, the deal called for Fiat to provide the technical wherewithal for the erection of a state-of-the-art car factory that eventually could annually produce 700,000 Soviet versions of the Fiat 124. The factory, situated coincidentally in Tol'iatti, the Volga-river city named after the Italian communist who had died in 1964, began serial production of the Lada (known in the USSR as Zhiguli, after the hills on the right bank of the Volga) in 1972.[13] None of this made Khrushchev happy. "In the first place," he noted in his memoirs, "a Fiat is a product that only a limited quantity of people can use. In the second place, we already have pretty good cars of our own – our Zaporozhets, our Moskvich, our Volga, to say nothing of our classier cars..."[14]

Pretty good or not – and the consensus among people who know a lot more about car performance than I do is that they left a lot to be desired – not enough were being made available to satisfy the longing for personal mobility and convenience, for getting to the dacha on weekends, and for other purposes. The case for expanding individual ownership of automobiles rested on their identification as "personal property" no different in kind from refrigerators, televisions, and vacuum cleaners. "Pity the poor automobilist" (in Russian, *avtoliubitel'*, a term that combined notions of amateur and enthusiast and managed thereby to serve as a euphemism for owner). This was the message of an article appearing in *Izvestiia* in January 1965, a few months after Khrushchev's forced retirement. "I'm an engineer, and it took me ten years to come up with the money for this car," the driver of a Zaporozhets complained when he stopped late one evening to give a lift to the reporter. "And here's what I don't understand …. It baffles me why when a person buys a television, a piano, a carpet or other junk it's called the growth of well-being (*blagosostoianie*). But deny yourself all these charms, go into debt and obtain the most modest automobile or even win a Moskvich in the lottery, and you immediately become a suspicious private person (*chastnik*)." To be a chastnik meant to endure rude treatment by police who dismissed "hooliganism" (randomly inflicted damage) against individually owned cars with the comment that "you must understand that private persons are not liked here," and who were known to stop drivers on Sunday to fine them for driving dirty cars. And where was one to wash one's car? Not in the courtyard - the community (*obshchestvennost'*) wouldn't permit it. The nearest carwash is 15 kilometers away and you would have to wait at least three hours for your turn. As for parking, at nine rubles a month a parking place in the open air cost more than a two-room apartment with central heating and hot water.[15]

Clearly it was time to change attitudes toward and improve conditions for car owners. "Older citizens," *Izvestiia* observed in March 1966, "remember a time not too long ago when wrist watches and bicycles were luxury items, to say nothing of radio receivers, televisions, and vacuum cleaners. But now these things have entered into daily life." So too would automobiles.[16] "Especially in connection with the rapid development of technology and the growth of production, the car undoubtedly will become more accessible and cease to be regarded as a luxury item," another article from August 1966 promised.[17]

And so they did, though never as much so as refrigerators, televisions, and vacuum cleaners which approximately 90 percent of Soviet households possessed by 1980.[18] Car ownership stood at about 5.5 million in 1975 rising closer to 10 million by 1985.[19] This corresponded to an increase in the ratio of cars to people from 26 per thousand to 45 per thousand in 1985, or approximately 5 percent of households in 1975 in possession of a car but 15 percent of households in 1985. Of course, densities varied from republic to republic as well as within each of them. If the Baltic republics were at the high end with roughly twice as many cars per person as the all-Union average, Moldavia in the southwest and the Central Asian republics fell below it.[20] Personal ownership of cars remained quite low in kolkhozes and among sovkhoz workers compared to urban residents. Though evidence is mostly impressionistic, it appears that white-collar workers/*intelligenty* were more likely to own a car than blue-collar workers.[21]

According to Soviet economic practice, goods were not so much sold as distributed. Insofar as consumers obtained both items through the distribution mechanisms of their trade unions and had little choice with respect to models, colors, and other features, refrigerators and cars resembled each other. Insofar as it usually took much longer to obtain a car than a refrigerator – the length of time creeping upward from six to eight and even ten years by the 1980s – they did not.[22] The difference between cars and domestic appliances was not just differential density of ownership or the time it took to acquire each item. A Leningrad-based study of the inventory of engineering workers from the early 1970s placed cars in the same category as grand pianos because approximately the same percentage of households possessed each, but one would be hard-pressed to see any other similarity between the two items.[23]

As far as technical properties are concerned, cars and refrigerators actually share important characteristics. "Like the automobile," Victoria de Grazia has noted, "the refrigerator required an electrical system and a compressor for the cooling system." William Durant, who sold his fledgling refrigerator company (Frigidaire)

Fig. 1 Soviet refrigerators

to General Motors in 1919, once described cars and refrigerators as essentially the same item: metal boxes with motors inside. Perhaps this was why in addition to producing a line of heavy trucks and the country's most prestigious limousines, ZIL (Zavod imeni Likhacheva) turned out refrigerators (Fig. 1).[24] And if vacuum cleaners could be designed to remind the prospective purchaser of rocket ships, then the styling of refrigerators could resemble that of automobiles.[25] But in terms of the complexity of legal issues provoked by their ownership and disposition, it is the apartments and dachas containing refrigerators (and, occasionally, pianos) that resembled cars. As with these dwelling places, Soviet jurists had to make Solomon-like judgments about the disposition of cars and cooperative garage shares in divorce cases, the legality of presenting a car as a gift to an unrelated person, and the ins and outs of insurance and liability in cases of accidents.[26]

Producer and consumer goods

What most distinguished automobiles, though, was not their legal standing but rather the fact that so many were used by their owners for income-generating purposes. The distinction was crucial to Soviet legal theory, which defined personal (*lichnaia*) property as "that which is destined exclusively for the personal needs of the owner or his family." Private (*chastnaia*) property by contrast was property "used for profit, enrichment, or earnings."[27] "Large numbers of Soviet motorists ... drive out to the country to steal cabbages from collective farms, hire their car out for taxi service or buying up scarce foods," reported an American academic couple in *The New York Times* in 1966.[28] They thereby crossed the legal line between the two forms of property and, as the Americans noted, were engaging in illegal activities. In effect, they were converting an article of personal consumption into a producer good and personally – or rather, privately – reaping the profit. Motorists undoubtedly took risks in doing so, but the ordinariness of picking people up for a mutually agreed-upon price strongly suggests that the police could not be bothered. Still, the taint of flouting legal as well as ethical prohibitions remained strong among car owners, strong enough to cast cars as dubiously legal, personally corrupting, and socially disruptive objects in quite a few Soviet films of the Khrushchev and Brezhnev eras. Comedies in particular could get away with exposing some of the social and political ambivalence about cars in a way that more serious dramas could not.

In the 1958 comedy, *A Driver by Accident (Shofer ponevole)*, Ivan Petrovich Pastukhov, the driver of the title, takes the wheel after his chauffeur who also happens to be named Ivan Petrovich suffers back spasms that require his hospitalization. Each inevitably is mistaken for the other, but it is the accidental driver's adventures in the car he can barely keep on the road that provides much of the humor.[29] Audiences could take away two diametrically opposed messages: assuming the role/identity of a professional driver is asking for trouble, and, what an idiot this guy is! I would drive much better than he. In *Three Plus Two (Tri plius dva)* from 1963 (Fig. 2), one of the three guys tells his friend who is on his back underneath his car, "You poor slave of four wheels! How many times must I teach you that machine must serve man, and not the reverse!"[30] This remark, said in a tone of mock seriousness, could be interpreted as both endorsing the ideologically charged hostility to private ownership of cars characteristic of the Khrushchev era and lampooning it. Most Soviet viewers probably realized that only thanks to one of the guys owning a car did the three of them get to camp along

Fig. 2 *Three Plus Two (Tri plius dva)*, 1963

the Black Sea coast as "wild tourists" – itself a rather controversial category – and meet the two women who also have motored down from Moscow.[31] Then again, of the three, it is the slave-to-the-machine car owner who is left out when the other two pair off with the two female beach lovers.

The two best-known comedic movies from the Brezhnev era in which cars had leading roles were directed by El'dar Riazanov. In his 1966 film *Look Out for Your Car! (Beregis' avtomobilia)* the great Soviet actor Innokenty Smoktunovskii plays Iurii Detochkin, an avenging angel who steals cars from their nefarious owners, sells them to honest people, and donates the money to orphanages. Justice – though not law – could be seen to have been served until Detochkin goes too far by stealing a Volga from a physicist, that is, someone above reproach (Fig. 3).[32] For this crime, Detochkin is sent to prison, but at the very end of the film we see him released and reunited with his girlfriend apparently cured of his "pathological" aversion to shady car owners. In 1979 Riazanov returned to cars as corrupters of morals but this time also as sources of antagonism among workmates and friends. In *Garazh (The Garage)*, a group of

Fig. 3 *Look Out for Your Car!* (*Beregis' avtomobilia*), 1966

museum employees discovers that they need to eliminate four of their number from the coveted garage cooperative because there are not enough spaces for their cars. But how are they going to do it without wrecking a lot of friendships, not to mention the collective's *esprit de corps*?

I am unaware of a Soviet movie in which a refrigerator or any other domestic appliance plays a major role, though televisions appear in many and sometimes help to move the plot along. A biography of televisions in the late Soviet period also presumably would contain references to the propensity of several models to explode.[33] In this respect – defective manufacturing of consumer goods – they would resemble cars and indeed many of the kitchens built for new apartment dwellers. The reasons for the low quality were many and well known.[34] Some were structural, such the lack of quality-control which virtually ensured that defects in materials would be passed onto and cause problems in the next stage of the production process; the importance of quantitative indices in plan fulfillment which tended to marginalize substantive criteria; and the lower priority accorded to consumer goods compared to military-industrial and other strategically important sectors of the economy. Others had to do with the lack of significant incentives among workers or the weakness of correspondence between effort and reward.

The more components and other resources an article contained, the greater the number of administrative units involved in providing the wherewithal to obtain them. Focusing on kitchen equipment during the Khrushchev era, Susan Reid has written that "in the mismatch of one ostensibly coterminous surface with another lay the discontinuities of an entire economy... [T]he kitchen, where the products of various industries and services came together in a single small space, was the site where such contradictions became most palpable."[35] Just as countertops rarely aligned with stove tops, or refrigerators with the space designed to accommodate them, so car body production did not coincide with tire supply, batteries, or just about anything else. One ministry or sub-ministerial *glavk* presided over the production of spark plugs, while another arranged for and monitored the production of cloth for upholstery. While highly desired by the public, cars and their production lacked the highest priority in the state's ordering of things and thus, like countertops, did without effective coordinating mechanisms in the party-state bureaucratic machine.

Skirting the law

Cars *were* like refrigerators and televisions in that owners either could repair them by themselves if they were so mechanically inclined and had access to the necessary parts, or they could pay someone else to fix them. Despite the promise of VAZ to replicate Fiat in providing a network of stations to service the vehicles they produced, such venues never catered to more than a small percentage of car owners.[36] They and the facilities intended to service other models also were notoriously understaffed, poorly equipped and unreliable. Indeed, stories of cars being cannibalized while their owners waited for them to be repaired became part of the gallows humor associated with "auto enthusiasm" (*avtoliubitel'stvo*).[37] The "someone else" thus often meant a pensioner or mechanic working on the side. But whether motorists did the job themselves or had it done by a moonlighter, securing the parts for the job was never easy and often involved skirting the law.

Parts were in notoriously short supply partly as a result of bad coordination among different production units and their supervising bodies, partly because priority was given to fleets owned by state institutions, and partly because planners systematically underestimated the longevity of cars and therefore the demand for parts. Whatever the causes, three-quarters of auto owners surveyed nationally in 1968 cited a shortage of parts among the difficulties they faced. Fourteen years later, in 1982, "more than" 160 car parts were reported to be in short supply throughout the country. Spare parts production inexplicably fell by a reported 9 percent that year compared to 1980, while the stock of cars had increased by 22 percent in the interim.[38] Managers of stores hectored by the press for lacking supplies of parts complained of hoarding and panic buying by speculators and second-hand dealers (*perekupshchiki*), but, if true, this was only symptomatic of a larger problem.[39] Little wonder that among the many songs composed by Iurii Vizbor that commented on everyday life was one about the owner of a Pobeda who used his wife's sewing machine for spare parts, and another in which the hero procures two fish, exchanges them for two tickets to the Taganka theater, and only then obtains the parts he needs for his car.[40]

It is here, at the point where motorists crossed over into the shadow/grey/on-the-side/ or second economy to obtain parts, fuel, garage space, and repair services, that we must again distinguish cars from refrigerators and other domestic appliances.[41] Cars in the late Soviet period had greater "knock-on" effects with respect to off-the-books, semi-legal, and illegal activity than any other durable good. According to British economist Peter Wiles, road transport (essentially, fuel consumption) figured among the activities "most affected" by second-economy activities, but along with building repairs, car repairs were "in a class by themselves" where "there seem to be few uncorrupt transactions."[42] In short, their contribution to the second economy was far in excess of refrigerators, vacuum cleaners or televisions, even if in terms of physical units cars were not nearly as numerous.

Parts could be procured almost anywhere that suppliers and purchasers agreed to meet – at technical service stations where supplies intended for ordinary customers went missing; in auto towns such as Tol'iatti where, in the mid-1980s, camshafts officially priced at 23 rubles were sold "among speculators" for 200-250 rubles and Cardan shafts that sold in the stores (if the stores had any) for 6.5 rubles went for 50-60 rubles; and on the outskirts of towns sometimes along railroad sidings or on abandoned lots such as near the Dmitrov highway north of the Moscow Ring Road. There, illicit suppliers – whom the main character in a novel about a desperate car owner refers to as "unofficial members of the priestly sect of Automobile Longevity" – would lay out their wares on the ground to be inspected by flashlight in the wee hours of the night.[43] As with using their cars to make money, motorists were running something of a risk to spend it in this manner, but their need for wheels usually outweighed their fear of purchasing *brak* (defective parts) or getting caught by the police.

A whole cottage industry developed in the West around studying second economic activity in the USSR, including activity related to cars. One such study from 1977 estimated that in 1972 cars owned by individuals consumed approximately 500 million liters of gasoline "on the side," primarily via coupons that truck drivers sold to motorists for use at gas stations, or by directly siphoning gas from the trucks. The equivalent figure for 1982 amounting to three-quarters of all fuel consumed by private automobiles was 7.5 billion liters. Another study dealt with the second-hand car market which was far more robust and involved considerably higher prices than those officially announced in the state-run commission stores. Indeed so vibrant was the market for used cars that "the average ruble price ... was often higher than the price at which [they] had originally been sold."[44] In this respect as well cars did not resemble refrigerators.

Cars, space, and gender

What was the allure of the automobile that would justify such sacrifices? Like cars the world over, the Soviet automobile was a source of prestige, something stressed by people with whom I did interviews for *Cars for Comrades*. It also gave owners greater control over their time and enabled them to reach more easily destinations such as dachas and relatives living beyond city limits. In addition, cars provided their owners and members of their family with private space additional to the often quite minimal amount afforded by family apartments. Here, I am using "private" not as Soviet law defined it but rather in the double sense of being at the discretion of the individual rather than the collective, and of being hidden rather than transparent or out in the open.[45] As Jean Baudrillard observed in a very different cultural context, "The car rivals the house as an alternative zone of everyday life: the car, too, is an abode, but an exceptional one; it is a closed realm of intimacy, but one released from the constraints that usually apply to the intimacy of the home, one endowed with a formal freedom of great intensity."[46] Not until the post-Soviet era would Muscovites have the opportunity to replicate the Parisian experience described by Kristen Ross of peaceful solitude in the midst of a traffic jam, but who needed traffic jams to sit in one's own (stationary) car and shut out the rest of the world?[47]

The fact that cars did not live in the household but were domiciled at some – often considerable - distance from where their owners lived is yet another way of distinguishing them from domestic appliances. Just as the Soviet gender order coded domestic space and the use of the equipment located therein as feminine, so the courtyards and garages where owners kept their cars became

Fig.4 Garages in Makhachkala

identified as masculine space (Fig. 4).[48] This spatial-gender division was far from unique, although the ubiquity of the "double shift" in late Soviet public discourse and the unusualness of female ownership of cars lead one to think that the division assumed particularly sharp proportions in the Soviet Union.[49] Elsewhere I have described the garages and sheds where Soviet (urban) motorists kept their cars as "alternative living rooms" that "provided a car-centered milieu for male sociability" and bonding.[50] The bonding was above all with the car itself but it also could be intra-familial – between fathers and sons (or in the absence of sons, occasionally daughters) – or it could occur among fellow car owners in the neighborhood. Hoping to pick up a thing or two about cars, young boys living in the same apartment block would gravitate to these places and thereby grow into what the Swedish ethnographer, Ulf Mellström, has called "technical male sociability." Conversation could be about cars, but about other things too, especially things that would not be discussed in the presence of women. Substantial quantities of alcohol and cigarettes could be consumed.[51]

Soviet cars, while not the most reliable, were relatively easy to fix. This was fortunate for, as the Russian historian Marina Zezina has noted, "in the absence of a developed system of car servicing, the responsibility for everyday technical servicing and car maintenance continued to rest on the shoulders of car owners."[52] Or, in the words of a Soviet transportation expert participating in a roundtable discussion in 1976 on "motorization in a developed socialist society," "Car enthusiasts are compelled to raise their own technical culture ... ." Obviously trying to put the best face on the abysmal state of repair services in the Soviet version of a developed socialist society, the expert referred to this compulsion as "a positive development."[53] But we should not dismiss the notion that, though time-consuming, maintaining and fixing one's own car could be a pleasurable and rewarding experience. It was not only that working on the car gave men a ready-made excuse to absent themselves from other domestic responsibilities, though the analogy used by one informant is telling. "In winter," he told me, when it was really cold, if you wanted to use your car, you had to warm it up before you went to bed, and then at 4:00 a.m. and then again at 8 – like feeding a baby."[54] Cars in this sense were very personal property, quite unlike refrigerators.

Conclusions

Cars and refrigerators have little in common except that both were cited as key indices of "material betterment" and "cultural-community purpose" in annual statistical collections on the national economy as well as in sociological journals.[55] The inexorable growth in their numbers, like those of vacuum cleaners, television sets, washing machines and other domestic appliances implied that the USSR was getting ever closer to the situation of sufficiency if not abundance vouchsafed by its political leaders. The rate of growth was indeed impressive, suggesting that the historical gap in personal consumption between the Soviet Union and the advanced capitalist countries was diminishing.

Upon closer inspection, the statistics were, if not illusory, then revealing of only one dimension of the complex relationship between individuals or families and material goods and the extent to which people were encouraged to believe they were entitled to these items. As already noted, the rate of ownership of automobiles was found to be roughly equivalent to that of grand pianos among working-class households in the early 1970s. Nearly ten years later, three times as many working-class households owned a car as a piano.[56] But these findings indicate nothing about "demand," or more meaningfully, desire.[57] As fast as VAZ and other car manufacturers turned out their diminutive four-wheelers, the queues of aspiring owners grew faster still. This was democracy, Soviet-style. Not exactly encouraging such a torrential wave of desire for personal mobility, the authorities nevertheless condoned it – and thereby the bribery, wheeling-and-dealing, shady operations, on-the-side machinations, and other activities by no means unique to cars but more closely associated with them in the Brezhnev era than, well, than refrigerators.

Notes

1 See respectively Kristen Ross, *Fast Cars, Clean Bodies: Decolonization and the Reordering of French Culture* (Cambridge MA: The MIT Press,

1996), 19; John Urry, "Automobility, Car Culture and Weightless Travel: A discussion paper," 1, Department of Sociology, Lancaster University, Lancaster LA1 4YN, UK, at http://www.comp.lancs.ac.uk/sociology/papers/Urry-Automobility.pdf (accessed April 4, 2008); Roland Barthes, *Critical Essays*, trans. Richard Howard (Evanston: Northwestern University Press, 1972), 88; David Gartman, *Auto Opium: A Social History of American Automobile Design* (London: Routledge, 1994); Tom McCarthy, *Auto Mania: Cars, Consumers, and the Environment* (New Haven: Yale University Press, 2007); and *Autopia: Cars and Culture*, ed., Peter Wollen and Joe Kerr (London: Reaktion, 2002).

2   Igor Kopytoff, "The Cultural Biography of Things: Commoditization as Process," in *The Social Life of Things: Commodities in Cultural Perspective*, ed. Arjun Appadurai, (Cambridge UK: Cambridge University Press, 1986), 68.

3   Susan E. Reid, "Who Will Beat Whom?: Soviet Popular Reception of the American National Exhibition in Moscow, 1959," *Kritika: Explorations in Russian and Eurasian History*, 9, no. 4,(2008): 862, 898; *Idem.*, "Sites of Convergence: The USSR and Communist Eastern Europe at International Fairs Abroad and Home," paper presented at Sites of Convergence conference, Budapest, May 28-30, 2009.

4   Susan E. Reid, "'Our Kitchen Is Just as Good': Soviet Responses to the American Kitchen," in Ruth Oldenziel and Karin Zachmann, ed., *Cold War Kitchen: Americanization, Technology, and European Users* (Cambridge MA: MIT Press, 2009), 83-112, quotation at 83. Recent scholarship on the Soviet fashion industry suggests a similar dynamic. See Larissa Zakharova, "Kazhdoi sovetskoi zhenshchine – plat'e ot Diora! Frantsuzskoe vliianie v sovetsoi mode 1950-1960-kh gg." in *Sotsial'naia istoriia Ezhegodnik*, 2004, 339-67.

5   See Walter L. Hixson, *Parting the Curtain: Propaganda, Culture, and the Cold War, 1945-1961* (New York: St. Martin's, 1997), 199-203.

6   For earlier negative comments about American cars' excessively powerful engines and "uneconomical" bodies, see *Avtomobil'naia i traktornaia promyshlennost'*, no. 8 (1956): 39-46; no. 10 (1956): 43-46.

7   Kommunisticheskaia partiia Sovetskogo Sojuza. S"ezd 1956, Moskva, *Stenograficheskii otchet*, 2 vols. (Moscow: Gosizdat, 1956), 1: 51.

8   *Za rulem*, no. 12 (1959): 8-9, inside cover.

9   *Pravda*, 14 June 1960, 4. See also *Za rulem*, no. 8 (1960): 17-19; no. 3 (1962): 12-13.

10   Muriel Reed, "Avec la nouvelle société russe en vacances j'ai gouté aux délices de Sotchi," *Réalités*, no. 213 (1963): 59-60.

11   *Izvestiia*, 30 Aug.1961, 3. This fantasy seems to have been of fairly long duration. Milla Fedorova refers to a history lesson in her Soviet

high school class (during the 1970s at the earliest) in which her teacher claimed that under full Communism "there would be no money and anyone would be able to go to a store and simply take what he/she needed. 'Even a car?' – asked an unbelieving voice. The class burst out laughing, and the teacher was furious." Review of *Cars for Comrades* in *Slavic and East European Journal*, 54, no.1 (2010): 205.

12   Nikita Khrushchev, *Khrushchev Remembers: The Last Testament*, trans. Strobe Talbott (Boston: Little Brown and Company, 1974), 160.

13   For more on the deal and the VAZ factory that eventuated from it, see Lewis H. Siegelbaum, *Cars for Comrades: The Life of the Soviet Automobile* (Ithaca: Cornell University Press, 2008), 88-109. For a collectively authored history of VAZ, see R. Pikhoia *et al. AVTOVAZ mezhdu proshlym i budushchim. Istoriia Volzhskogo avtomobil'nogo zavoda, 1966-2005 gg.* (Moscow: RAGS, 2006).

14   Khrushchev, *Khrushchev Remembers*, 159.

15   *Izvestiia*, 28 January 1965, 3.

16   *Izvestiia*, 4 March 1966, 3; 5 March 1966, 3.

17   *Izvestiia*, 18 August 1966, 5.

18   The proportion of Soviet households reported as owning televisions and refrigerators rose respectively from 24 and 11 percent in 1965, to 74 and 65 percent in 1975, and 92 and 89 percent in 1982. See Table 2.6 in David Lane, *Soviet Economy and Society* (Oxford: Blackwell, 1985), 58. For references to these items in connection with automobile ownership, see D. P. Velikanov, "Avtomobil' i my," *Literaturnaia gazeta*, 19 March 1971, 12; *Pravda*, July 24, 1971, 3; Leonid Likhodeev, *Ia i moi avtomobil'* (Moscow: Sovietskii Pisatel', 1972), 17-19 ("Do you have a TV, do you have a refrigerator? So, there will be a car."), and G. N. Andrienko, "Legkovoi avtomobil' v sem'e," in *Ekonomika i organizatsiia promyshlennogo proizvodstva* (Kiev, 1985), 106.

19   TsSU SSSR, *Narodnoe khoziaistvo SSSR v 1985* (Moscow: Gos. stat. izd-vo, 1986), 446. Toli Welihozkiy, "Automobiles and the Soviet Consumer," in *Soviet Economy in a Time of Change, a Compendium of Papers submitted to the joint Economic Committee, Congress of the United States* (Washington, D. C.: US Government Printing Office, 1979), 818 cites a figure of 7.3 million vehicles by 1979, of which 80 percent (5.8 million) were owned by individuals.

20   William Pyle, "Private Car Ownership and Second Economy Activity," *Berkeley-Duke Occasional Papers on the Second Economy in the USSR*, no. 37 (Washington, D.C., 1993), 49, and A. Arrak, "Ispol'zovanie avtomobilei lichnogo pol'zovaniia," *Voprosy ekonomiki*, no. 7 (1978): 134; *Izvestiia*, 14 August 1988, 3.

21   Andrienko, "Legkovoi avtomobil'," 111.

22   John M. Kramer, "Soviet Policy Towards the Automobile," *Survey*, 22, no. 2 (1976): 20-21; Welihozkiy, "Automobiles and the Soviet Consumer," 822-23.

23   Ivan Trufanov, *Problems of Soviet Urban Life*, trans. James Riordan (Newtonville, Mass.: Oriental Research Partners, 1977), 92-93.

24   Victoria de Grazia, *Irresistible Empire: America's Advance through Twentieth-Century Europe* (Cambridge UK: Belknap Press, 2005), 206; Siegelbaum, *Cars for Comrades*, 28-29.

25   Susan E. Reid, "This is Tomorrow! Becoming a Consumer in the Soviet Sixties," p. 30 of draft presented at 2010 Fisher Forum conference on "The Socialist 1960s: Popular Culture and the City in Global Perspective," 24-26 June 2010. I. V. Narskii reports that his grandparents' apartment in Gor'kii contained a ZIL-Moskva refrigerator "with a handle and an opening for a key like the door of an automobile." This was in the mid-1960s. See I. V. Narskii, *Fotokartochka na pamiat': Semeinye istorii, fotograficheskie poslaniia i sovetskoe detstvo (Avtobio-istorio-graficheskii roman)* (Cheliabinsk: Entsiklopediia, 2008), 45.

26   For such cases, see *Soviet Statutes & Decisions*, 22, no. 3 (1986): 54-57; E. I. Aiueva, "Sdelki grazhdan po rasporiazheniiu legkovymi avtomobiliami," *Sovetskoe gosudarstvo i pravo*, 9 (1974): 109-14; V. M. Zharkov, "Strakhovanie grazhdanskoi otvetstvennosti vladel'stev avtotransporta v SSSR," in *Problemy sovershenstvovaniia sovetskogo zakonodatel'stva*, 23 (Moscow, 1982): 154-64.

27   *Izvestiia*, March 4, 1966, 3. For two elaborations of the distinction, see Marcie Cowley, "Negotiating Soviet Inheritance Law, 1917-1965," Ph.D. dissertation, Michigan State University, 2009; Charles Hachten, "Property Relations and the Economic Organization of Soviet Russia, 1941-1948," Ph.D. dissertation, University of Chicago, 2005.

28   Donald D. Barry and Carol Barner Barry, "Happiness is Driving Your Own Moskvich," *New York Times Magazine*, April 10, 1966, 48.

29   *Shofer ponevole* (Nadezhda Kosheverova, dir., 1958, Lenfil'm). The screenplay was by Sergei Mikhalkov, children's story writer, co-author of the words to the Soviet national anthem.

30   The film was based on *Wild Tourists (Dikari)*, a play from 1959 by Sergei Mikhalkov. See his *Teatr dlia vzroslykh* (Moscow: Iskusstvo, 1979), 329-78.

31   See Christian Noack, "Coping with the Tourist: Planned and 'Wild' Mass Tourism on the Soviet Black Sea Coast," in *Turizm: The Russian and East European Tourist under Capitalism and Socialism*, Anne E. Gorsuch and Diane P. Koenker, eds. (Ithaca: Cornell University Press, 2006), 281-304

32   David MacFadyen, *The Sad Comedy of El'dar Riazanov: An Introduc-*

tion to Russia's Most Popular Filmmaker (Montreal: McGill-Queen's University Press, 2003), p. 113. For the script of the film, see Emil' Braginskii and El'dar Riazanov, *Tikhie omuty* (Moscow: Vagrius, 2000).

33   Exploding televisions emerged in the western media during perestroika as possibly "the gravest problem facing Western companies hoping to advertise on television, according to an article appearing in the Business section of *The New York Times*, May 23, 1990.

34   This was of course the case not only in the USSR, but throughout the Soviet bloc. For an insightful analysis of some of the cultural consequences of indifferently-made goods, see Krisztina Fehérváry, "Goods and States: The Political Logic of State-Socialist Material Culture," *Comparative Studies in Society and History*, 51, no. 2 (2009): 426-59.

35   Susan E. Reid, "The Khrushchev Kitchen: Domesticating the Scientific-Technological Revolution," *Journal of Contemporary History*, 40, no. 2 (2005): 314. On the "bureaucratic maze," Moshe Lewin's term for this phenomenon, see his *The Soviet Century* (London: Verso, 2005), 342-60.

36   *Izvestiia*, April 13, 1972, 4; *Za rulem*, no. 2 (1978): 11; R. D. Kisliuk, "Otkrytie avtoservisa v strane. Sozdanie novykh otnoshenii 'chelovek – avtomobil',"' in *Istoriia OAO "AVTOVAZ": uroki, problem, sovremennost'*, ed. R. G. Pikhoia (Tol'iatti: AVTOVAZ, 2005), 261-64.

37   See for example *Pravda*, 24 July 1971, 3; *Izvestiia*, 9 September 1971, 3; Nataliia Il'ina, "My remontiruem avtomobil'," *Literaturnaia gazeta*, February 21, 1973, 12; P. Volin, "Kogda techet 'Volga'," *Literaturnaia gazeta*, 20 September 1978, 12; *Za rulem*, no. 9 (1978): 6; no. 1 (1986):18-19; no. 4 (1986): 15; no. 6 (1986): 6; no. 9 (1986): 15; no. 11 (1986): 7.

38   *Za rulem*, no. 3 (1968), back page; no. 4 (1968): 17; no. 5 (1968): 12; Andrienko, "Legkovoi avtomobil', 109, 115.

39   *Za rulem*, no. 4 (1978): 36-37.

40   Maria R. Zezina, "The Introduction of Motor Vehicles on a Mass Scale in the USSR: from Idea to Implementation," in *Towards Mobility. Varieties of Automobilism in East and West*, Corinna Kuhr-Korolev and Dirk Schlinkert, eds. (Wolfsburg: Volkswagen AG, 2009), 49.

41   The canonical article on the subject is Gregory Grossman, "The 'Second Economy' of the USSR," *Problems of Communism*, 25, no. 5 (1977): 25-40. For a typological definition of the second economy and its interdependence with the official economy, see F. J. M. Feldbrugge, "Government and Shadow Economy in the Soviet Union," *Soviet Studies*, 36, no. 4 (1984): 528-43.

42   Peter Wiles, "What We Still Don't Know About the Soviet Economy," in *The CMEA Five-Year Plans (1981-1985) in a New Perspective: Planned and Non-Planned Economies* (Brussels: NATO, 1982), 129.

43   Pikhoia et al., *AVTOVAZ mezhdu proshlym i budushchim*, 250-51;

Za rulem, no. 1 (1986): 18-19; author's interview with Sasha, 13 September 2004, Moscow; James M. Laux, *The European Automobile* Industry (New York: Twayne, 1992), 209; Likhodeev, *Ia i moi avtomobil'*, 208.

44   See respectively Welihozkiy, "Automobiles and the Soviet Consumer," 849; M. Alexeev, "Underground Market for Gasoline in the USSR," *Berkeley-Duke Occasional Papers on the Second Economy in the USSR*, no. 9 (Washington, D.C., 1987), 1-25; Pyle, "Private Car Ownership and Second Economy Activity," 42-45.

45   Jeff Weintraub, "The Theory and Politics of the Public/Private Distinction," in *Public and Private in Thought and Practice: Perspectives on a Grand Dichotomy*, ed. Jeff Weintraub and Krishan Kumar (Chicago: University of Chicago Press, 1997), 4-5.

46   Jean Baudrillard, *The System of Objects* (London: Verso, 1996), 67.

47   Ross, *Fast Cars, Clean Bodies*, 54-55.

48   On the concept of gender orders see R. Connell, *Gender and Power: Society, the Person, and Sexual Politics* (Cambridge UK: Cambridge University Press, 1987), 92-100. On its application to Soviet (and post-Soviet) Russia, see Sarah Ashwin, "Introduction: Gender, State, and Society in Soviet and Post-Soviet Russia," in *Gender, State, and Society in Soviet and Post-Soviet Russia*, ed. Sarah Ashwin (London: Routledge, 2000), 1-29.

49   The "double shift" or "double burden" is the subject of an immense literature. For a comprehensive overview, see Tatyana Mamonova, ed. *Women and Russia: Feminist Writings from the Soviet Union* (Boston: Beacon, 1984). For the paucity of women behind the wheel, see Corinna Kuhr-Korolev, "Women and Cars in Soviet and Russian Society," in *The Socialist Car: Automobility in the Eastern Bloc*, ed. Lewis H. Siegelbaum (Ithaca: Cornell University Press, 2011).

50   Lewis H. Siegelbaum, "On the Side: Car Culture in the USSR, 1960s-1980s," *Technology and Culture*, 50, no. 1 (2009): 18.

51   Ulf Mellström, *Masculinity, Power and Technology: a Malaysian Ethnography* (Aldershot: Ashgate, 2003), 115. For Russian examples, see Rebecca Kay, *Men in Contemporary Russia: The Fallen Heroes of Post-Soviet Change?* (Aldershot: Ashgate, 2006), 79, 91-92, 133; and the interview with Vladimir Arkusha, associate editor, about his early acquaintance with cars in the 1960s and '70s in *Za rulem*, no. 3 (2002): 132-34. I also am drawing on personal observation in Moscow and Tol'iatti.

52   Zezina, "Introduction of Motor Vehicles," 53.

53   V. T. Efimov and G. I. Mikerin, "Avtomobilizatsiia v razvitom sotsialisticheskom obshchestve," *Sotsialisticheskie issledovaniia*, no. 1 (1976): 13

54   Telephone interview with Vadim, 9 June 2004.

55   See annual volumes of *Narodnoe khoziaistvo SSSR* issued by the Central Statistical Administration and articles such as V. Kh. Bigulov, A.

O. Kryshtanovskii, and A. S. Michurin, "Material'noe blagosostoianie i sotsial'noe blagopoluchie: Opyt postroeniia indeksov i analiz vzaimosvi-azi," *Sotsiologicheskie issledovaniia*, no. 4 (1984): 88-93; M. E. Pozdniakova, "Obespechennost' naseleniia predmetami kul'turno-bytovogo naznache-niia," *Sotsiologichekie issledovaniia*, no. 3 (1987): 59-61.

56   Pozdniakova, "Obespechennost'," 60.

57   On the difference between these two categories, see Siegelbaum, *Cars for Comrades*, 222-23.

9

Texting the Body: Soviet Criminal Tattoos

by Helena Goscilo

> My body is my journal, and my tattoos are my story.
> Johnny Depp

> I know from experience that there's always some-
> thing terribly flawed about people who are tattooed
> [...] Most people who are tattooed, it's the sign of
> some feeling of inferiority, they're trying to establish
> some macho identification for themselves.
> Truman Capote[1]

The body as sign

Tattoos constitute a subcategory of the universal practice of body marking, its history in the Western tradition, roughly summarized, charting a jagged course from divine-evidentiary to social-communicative, to decorative-erotic: in other words, devolution from a manifestation of the Prime Mover or First Cause for the believer to ornamentation for the unwittingly conformist individual.[2] Clinton Sanders characterizes the history of tattooing as evolving "from deviance to art" (32). Across the world and throughout millennia, tattoos have served as symbols of religious and spiritual devotion, marks of status and rank,[3] rites of passage, amulets and talismans, proof of membership, acknowledgment of bravery, pledges of love, sexual lures, symbols of fertility, punishment, and signs of outcasts,

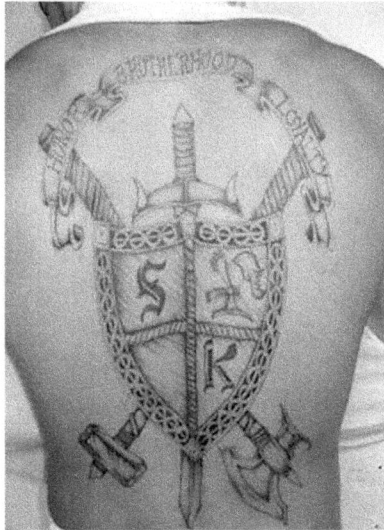

Fig. 1. Saxon Knights' Shield tattoo, declaring membership in and adherence to the principles of the Saxon Knights, 2008. Courtesy of Camocon on Wikimedia Commons.

slaves, and convicts ("Tattoo")(Fig. 1).[4] Any analysis of Western body modification must take into account the latter's alleged inseparability, since time immemorial, from the spirit/soul/thought/emotion that resides within it.[5] According to that notion, the *exterior* is the visible, tangible shell that encases and reflects aspects of the *interior*, which comprises the invisible, immaterial substance (variously troped as air, light, fire, moth, etc.) that informs morality and demeanor during life and leaves the shell only upon death. Sundry concepts, both religious and secular, of the human body as an entity offering insight into character and moral values boast a robust tradition dating back to the ancient Greeks.[6] Pseudo-scientific theories of the body's legibility enjoyed particular popularity in German-speaking countries during the late eighteenth and nineteenth centuries, as attested by the Swiss pastor-physiognomist Johann Caspar Lavater (1741-1801)[7], the German phrenologist Franz Joseph Gall (1758-1828),[8] and Ernst Kretschmer (1888-1964), a psychiatrist who posited typologies based on the continuity between body and mind.[9] Though later discredited, in their day all three exerted an incalculable influence throughout Europe.[10]

A preliminary glance at narratives about the divine-eviden-tiary trajectory in body marking reveals that Christ's stigmata, perhaps the most renowned body markings in recorded cultural history, purportedly offered palpable evidence of divinity and its omnipotence. Yet they also functioned as a miraculous, arbitrary sign not unlike Zeus' eagle in classical epics. They provided em-pirical corroboration, on the one hand, and faith-dependent mes-sage, on the other. Such ambidextrous signs operate on the vertical or otherworldly axis. They engage timelessness or what Mikhail Bakhtin calls "synchronized diachrony," transcending the linearity of logic or the comprehensible, and enlisting the physical/visible to affirm the spiritual/invisible.[11] In a sense they allay uncertainty, reassuring skeptics whose temporary doubt operates within a com-prehensive psychological framework of belief. In religious myths, miracles entailing the instant elimination of hideous marks (e.g., on lepers' bodies), not unlike the punitive imprinting on Cain's fore-head, belong to this category.[12] God, in fact, may be somewhat blas-phemously viewed as the first tattoo artist via remote control, who rendered his unappealable judgment legible and who, according to the Bible, decreed this procedure His exclusive prerogative. As 'recorded' in the Old Testament, His prohibition to humankind de-creed, "You shall not make any cuttings in your flesh on account of the dead or tattoo any marks upon you: I am the Lord" (Lev 19: 28).

Literature appropriated this semiotics of divine will in inter-mittently visible praxis—substantiated, for example, by the tor-menting "A" embossed on Arthur Dimmsdale's hypocritical flesh in Nathaniel Hawthorne's *Scarlet Letter* (1850) and by the brand on Mina Harker's forehead in Bram Stoker's *Dracula* (1897).[13] In such a cultural context, early Russian popular belief in the "marks of the Tsar"—recreated in Pushkin's novel *Kapitanskaia dochka* (*The Captain's Daughter*, 1836) and in *Russkii bunt* (*Russian Revolt*, 2000), Aleksandr Proshkin's screen version of Pushkin's text—makes perfect sense, for the Tsar (like British and French kings endowed with "divine right") descended directly from God and occupied the niche just below Him in the cosmic hierarchy. The ruler bore God's mysterious, authoritative stamp of election. Accordingly, though with the valence reversed, a disquieting percentage of Russia's population interpreted Mikhail Gorbachev's birthmark, promi-

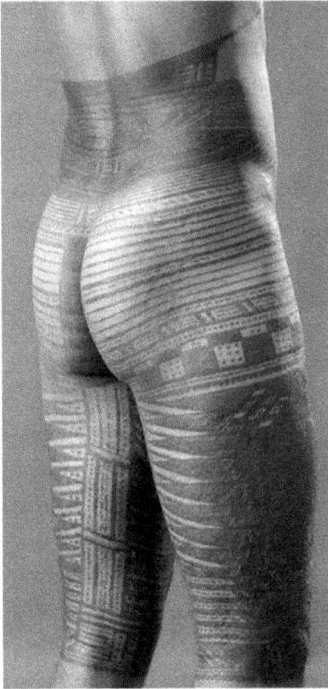

Fig. 2. Traditional Samoan tattoo, 2002. Courtesy of CloudSurfer on Wikimedia Commons.

Fig. 3. A Maori chief, with full facial moko. Sketched by Sydney Parkinson in 1769, published in 1784. Courtesy of Parkinson, Sydney. *A Journal of a Voyage to the South Seas* (London: 1784), plate.

nently centered on his forehead but airbrushed out of most Soviet photographs, as a mark of the Devil—politically, the irredeemable and corruptive evil of Western capitalism and democracy.[14]

Ritualistic body markings, especially widespread among tribal cultures, blend the metaphysical with the social; they accompany rites, often of an initiatory nature (Schiffmacher 11), that tacitly or expressly invoke superior forces while also regulating and uniting a community (Figs. 2-3). Typically these decorations and mutilations are apotropiac, i.e., they court safety and protection from evil or misfortune (not unlike propitiatory sacrifices to the gods in the ancient Graeco-Roman world) and defy comprehension by anyone outside the given group.[15] Yet, however inscrutable, ultimately body marks metamorphose all of us into semioticians or herme-

Fig. 4. An aesthetically beguiling tattoo with traditional Chinese imagery of cherry blossoms and koi (fish), 2008. Courtesy of Tattoo Temple, Joey Pang, on Wikimedia Commons.

neuts. Even the contemporary trend of body art as an aesthetic, decorative practice, which revives ancient habits, urges interpretation (however speculative) of identity, allegiance, or stylistic preference (Fig. 4). We cannot resist the 'need to read.' Contemporary tattoos, for instance, frequently signal forms of membership in a more or less 'closed' unit or community (be it a club, a street gang, various branches of the armed forces, etc.), the way branding of animals formalizes ownership. Both register forms of belonging.[16] Projected against this background, my essay targets a hermeneutically richer but taxonomically perhaps more circumscribed or uniform sphere: criminal body markings—more specifically, Soviet prisoners' tattoos.

The longstanding liaison of crime and tattoo

The criminal bearing the mark of punishment on his forehead originates with Cain the fratricide in the Book of Genesis.[17] According to Gospel narratives, the next mythically momentous case of punitive body signs was Christ's crucifixion, which placed him between two criminals on flanking crosses. Since the word "stigmata" is the plural of "stigma" (στίγμα), the Greek for "tattoo mark," anyone intent on a secular reading of the crucifixion could posit Christ as the most famous tattooed prisoner executed for alleged crimes, who posthumously revealed his "marks of shame" (in Russian, *kleima*) as testimony, just as the survivors of modern-day concentration camps can display the numbers etched into their flesh as concrete evidence of their experience.[18] Both a form of violent humiliation and a practical mode of bookkeeping, these numbers ally camp prisoners with the branded cattle whom they resembled during forced en masse transportation to the gas chamber and the unknown. The phenomenon acquired a modern update in James Cameron's 1984 film, *The Terminator*—an apocalyptic caution against overreliance on technology that imagines a futurist camp administered by machines, where Kyle Reese, a resistance fighter battling the machines' supremacy, has a barcode burned into his wrist. Like Christ and Nazi camp survivors, he corroborates his autobiographical claims by exposing his bodily mark. The pertinence of *The Terminator* to criminal tattoos may be deduced from the popularity among contemporary Russian prisoners of a tattoo duplicating the cyborg terminator's famous words, "I'll be back," rendered in English—a threat-by-association and simultaneously a fitting promise by recidivists or those uninterested in future rehabilitation.

As an institutional system, the inseparability of genuine or imputed criminality and tattoos boasts a long history,[19] in the West, reportedly extending back to the ancient Romans, who referred to their practice of designating dangerous prisoners as *deformare stigmatum notis* (disfiguring by marks of tattoos)—a custom likewise observed by the Japanese and the Mexican Aztecs (Jelski 184-185). Despite the fourth-century Roman Emperor Constantine's ban on facial tattoos as despoiling what was 'made in God's image' (literally, "which has been fashioned in the likeness of the divine beauty"[20]) (Lineberry; Gustafson 86), tattooing and branding

Fig. 5. Aptly designated as "modern primitive," 2006. Courtesy of User Nicor on Wikimedia Commons.

thrived during the Middle Ages, and the practice of placing tattoos on the face, particularly the forehead, survives to this day (Fig. 5).[21] Thieves, prostitutes, money forgers, and cardsharps in Europe underwent branding, primarily as a means of identification and official sanction. The late medieval era refined the process by typological differentiation, stamping a boat hook on navy deserters, horns on poachers, and so forth (Jelski 185). During the late eighteenth century thieves in France bore a lily with the letter "V" for *voleur* on their shoulders. According to one scholar, the practice of branding convicts that originated with Peter the Great was solidly established "in the Russian penal lexicon" by the early nineteenth century (Schrader 180-181), and was extended to fugitives by an edict of Nicholas I in 1845 (Schrader 180-181).[22] Until 1864 prisoners exiled to Siberia had the letters "KT" (for *katorzhnik*) burned or tattooed on their bodies (Jelski 186).[23] Similarly, prisoners transported from Britain to Australian penal colonies between 1787 and 1867 (a period roughly overlapping with the heyday of Lavater's and Gall's influence) bore the tattoo "D," for deserter, on their foreheads or other marks intended to signify disgrace and social ostracism ("Criminal Tattoo"; Jelski 186). Fascinatingly, this institution underwent a *volte-face*, whereby the governmental procedure of imposing distinctive marks of ignominy on criminals became co-opted by the latter, who transformed a relatively simple, legible mode of identification, control, and condemnation into their own highly complex semiotic system—above all, in Soviet Russia.[24]

Soviet criminal tattoos as a linguistic system

While Soviet prisons and camps degraded the human body to its most primitive state, on the one hand, on the other, they tolerated inmates' own elaboration of an intricate language indelibly inscribed on the state-regimented body.[25] The practice of tattooing in the criminal milieu instantiates what the Russian semiotician Iurii Lotman calls "legitimized anti-behavior," though one could conceivably label it an "illegitimate" revision of conventional social conduct, with its own rigorous stratification, "laws," rituals, and symbols. Literally and metaphorically stripped to its minimum, here the body becomes a blank slate on which the incarcerated codify and write the principles governing their inner community, thereby reappropriating their bodies.[26]

This procedure eerily plays out the scenario of Franz Kafka's "In the Penal Colony" (1916), from which it diverges in several respects, while sharing the cardinal actuality of semantically loaded body inscription. Whether Kafka's characteristically enigmatic narrative implies the futility of "all our attempts to redeem the body for the signifying process, to make its naturalness into a cultural product," as Peter Brooks tentatively proposes (Brooks 286), and "portrays the process of enculturation as a torturous marking of the body" (Mascia-Lees and Sharpe 146), which is "totally imprinted by history" (Foucault 148), remains an open question. Regardless of which interpretation one favors, the prisoner's body in Kafka's tale manifestly succumbs to forcible imprinting by totalitarian dictate. For Soviet prisoners, however, who elected and, with remarkable effort and ingenuity, themselves secretly executed each painstaking (and painful) operation,[27] tattooing not only formally registered the incorporation of inmates into the criminals' self-regulated social system, but also afforded the sole possible gesture of independence from their wardens and the Soviet system.[28]

Paradoxically, only the circle of initiates—the prisoners themselves—possessed the tools to interpret these ambulatory texts; for the tattoos, whether confined to images or combined with words, comprised a minority language within a larger, culturally dominant milieu that the minority excluded from its linguistic system. Such anomalous circumstances instanced inversion; they turned Outsiders—those outside The Law—into literal and figurative Insiders, who forged their own laws. This insider language could not be censored or eliminated by legal authorities without the wholesale liquidation of the bodies on which it was imprinted. That paradox seems to corroborate what on first glance strikes one as contestable claims in Aleksandr Solzhenitsyn's *First Circle* (*V kruge pervom* 1968) and Andrei Siniavskii's *Voice from the Chorus* (*Golos iz khora* 1973): namely, that under Soviet rule only prison offered a measure of liberty.[29] Whatever the validity of such a counter-intuitive view, incarceration indisputably distanced the citizen in the cell from the univocal Soviet-speak multitudes, for whom the insiders' body signs constituted indecipherable hieroglyphics. Moreover, "false tattoos" (those departing from the criminal code) were punishable by death, carried out by inmates in consonance with their *sui generis* variant of conventional legal systems (Plutser-Sarno "All power..." 35)—principles likewise incomprehensible to outsiders. Within the Soviet Union, prison constituted a microcosm with its own strictly defined social structure, regulations, and language; while the verbal language slowly seeped into everyday Soviet discourse, its visual counterpart remained cryptic to those outside the penitentiary. Viewed by some as part of a deviant subculture, the tattoos that oversaw conduct in the Soviet jails and prisons may be seen as a sign system that resisted the power inhering in conventional social institutions ostensibly administering justice but *de facto* mired in sundry modes of corruption.[30]

Whereas during the late Soviet period Solzhenitsyn's novels and a few dictionaries introduced readers to prisoners' jargon,[31] post-Soviet Russia has witnessed several attempts to organize and decode prisoners' body-talk. Danzig Baldaev (1925-2005), whose *Tatuirovka zakliuchennykh* (*Prisoners' Tattoos* 2001) remains the single largest-scale illustrated study, is the chief documentarian of the phenomenon. One of several publications by Baldaev about prisoners' system of signification, the volume singularly instances an official's voluntarily assumed role of inmates' historical witness, language-learner, and publicity agent. Baldaev was of Buriat-Mongol descent, with a paternal grandfather who died in prison. A former art student and long-time investigator employed for 33 years by the MVD (Ministerstvo Vnutrennikh Del [Ministry of the Interior]), Major Baldaev worked primarily as a guard in the notorious Kresty prison in St. Petersburg, with its solitary confinement cells. He heeded his ethnographer father's advice to record prisoners' tattoos as a significant compendium of folklore materials, and traveled to camps and prisons across the country, tirelessly accumulating data and reproducing the relevant visuals. His numerous copies of the tattoos appear not only in the first book, but also in three Anglophone collections subsequently published by the maverick Fuel press.[32] These books afford an illuminating if endlessly challenging glimpse into Soviet prisons' inner culture, aided by the explanatory essays of the knowledgeable if hyperbolic Aleksei Plutser-Sarno, a leader in the radical art collective called Voina (War), who in 2010 supposedly fled to Estonia, but the following year surfaced in Prague, where he resumed his subversive activities.[33]

Reading the signs

Prisoners' tattoos functioned as a passport, an autobiography, a "case file," an index of social standing, a uniform hung with medals and ribbons, and also as a political or emotional statement (Plutser-Sarno "The Language..." 27). [34] Within this clandestine communication, which derived from and codified a complex social structure, any initiate could 'read' a fellow prisoner simply by witnessing him or her undress, shower, and so forth.[35] As the epigraphic assertion attributed to Johnny Depp implies, the textualized body rendered oral exchange of life history, philosophy, and attitude superfluous, for nakedness 'told all.' Multiplicity of terms for the tattoo, in fact, paralleled the diversity of its functions: *reklama* (ad), *regalka* (regalia or professional I.D., indicating criminal specialty), *raspiska* (painting), *kleimo* (brand or mark of shame), and *portachka* (amateur tattoo) (Plutser-Sarno in Baldaev 2001, 8). These texts defined every inmate's niche in the hierarchy established within each camp and prison, not unlike insignias on military uniforms denoting ranks.

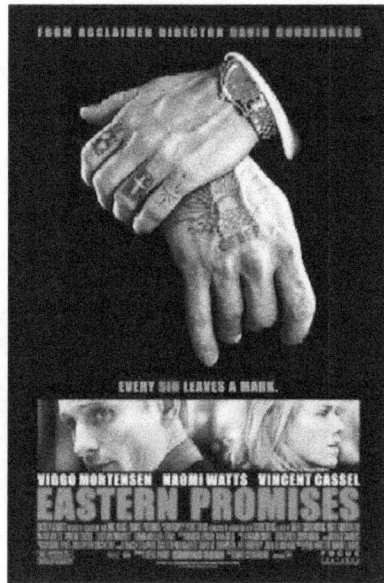

Fig. 6. The hands of the purported Thief in Law Nikolai Luzhin (aka Viggo Mortensen) in David Cronenberg's *Eastern Promises* (2007).

Epaulettes tattooed on prisoners' shoulders, in fact, functioned as official recognition of high status, just as in the eighteenth century they were the distinguishing feature of an officer.

The Code of Thieves (*Vorovskoi zakon*)[36] dictated how prisoners earn their status in the community and, accordingly, their right to bear particular tattooed images. An untattooed prisoner lacked status, hence suffered the derogatory label *petushok* (faggot, lit. little cock/cockerel), for his body was perceived as "weak," "unauthoritative," and "unmanly" (Plutser-Sarno "'All power...'" 49). By contrast, the densely tattooed body elicited respect as *frak s ordenami* (tail coat with medals/orders). Tattoos appeared on any and all parts of the body, but were concentrated on hands, shoulders, torso, back, stomach, hip, and buttocks (Fig. 6). Location, serving as a linguistic context, determined meaning. A woman's head imprinted on the stomach signaled a prostitute—a prisoner providing sexual service to inmates—but on the chest it symbolized the initiation of an under-age *zek* (i.e., *zakliuchennyi*, camp prisoner) (Plutser Sarno "The Language..." 31). Hands—obviously, as the instrument of crime and as the ever-exposed part of the body—bore highly condensed and codified signs: typically they conveyed the prisoner's history of past convictions, type of offenses, and level of authority

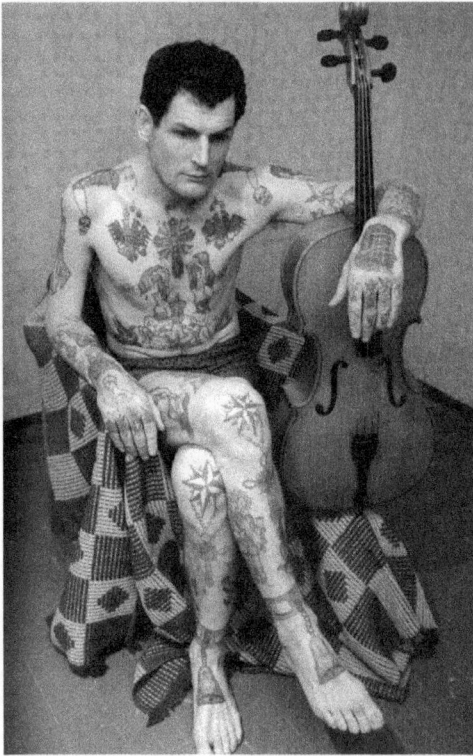

Fig. 7. An authoritative criminal, as attested by the plethora of tattoos. Photograph in *Russian Criminal Tattoo Encyclopedia*, vol. 1 (London: FUEL, 2001), p. 93. © FUEL / Sergei Vasiliev. From the *Russian Criminal Tattoo Encyclopaedia*.

within prison (Lambert *Mark of Cain*). For instance, the enlightened viewer instantly understands that the hands of the Russian mafia enforcer Nikolai Luzhin (Viggo Mortensen) in David Cronenberg's *Eastern Promises* (2007) testify that Luzhin has traveled through the zone (*zona*, the colloquial Soviet term for the prison system) (Fig. 7).[37] Moreover. the tattoos on his chest, shoulders, and knees in the episode set in the *bania* (sauna) provide copious specifics about his status during incarceration. Indeed, a website devoted to decoding Luzhin's tattoos reveals viewers' fascination with this recondite symbol-based language.[38] Most importantly, the crucified Christ on Luzhin's chest certifies his rank as "a prince of thieves" (legitimate thief/*Vor v zakone*, lit. Thief in Law), while the church and cupolas on his back indicate that he served three prison terms, of which one lasted three years. The stars that viewers witness being imprinted on his knees signal a refusal on the wearer's part to bow to any authority outside the Thieves' Law.[39]

Fig. 8. A tattoo on the right side of a
prisoner's chest at the Zima Corrective
Labor Colony in the Irkutsk Region
during the 1960s. The cupolas, wings,
skull and dagger convey their wearer's
criminal history and elevated status in
the prison hierarchy. The accompanying
text identifies him as a "criminal boss
convicted under article 146 of the 1960
Criminal Code of the RSFSR." According
to him, from the 1930s to the 1960s, "the
town of Zima marked the start of an un-
broken line of corrective labour camps,
corrective labour colonies and educa-
tional labour camps, stretching along
the Trans-Siberian railway as dense 'as
beads strung on a thread.'" Drawing and text by Danzig Baldaev, *Russian
Criminal Tattoo Encyclopedia*, vol. 1 (London: FUEL, 2001), p. 172. © FUEL
/ Danzig Baldaev. From the *Russian Criminal Tattoo Encyclopaedia* Volume
I (FUEL Publishing 2003).

That law dictates the specifics of criminal life, encompassing the
rejection of any and all family; subsistence exclusively on whatever
means have been acquired through thievery; non-betrayal of ac-
complices in a crime; complete rejection of authorities, the military,
and communal organizations; an excellent command of criminal
jargon (*fenia*); the right to gamble only when able to cover losses;
mandatory retention of rational judgment when imbibing alcohol,
and many more.[40] What the code confirms is that within prison,
criminals not only continue but systematically reinforce their anti-
social proclivities, which the collectively adopted set of strict man-
dates legislates as proper conduct. These regulations are the criminals' inverted version of a legal code, the violation of which incurs
punishment ranging from rape and forcible tattooing to death.

Tattoos that the uninitiated might equate with avowals of religi-
osity, love, or political affiliation often carry dramatically different
meanings that are context-dependent: for instance, among visual
images, a church cupola most frequently represents a conviction,
and multiple cupolas, a recidivist's record of incarceration (Fig. 8).
One of the most ubiquitous tattoos, the cat denotes a thief, individ-

ualized through additional details, and suggests success, caution, patience, and mercilessness. The word KOT (CAT) during the 1960s was an acronym for "Korennoi obitatel' tiurmy" (Native prison resident) (Baldaev 2001, 39). A skull usually means authority and/ or death, but when combined with a crown, it signals a desire for power, and if pierced by a knife, it unambiguously identifies its wearer as a murderer. Among polysemous signs, the snake represents a deadly fate, but also the wisdom of thieves' laws. Crosses figure richly in the sign system, depending on context: some denote the thief, whereas others inscribe vows of revenge, while still others fulfill the standard role of a religious talisman (Plutser-Sarno "The Language..." 35-39). Analogously, the Madonna—and various familiar Renaissance Madonnas, such as da Vinci's or Raphael's, decorate many a chest—may reference an inmate who was born and has spent his (or, more rarely, her) entire life in the zone. But it also may inscribe a vow of loyalty to a criminal caste or the belief that the Mother of God (*Bogomater'*, typically associated in the Orthodox tradition with merciful intervention) will save the wearer (Lambert 2003, 29). Perhaps the multiple meanings of a simple dot best illustrate the significance of a tattoo's placement: beneath the eye or near the mouth, such a simple mark identifies the passive homosexual (Baranovskii 266); on the nose, it is synonymous with 'stoolpigeon'; and on the chin, it warns that the wearer is a 'rat' (*krysa*) who steals from his mates.

Images of Lenin, Marx, Engels—which have lost relevance in recent decades—earlier functioned as sui generis bullet-proof vests, for prisoners knew that guards would not risk shooting at one of the Marxist leaders, just as European sailors in the past reportedly tattooed the crucifixion on their backs to avoid flogging, since that punishment would entail defacing the image of Christ—in itself a crime (Schiffmacher 12).[41] Here, quite obviously, the inmates craftily turned the taboos of official ideology against its representatives. In Pavel Chukhrai's film *Vor* (*The Thief* 1997), the tattoo of Stalin on the chest of the larcenous protagonist, Tolian, indicates not, as he claims, his status as Stalin's son, but his having spent time as a "legitimate thief" in the zone.

Among verbal tattoos, variants of "Mama," in such poetic pseudo-masterpieces as "Mat' moia, prosti menia!" (Mummy-y, forgive

me!) or "Ne zabudu mat' rodnuiu!" (I'll not forget my own dear
Mother!), could document the immemorial filial devotion and appeal to Russia's stoic maternity, but other "mother" tattoos signified
only within a purely criminal system. They often professed loyalty
to the older female criminal who headed a group of thieves, hid
their ill-gotten gains, and both observed and reinforced longstand-
ing criminal traditions. Her status explains why thieves deemed
the oath "Klianus' mamoi!" (I swear by Mom) binding (Plutser-
Sarno 2001, 10-11). As with the Italian mafia, the criminal network
adopted the structure and nomenclature of the family, also favored
by Stalin's rhetoric (i.e., the state as The Big Family). The endur-
ance of this discourse is attested by the continued use of the word
bratva and such post-Soviet films as Aleksei Balabanov's films *Brat*
(*Brother* 1997) and *Brat-2* (*Brother-2* 2000), where brotherhood car-
ries the double meaning of a bona fide blood tie and membership in
a criminal gang prepared to take on anyone opposing it.[42] A kindred
ambiguity marks the maternal nomenclature in Denis Evstigneev's
film *Mama* (1999), the title referencing not only the biological mother of four adult yet submissive sons, but also her criminality and
despotic control over them.[43]

Politically subversive word play figured prominently in the
tattoos' semiotics, based on prisoners' categorical rejection of any
authority outside the criminal hierarchy, which has led one com-
mentator to liken their tattoos to "a mass media complex purveying
propaganda opposed to the authorities" (Plutser-Sarno "'All power…'" 37). Prisoners, often in crude or obscene modes, opposed all
official enterprises, discourse, and iconography. Ironic ambiguity
or challenges (known as *oskaly* [grins] addressed to the authorities)
informed numerous abbreviations, which inverted the standard
denotation of canonical acronyms. BOG [GOD], for instance, means
"Budu Opiat' Grabit'," (I'll steal again); MIR [PEACE/WORLD] de-
fiantly announces "Menia Ispravit Rasstrel" (Only being shot will
set me straight) (Fig. 9), while NKVD, an acronym for the early version of the KGB, expresses the sentiment "Net Krepche Vorovskoi
Druzhby" (There's no friendship stronger than that of thieves/crim-
inals) (Plutser-Sarno 2001, 7). Lenin's face often accompanied the
word VOR because the three letters coincided with Lenin's fame as
"Vozhd' Oktiabr'skoi Revoliutsii" (Leader of the October Revolu-

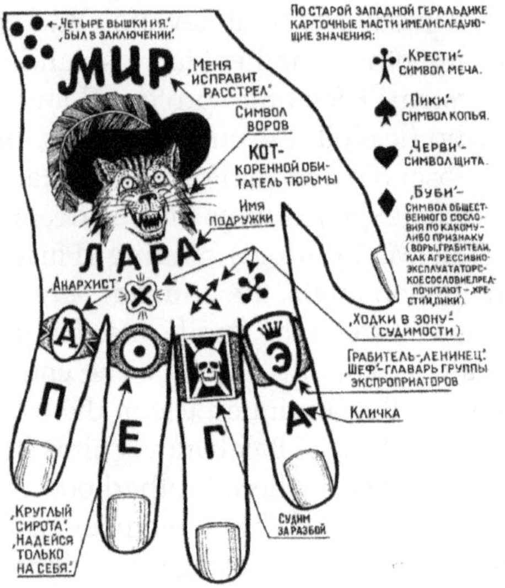

←ЧЕТЫРЕ ВЫШКИ Н.Я.
,БЫЛ В ЗАКЛЮЧЕНИИ.

МИР ,МЕНЯ ИСПРАВИТ РАССТРЕЛ

СИМВОЛ ВОРОВ

КОТ- КОРЕННОЙ ОБИ- ТАТЕЛЬ ТЮРЬМЫ

ИМЯ ПОДРУЖКИ

ЛАРА

,АНАРХИСТ

А   О   Э

П   Е   Г   А

,КРУГЛЫЙ СИРОТА: ,НАДЕЙСЯ ТОЛЬКО НА СЕБЯ!

СУДИМ ЗА РАЗБОЙ

ПО СТАРОЙ ЗАПАДНОЙ ГЕРАЛЬДИКЕ КАРТОЧНЫЕ МАСТИ ИМЕЛИ СЛЕДУЮЩИЕ ЗНАЧЕНИЯ:

,КРЕСТИ- СИМВОЛ МЕЧА.

,ПИКИ- СИМВОЛ КОПЬЯ.

,ЧЕРВИ- СИМВОЛ ЩИТА.

,БУБИ- СИМВОЛ ОБЩЕСТ- ВЕННОГО СОСЛО- ВИЯ ПО КАКОМУ- ЛИБО ПРИЗНАКУ (ВОРЫ,ГРАБИТЕЛИ, КАК АГРЕССИВНО- ЭКСПЛУАТАТОРС- КОЕ СОСЛОВИЕ,ПРЕ- ПОЧИТАЮТ-,КРЕ- СТИ,ПИКИ).

,ХОДКИ В ЗОНУ- (СУДИМОСТИ)

ГРАБИТЕЛЬ-,ЛЕНИНЕЦ: ,ШЕФ-ГЛАВАРЬ ГРУППЫ ЭКСПРОПРИАТОРОВ

КЛИЧКА

Figure 9. Astonishing condensation of biographical data on a prisoner's hand via a " widespread criminal finger-ring tattoos." The five dots on the top left indicate that the wearer, nicknamed Pega, has been in prison; the cat's head indicates his identity as a "native inhabitant of prison"; the crosses on the knuckles show that he has spent three separate sentences in the 'zone.' The symbols on his four fingers testify that he is a 'Leninist' bandit, heading "a group of expropriators" (forefinger) and convicted for brigandage (middle finger). A "complete orphan" (third finger), he is an anarchist (little finger). Of the symbols for the four suits in cards, thieves and robbers favor clubs (=sword) and spades (= spear). Drawing and text by Danzig Baldaev, *Russian Criminal Tattoo Encyclopedia*, vol. 1 (London: FUEL, 2001), pp. 206-07. © FUEL / Danzig Baldaev. From the *Russian Criminal Tattoo Encyclopaedia* Volume I (FUEL Publishing 2003).

tion). Since prisoners acknowledged no authority outside their own code, they uniformly execrated democrats, socialists, communists, etc. and did not distinguish between political leaders and Satan or petty demons. All constituted implacable enemies. Thus the hoof-and-tailed Lenin as the *pakhan* (chief figure among the Thieves in Law) of the Communist Party rests on a sickled moon beneath a deathly sun, while other heads of state appear in satirized, degraded forms. Stalin similarly is cast as Satan, a vampire, or bat (Plutser-Sarno "The Language..." 41) (Fig. 10). The iconography of Soviet power in general underwent new, demonized, and often obscene reconfigurations, which varied little from leader to leader in what one might call phallocentric representations—i.e., ones in which the phallus occupies center stage.

Figure 10. Stalin as murderer, vampire, and ghoul in a tattoo copied by Danzig Baldaev at the Interior Inter-Regional Hospital in 1979. A native of Tambov, its wearer spent more than forty-two years in various places of detention. The tattoo is identified as "The Great Cannibal—the organizer of the Great Terror," with a punning text that ironizes Stalin's reputed assertion, "We were born to make fairy tales a reality" (My rozhdeny, chtob skazku sdelat' byl'iu). That apodictic claim is recast as "We were born to make Kafka a reality" (My rozhdeny, chtob Kafku sdelat' byl'iu). Drawing and text by Danzig Baldaev, *Russian Criminal Tattoo Encyclopedia*, vol. 1 (London: FUEL, 2001), p. 233. © FUEL / Danzig Baldaev. From the *Russian Criminal Tattoo Encyclopaedia* Volume I (FUEL Publishing 2003).

Chauvinism and anti-Semitism figured repeatedly in tattoos, as did misogyny, contempt for male weakness, and death imagery specific to the camps, especially Kolyma. Sexual visuals rarely symptomatized eroticism, but sooner conveyed the debasement of the tattoo-wearer, who frequently had undergone punitive tattooing against his will in an act of violence. Forcible tattooing was part of the compulsory punishment for stoolpigeons, those who reneged on their gambling debts, and those incarcerated for sexual crimes. Such visible signs of ostracism from the privileged section of criminal society marked those who were "soiled" (*neprikasaemye*). These outcasts performed the dirtiest jobs and were exiled to special corners of the prisoners' living space (Plutser-Sarno "'All power...'" 39), accepting the judgment of the thieves' code, which could also pass death sentences on those guilty of infractions.[44]

In comparably ambiguous terms, nationalism evoking Russian mythology and folklore found materialization in reworked images cherished via collective memory, just as sacrosanct Soviet icons re-

Figure 11. A common tattoo in the camps during the 1950s and 1960s, the visual mocks the hortatory Civil War poster by Dmitrii Moor [Figure 12], replacing an appeal to national pride and duty with cynical contempt for naïve credulity in Soviet propaganda. The accompanying text, in Andrew Bromfield's translation (slightly adjusted), reads: "You little Soviet shit, you're still kowtowing, ass-licking, and flogging away for the CPSU, and being paid zero point fuck-all, and you want to be a cripple? Think about it!" Drawing and text by Danzig Baldaev, *Russian Criminal Tattoo Encyclopedia*, vol. 1 (London: FUEL, 2001), p. 242. © FUEL / Danzig Baldaev. From the *Russian Criminal Tattoo Encyclopaedia* Volume I (FUEL Publishing 2003).

Figure 12. Tapping into the male viewer's conscience, Dmitrii Moor's famous 1920 enlistment poster queries whether he has enlisted. The concept was probably inspired by the 1914 British poster announcing "Your Country Needs You," paralleled by the American James Montgomery Flagg's ubiquitous "I Want You for U.S. Army," recruiting volunteers during World War I. All four images rely on the accusatory finger pointing at whoever sees the visual. Courtesy of Aleksandr Vislyi, Russian National Library, Moscow.

cast in an ironic, cynical vein (Fig. 11-12), likewise enjoyed popularity. In general, the humor and cynicism of prisoners' tattoos placed
them squarely within folklore paradigms, alongside *chastushki* and
the frankly lewd folktales that Russian censorship excluded from
A. N. Afanas'ev's classic three-volume collection, *Narodnye russkie
skazki* (*Russian Folktales* 1855-63). The racy tales were published
in Geneva as *Russkie zavetnye skazki* (*Russian Secret/Forbidden Folktales* 1872), and reissued in Moscow more than a century later (by
Russkii knizhnyi dvor in 1992; by Ladomir publishers in 1994 and
1997). Criminal tattoos share with folktales both oral transmission
and absence of censorship by anyone except the immediate community—in this case, the incarcerated.[45]

Devaluation and de-signification of the sign

Post-Soviet revelations of previously suppressed Soviet-era practices reveal the extent to which the criminality that permeated Soviet culture enriched its systems of signification. As an extortionist
who has spent twelve years in the zone observed, "Formerly, every
tattoo meant something but now each person pastes whatever he
can" (Lambert 2003, 17). Succumbing to nostalgia for lost empire
and its recently transvalued conventions, the 1990s reclaimed, as
part of culture's ready-made, sundry criminal genres and discourses, now bleached of political subversion, yet still vaguely and tit-
illatingly redolent of prohibition. Such stylization (as opposed to
politicization) marked sartorial fashion, glossy magazines, and the
early recordings of the musical group Liube, even as the *detektiv*
(contemporary Russia's idiosyncratic version of mystery/crime
novels) reigned supreme in the publication and sale of books, with
Aleksandra Marinina, Boris Akunin, and Dar'ia Dontsova heading
a prolific pack of best-selling authors. And, as the case of former
Mayor Iurii Luzhkov and the most recent parliamentary elections
have demonstrated, criminality was and remains a standard *modus
operandi* for national and local politicians.

Although the overall picture of Russia during the last two decades conjures up a society in thrall to crime and accelerated enrichment by any and all means, it also reveals the post-Soviet fascination with what Russians, in a poignantly erroneous citation from
English, call "the happy end"—the sunny resolution of problems

identified with American cinema. Perhaps the term appeals because on a micro-level it evokes the Soviet "radiant future" that
never eventuated, and, unlike that ever-receding utopia, possesses
the seductive appeal of accessibility. In any case, intimations of
"the happy end," curiously, characterize some Soviet prison tattoos, indicating that romance—or perhaps the desire for it—thrived
within the walls of punitive institutions. Indeed, prisons and camps
not only failed to snuff out romantic bonds, but in some cases pro-
moted them. Ironically, the zone was the sole environment in the
Soviet Union that tolerated same-sex love, which could be openly
practiced without fear of reprisal. Whereas among male prisoners
sodomy-rape punished violators of the Thieves' Law, and 'losers'
were forced to service their more powerful inmates, lesbian bonding was voluntary and apparently provided succor. According to
one female prisoner, "everything happens by consent" in the wom-
en's colony, to which rape is utterly alien (Lambert 2003, 61, 69).
Perhaps that explains why female inmates, who currently comprise
five percent of the approximately million prisoners in Russia (Lambert 2003, 56), and whose bodies tend to bear fewer tattoos than
men's,[46] sometimes opt for visuals and texts centered on love. One
upbeat conjugal image reproduced by Baldaev features cozy, domestic devotion: two cats snuggle up against each other, surrounded by barbed wire, which indicates the length of their sentences,
while a tulip and rose beside them register the years they spent in
the zone: she sixteen and he eighteen. "Saturn," the abbreviation
serving as a caption and testament to their love, avows, "Slyshish',
a tebia uzhe razliubit' nevozmozhno" (You know, it's impossible
now to stop loving you). Other female tattoos record the names
of lovers and, infrequently, display lesbian pleasure (Baldaev 2001
#716). Despite their commonalities, the women's sector in prisons
is less prone than the men's not only to physical violence, but also
to its reflection in bodily markings.

The numerous tattoos reproduced in Baldaev's volumes belong
to the Soviet era. During the 1990s, according to Alix Lambert's
2000 *Nightline* documentary on the Soviet and post-Soviet zone,
the hardy regime of prison tattoos suffered a semiotic sea-change.
Under the pressure of proclaimed market values, dollar signs and
sundry capitalist insignia destabilized the fabled tattoo iconogra-

phy of yore. Moreover, unlike their predecessors, who earned their privilege of head-to-toe tattoos through years of lawlessness, the New Russian criminals simply began buying their brands with bucks. Images clearly appropriated from American films and comics (for example, vampires) stylistically differ from the traditional Soviet repertoire, and they stand out as novelties. In a sense, innovations in the criminal linguistic system mirror transformations in the Russian language outside the penitentiary over the last two decades. Standard usage in conversations, on the internet, or in the media reveals a plethora of Anglophone borrowings from the discourse of business, technology, and sundry professional practices (e.g., воучер, гаджет, троллинг, воркшоп). While the likelihood of a decrease in crime within Russia in the next few decades seems remote, the gradual disappearance of tattoos that flourished under Stalin and even Brezhnev suggests that the body language of Thieves' Law will either vanish or, over time, change so fundamentally as to constitute an entirely different system of communication. Should that occur, the advice of Baldaev's father to preserve Soviet criminal tattoos as an instance of folklore in praxis (i.e., an evanescent cultural genre) will be wholly vindicated.

Notes

1   Johnny Depp, reportedly in conversation. Truman Capote, *Conversations with Capote.* Available at http://www.goodreads.com/quotes/tag/tattoos. Accessed 28 November 2011.

2   According to at least one source, tattooing has been a Eurasian practice since the Neolithic era, and in Japan since the Paleolithic. See "Tattoo" on Wikipedia, available at http://en.wikipedia.org/wiki/Tattoo, accessed 5 February 2007. Archeologist Joann Fletcher at the University of York in Britain, however, cites a later date of 5,200 BC, on the basis of the Iceman, discovered in 1991 (Lineberry). See also Gustafson 80.

3   Ancient writers referring to tattoos include Plato, Aristophanes, Herodotus and Julies Caesar, while in literature Pierre-Augustin de Beaumarchais in *Le Mariage de Figaro* (1784) and Victor Hugo in *Les Misérables* (1862) feature tattoos in scenes of recognition (Baranovskii 87). According to the Greek writer Herodotus (c. 450 BC), among Scythians and Thracians "tattoos were a mark of nobility, and not to have them was testimony of low birth" (cited in Lineberry). Similarly, tattoos were popular among the upper classes in early twentieth-century England, as attested by Lady

Randolph Churchill and George V, as well as in Russia, where Nicholas II apparently underwent the procedure (Baranovskii 68).

4   On Encyclopedia Britannica Online and Wikipedia. For more functions, see Schiffmacher *passim* and Sanders 1-35.

5   Others have remarked on the connection between the inner and outer selves. For instance, leaning on Foucault, Gustafson sees "the subjection and discipline of the body" as simultaneously "the subjection of the soul" (Gustafson 91) and reminds readers that Claude Lévi-Strauss maintained that the purpose behind tattooing among the Maori was "to stamp onto the mind all the traditions and philosophy of the group" (Gustafson 90; citing Claude Lévi-Strauss, *Structural Anthropology*, vol. 1 {1963} 257).

6   Broadly speaking, philosophies of the body may be grouped into two contrasting camps: one posits a continuity between body and soul/mind, whereas the other views them as antipodal and in perpetual conflict.

7   Lavater's antirationalist *Physiognomische Fragmente zur Beförderung der Menschenkenntnis und Menschenliebe*, 4 vol. (1775–78; *Essays on Physiognomy*, 1789–98) not only beguiled Goethe but proved exceedingly influential throughout Europe and played a fundamental role in literary portrayal.

8   Gall's *The Anatomy and Physiology of the Nervous System in General, and of the Brain in Particular, with Observations upon the possibility of ascertaining the several Intellectual and Moral Dispositions of Man and Animal, by the configuration of their Heads*, begun in 1809 and published in 1819, enjoyed great popularity throughout Europe, as evident in the theories of the Italian criminologist Cesare Lombroso (1835-1909) and the novels of Honoré de Balzac (1799-1850), but had its greatest impact in England and played a key role in Charles Darwin's choice of crew for his voyage on the *Beagle* in 1831. On Lavater, see the excellent article by John B. Lyon, "The Science of Sciences: Replication and Reproduction in Lavater's Physiognomics," *Eighteenth-Century Studies*, 40, no. 2 (2006): 257-77. As Lyon points out, Lavater's analyses of human physiognomies, which were published in two Russian editions, "resonated with Enlightenment ideals such as the readability of nature and the harmony of nature and reason" and "influenced literature and science for years to come" (257). On the impact of physiology in Russian literature, see Edmund Heier, "'The Literary Portrait' as a Device of Characterization," *Neophilologus*, lx, no. 2 (April 1976): 321-33; Helena Goscilo, "Lermontov's Debt to Lavater and Gall," *The Slavonic and East European Review*, 59, no. 4 (October 1981): 500-15.

9   Nominated for the Nobel Prize in 1929, Kretschmer published widely, and his *Körperbau und Charakter* (1921) perhaps most clearly articulates his notions of body types and character.

10   Sigmund Freud's assertion in *The Ego and the Id* (1923) that "the ego is first and foremost a body-ego" and the ideas of his pupil Wilhelm Reich erected a bridge between their predecessors and contemporary representatives of body psychotherapy. See Jacqueline A. Carleton, "Body, Self and Soul: The Evolution of a Wholistic Psychotherapy," *Journal of the International Society for the History of Islamic Medicine*, 2 (2002). Available at http://www.ishim.net/ishimj/2/06.pdf (accessed 5 November 2011).

11   See Mikhail Bakhtin, "Forms of Time and of the Chronotope in the Novel" in M.M. Bakhtin, *The Dialogic Imagination* (Austin: University of Texas Press, 1981), 84-258, especially 153-58.

12   At the same time, the mark protected Cain from being killed by passersby (Genesis, Book 4: 15), thereby fulfilling an apotropiac function.

13   Literary characterization, of course, relies on physical appearance as an index of the 'inner person,' whereby certain standard associations operate in varying degrees (e.g., dark as negative, light as positive), though often inflected by ever-evolving social circumstances and values. For instance, small white hands as emblematic of aristocratic status, indicating that their affluent owner had no need to work outdoors (e.g., Andrei Bolkonskii in Lev Tolstoi's *Voina i mir*), today doubtless would be replaced by tanned hands, suggesting the individual's wherewithal to spend time relaxing in sunny climes.

14   For pertinent analyses of body semiotics, see *The Body in Russian Culture. Studies in Slavic Cultures*, vol. III (Pittsburgh: University of Pittsburgh Press, 2002); Helena Goscilo, "Post-ing the Soviet Body as Tabula Phrasa and Spectacle," in *Lotman and Cultural Studies: Encounters and Extensions*, ed. Andreas Schönle (Madison: Wisconsin University Press, 2006), 248-96

15   In some cases the procedure of body marking has a medicinal function, warding off specific diseases. Women in ancient Egypt reportedly tattooed their bodies for therapeutic purposes, according to Joann Fletcher, "as a permanent form of amulet during the very difficult time of pregnancy and birth" (Lineberry). See also Baranovskii, 244-52.

16   Establishment of ownership in Graeco-Roman times likewise entailed the tattooing or branding of slaves. See Jones, Gustafson, *passim*.

17   Hence Alix Lambert's choice of title for her documentary, *Mark of Cain*.

18   Drawing on Eugen Kogon's study (wr. 1945), Gustafson catalogues the Nazi system of clarifying the nature of prisoners' crimes via such specifics as a pink triangle for homosexuals, a red triangle for political prisoners, and the Star of David—a yellow triangle superimposed over another such triangle—for Jews, with single letters indicating nationality or other categories. These were sewn on clothing, while serial numbers were tattooed on the left forearm (Gustafson 94).

19   According to the *Encyclopedia Britannica,* what may be interpreted as tattoos were found on Egyptian and Nubian mummies dating from approx. 2000 BC. Classical authors refer to their use in relation to the Greeks, Gauls, and ancient Britons.

20   Gustafson, 86.

21   For the difficulty of clearly differentiating tattooing from branding during earlier eras, see Jones, *passim.* A category of prisoners in the Soviet and Russian penal institutions who are degraded to sex slaves have the word SLAVE (*RAB*) forcibly tattooed on their faces (Lambert 2003, 12).

22   On the evolution of branding and tattooing from Tsarist to early-Soviet times, see Schrader, *passim.* Schrader argues that in the early twentieth century vagrants appropriated official inscriptions for their own communicative purposes, but supplies no specific dates for this period.

23   Gustafson mistakenly claims that the letters embossed on the cheeks and foreheads of those sentenced to hard labor were KAT (Gustafson, following J.T. Sellin, *Slavery and the Penal System* {New York: Elsevier, 1976}, 121). The word tattoo was introduced into English from Tahiti, where it was first recorded in James Cook's record of his expedition in 1769. Some scholars note that body marking became fashionable particularly among sailors and coalminers, for whom it doubtless functioned as protection against the risks intrinsic to their professions (Lineberry).

24   As Schrader remarks, convicts followed the example of vagrants in earlier times by transforming marks of "shame and deviance into that which endowed them with sovereignty," transvaluing the "juridical mark" into a sign of "ownership" (Schrader, 189).

25   Indelibly in the sense that if the tattoo is removed, usually with some acidic substances that causes excruciating pain, scars remain as permanent 'tracks' of the criminal's tattoos.

26   On this reappropriation as a critical reaction to modern commodification of the body, see Fisher (103-04).

27   Most publications on tattoos contain detailed information about the process of tattooing and the materials necessary for that operation. See Baranovskii, Jelski, Kosulin, and especially popular magazines such as *Skin Art,* which also advertise the requisite paraphernalia. Essentially, Soviet prisoners used any sharp item, such as a needle or a honed guitar string attached to a shaver, to introduce pigmentation consisting of soot produced from burnt shoe heels, mixed with urine, under prisoners' skin.

28   In 1919, the Cheka (Soviet state security service) established the system of prisons and forced labor camps, largely in Siberia and the desolate northern areas. The Stalinist Gulag became known as the zone, which subsequently became synonymous with prison. See Lambert 2000.

29   For both, that freedom was an inner state—in Siniavskii's case, a

spiritual liberation enabled through endless time for reflection, whereas for Solzhenitsyn, it resulted from total dispossession: "Freedom's just another word for nothin' left to lose," as articulated in the 1960s song "Me and Bobby McGee," composed by Kris Kristofferson and made famous by Janis Joplin, whose amended rendition figured prominently in the epilogue of Rainer Werner Fassbinder's *Berlin Alexanderplatz* (1980).

30   In light of the startling incommensurability between the nature of various crimes and the sentences meted out to their alleged or self-confessed perpetrators (for example, six and a half years for armed robbery and assault, two years nine months for theft, and a probable five-year term for stealing speakers, documented by Lambert 2003, 23, 51, and 53 respectively), it is difficult to accept the Soviet legal system as an instrument of justice. Apparently, the recidivist receives longer sentences with each conviction (Lambert 2003, 54). For more on the topic of arbitrary sentences, see Lambert 2003, chapter 3.

31   Meyer Galler and Harlan Marquess, *Soviet Prison Camp Speech: A Survivor's Glossary* (Madison: University of Wisconsin Press, 1972), supplemented by Galler in 1977; post-Soviet publications include D. S. Baldaev, V. K. Belko, I. M. Isupov, comp., *Slovar' tiuremno-lagerno-blatnogo zhargona*, Moscow: "Kraia Moskvy," 1992; V. Bykov, *Russkaia fenia* (Smolensk: TRAST-IMAKOM, 1994); and the two-volume set edited by D. S. Baldaev, *Slovar' blatnogo vorovskogo zhargona* (Moscow: KAMPANA, 1997).

32   Baldaev is a one-man cottage industry, following the three volumes titled *Russian Criminal Tattoos* with *Drawings from the Gulag* (London: FUEL Press, 2010), published after his death, which documents the horrors of life in the camps through Baldaev's own drawings. Alix Lambert, the edgy journalist responsible for the peculiar volume titled *Crime* (London: FUEL Press, 2008), produced an informative documentary titled *The Mark of Cain* ABC 2000) and the slim, densely illustrated volume *Russian Prison Tattoos* (Atglen, PA: Schiffer Pub., 2003). For names of criminal investigators in the Russian penitentiary system who preserve prisoners' tattoos so as to understand the visuals' meaning, see Lambert 2003, *passim*.

33   See Andrew Farquhar, "Russian Activist Alexei Plutser-Sarno Flees to Estonia," *Provisions*, 1 (December 2010), available at http://provisionslibrary.com/?p=5323 (accessed 5 January 2011); Ellen Barry, "Artist Playing Cat-and-Mouse Faces Russia's Claws," *New York Times*, 21 January 2011, available at http://www.nytimes.com/2011/01/22/world/europe/22voina.html?_r=2&hp (accessed 23 January 2011); Shaun Walker, "The artists who crossed the line," *The Independent*, 23 February 2011, available at http://www.independent.co.uk/arts-entertainment/art/news/the-artists-who-crossed-the-line-2222639.html (accessed 3 March 2011).

34   Alexei Plutser-Sarno's "The Language of the Body and Politics:

The Symbolism of Thieves' Tattoos" is a slightly revised version of his Russian article by the same title in Baldaev 2001, 7-12.

35   New Zealand's Maori, for whom embellishment ("moko") on the face registered high status, anticipated Soviet prisoners' body language, for their tattoo designs "conveyed specific information about their status, rank, ancestry and abilities" and has been described as "a kind of aesthetic bar code for the face" (Lineberry). In other words, there are several unexpected precedents for the social status accorded tattoos in the Soviet criminal system.

36   *Vor* (thief) is the generic label for a criminal, not just someone who steals.

37   In 1994, the then popular rock group Liube made an idiosyncratic film within a prison titled *Zona Liube*, structured around its music, and recorded such songs as "Belyi lebed'" (White Swan), alluding to the high-security prison in Siberia, which, according to some inmates, has the most brutal regimen of all penitentiaries in the country (Lambert 2003, 91).

38   See http://easternpromises.livejournal.com/47809.html.

39   For a full-body analysis, see the site.

40   See "Russian Organized Crime," available at http://www.fas.org/irp/world/para/docs/rusorg3.htm (accessed 19 December 2011). The site maintains that in early 1993, the Russian Ministry of Internal Affairs reported more than 5,000 crime groups operating in Russia, comprising an estimated membership of 100,000, with a leadership of 18,000.

41   A photograph of Viktor Tyriakin, who had spent 37 of his sixty years in prison, shows the Soviet leaders' tattoos on his chest, acquired several decades earlier; Evgenii Novikov, another long-time inmate in the zone, confirms that such images protected prisoners from being shot (Lambert, *Russian Prison Tattoos*, 48).

42   American fraternities, obviously, also rely on this rhetoric to emphasize bonds within the group.

43   On *Mama*, see Yana Hashamova, "Castrated Patriarchy, Violence, and Gender Hierarchies in Post-Soviet Film," in *National and Gender Identity in Russian Culture*, eds., Helena Goscilo and Andrea Lanoux (DeKalb: Northern Illinois University Press, 2006.), 196-224, especially 201-02.

44   In his response to the first draft of this chapter, David Goldfrank suggested a parallel between the *neprikasaemye* and the *dalits* ("untouchables"), who, in the sociologist Orlando Patterson's dual model of enslavement, belong to the extrusive (as opposed to the intrusive) category: i.e., fallen insiders expelled from normal participation in the community because of failure to observe its norms. See Orlando Patterson, *Slavery and Social Death: A Comparative Study* (Cambridge, MA: Harvard University Press, 1982), especially 40-41. Thank you, David.

45   On the prophylactic function of audiences in the oral performance of folklore, see Petr Bogatyrev and Roman Jakobson, "Folklore as
a Special Form of Creativity," tr., Manfred Jacobson, in Peter Steiner, ed.
The Prague School: Selected Writings, 1929–1946 (Austin: University of Texas
Press, 1982), 32–46.

46   Lambert notes that only about a third of female prisoners sport
tattoos, and rarely in the profusion visible on many male criminals' bodies (Lambert 2003, 44). As Fisher rights points out, "historically, men have
been much more likely to get tattoos than have women" and the two sexes
favor different locations on their bodies, with women preferring hips, buttocks, and breasts, while men are partial to visible areas, especially the
arms (99-100).

Works cited

Baldaev, D.S. *Tatuirovka zakliuchennykh. Al'bom.* St. Petersburg: Limbus Press, 2001.

___. *Russian Criminal Tattoo Encyclopedia.* Vol. I. London: Murray &
Sorrell FUEL, 2003, reprint 2009.

___. *Russian Crimintal Tattoo Encyclopedia.* Vol. II. London: Murray &
Sorrell FUEL, 2006.

Baranovskii, V. and I. Mel'nikov. *Iskussstvo tatuirovok.* Moscow: ZAO
"Slavianskii dom knigi," "Slovo," 2002.

Caplan, Jane, ed. *Written on the Body: The Tattoo in European and American History.* Princeton, NJ: Princeton University Press, 2000.

Caplan, Jane. "Introduction," in Caplan, *Written on the Body,* xi-xxiii..

"Criminal tattoo." *Wikipedia.* Available at http://en.wikipedia.org/
wiki/Criminal_tattoo. Accessed 5 February 2007.

El'skii, Andzhei [Andrzej Jelski]. *Tatuirovka.* Minsk: "MET," 1977.
(Trans. from Polish edition by Jelski, 1993).

Fisher, Jill A. "Tattooing the Body, Marketing Culture," *Body & Society,*
8, no. 4 (2002): 91-107.

Gustafson, W. Mark. "*Inscripta in Fronte*: Penal Tattooing in Late Antiquity," *Classical Antiquity* 16, no. 1 (April 1997): 79-105.

Holy Bible. Revised Standard Version. New York: Meridian Books,
1974.

Jones, C.P. "Stigma: Tattooing and Branding in Graeco-Roman Antiquity," *The Journal of Roman Studies,* 77 (1987): 139-55.

Kosulin, V.D. *Iskusstvo tatuirovki.* St. Petersburg: "DIAMANT"/"ZOLO-
TOI VEK," 2000.

Lambert, Alix. *The Mark of Cain.* Documentary, with Q&A session, on
Nightline titled "The Zone." ABC, 2000.

___. *Russian Prison Tattoos: Codes of Authority, Domination, and Struggle.* Atglen, PA: Schiffer Publishing Ltd. 2003.

Lineberry, Cate. "Tattoos: The Ancient and Mysterious History." Smithsonian. 1 January 2007. Available at http://www.smithsonianmag.com/history-archaeology/tattoo.html. Accessed 4 April 2008.

McGuirk, Justin. "A graphical lexicon of the skin art of Russia's convict classes impresses." *Icon* (May 2004).Available at http://www.icon-magazine.co.uk/issues/012/tattoo_text.htm. Accessed 5 February 2007.

___. *Crime.* London: Murray and Sorrell FUEL, 2008.

Mascia-Lees, E. and Patricia Sharpe, eds. *Tattoo, Torture, Mutilation, and Adornment: The Denaturalization of the Body in Culture and Text.* Albany, NY: State University of New York Press, 1992.

Miller, Jean-Chris. Ed. *Skin Art,* vol. 8, no. 66. Hoboken, NJ: Art & Ink Enterprises, n.d.

Plutser-Sarno, Alexei. "The Language of the Body and Politics: The Symbolism of Thieves' Tattoos" in *Russian Criminal Tattoos Encyclopedia.* Vol. I. London: Murray & Sorrell FUEL, 2003, reprint 2009. 27-53.

___. "'All power to the Godfathers!'" in *Russian Criminal Tattoos Encyclopedia.* Vol. II. London: Murray & Sorrell FUEL, 2006. 32-57.

Sanders, Clinton R. *Customizing the Body: The Art and Culture of Tattooing.* Philadelphia: Temple University Press, 1989.

Schiffmacher, Henk. Ed. *1000 Tattoos.* Hong Kong, Köln, etc.: Taschen, 2005.

Schrader, Abby M. "Branding the Other/Tattooing the Self: Bodily Inscription among Convicts in Russia and the Soviet Union" in Caplan, *Written on the Body* (see above), 174-92.

"tattoo." *Encyclopedia Britannica Online.* Available at http://www.britannica.com/EBchecked/topic/584263/tattoo. Accessed 6 August 2011.

"Tattoo." *Wikipedia.* Available at http://en.wikipedia.org/wiki/Tattoo. Accessed 5 February 2007.

10

Reality-TV: Реальность или ТВ?

Павел Лысаков

Реалити-ТВ, как заявляет этот термин, претендует на особые отношения с реальностью (т.е. непосредственно показывает реальность, в отличие от других телевизионных жанров). Начало эпохи Реалити-ТВ принято связывать с выходом в свет шоу *Большой Брат* (*Big Brother*, 1999), за которым последовал ряд других, как на Западе, так, наконец, и в России (*За стеклом*, 2001, и т.д.). При более пристальном рассмотрении жанра реалити, можно обнаружить, что он не так нов, как может показаться, и восходит, с одной стороны к документалистике, теленовостям и сериалам, с другой—к так называемым «безсценарным» телепрограммам. Анализ конструирования программного блока типичного «реального шоу» позволяет увидеть ряд элементов художественного и—шире—нарративного конструирования, которые присущи телевидению как медиуму и используются в других тележанрах, на передачу реальности не претендующих.

В известном смысле основы жанра реалити были заложены еще до изобретения телевидения, его предшественником в передаче движущегося образа--кино--причем задолго до того, как в последнем появился звук. С самого появления на свет кинематографа наметились два концептуальных подхода к созданию кинопроизведения: реалистический, «отражающий» реальность, подход Луи Люмьера и креативный, сознательно формирующий особую, несуществующую реальность, подход

Жоржа Мельеса.[1] Но даже в самых первых фильмах Люмьера заснятая документальная реальность (выход рабочих с фабрики через проходную, прибытие поезда на станцию) проблематична, поскольку она превращается для зрителя кинотеатра в спектакль, т.е. становится шоу на материале реальности, отраженной медиумом кинематографа. Уже у Люмьера намечается отход от подлинно документальной реальности: во многих фильмах, рисующих обычные бытовые сцены, чтобы достичь оптимального результата, на съемках проигрывается по нескольку дублей.[2]

На третьем десятилетии существования кинематографа молодой российский документалист и пропонент запечатления на пленку «жизни врасплох» Дзига Вертов позволяет себе вставлять в сводку киноновостей игровые эпизоды[3]; исследователи его творчества отмечают наличие в кинотексте осознанно сконструированного аргумента.[4] В знаменитом *Человеке с киноаппаратом* (1929) есть сцены, в первую очередь, с участием оператора Михаила Кауфмана, поставленные специально в расчете на камеру, а монтаж кадров, полученных путем документальной съемки, в том числе скрытой камерой, совершенно не пытается себя скрыть и в большинстве случаев имеет откровенно художественный характер. Из последних ярких кинематографических примеров использования заснятой реальности в художественных целях и драматизации отснятых документальных эпизодов в процессе конструирования из них цельного текста можно привести французские фильмы *Микрокосмос* (*Microcosmos: Le peuple de l'herbe*, 1996) и *Птицы* (*Le peuple migrateur*, 2001).

Как ни парадоксально это может звучать, но телевизионное реалити-шоу в современном понимании также изобретено кинематографом. В итальянском футуро-фантастическом фильме *Десятая жертва* (*La decima vittima*, 1965) рассказывается о некоей смертельной Игре, в которой участвует Охотник и не знающая его Жертва. Охотник, выйдя на Жертву, совершает убийство перед камерами; жертве предоставлено право защищаться и может получиться так, что будет убит Охотник. Отснятый материал затем используется в телевизионной рекламе. Фильм не только иллюстрирует один из основных жанров реалити-шоу (игра на выбывание, заснятая на пленку), но и указывает на связь реалити-шоу с рекламой и маркетингом. К последнему мы еще вернемся.

Собственно на телевидении историю жанра реалити можно проследить уже с семидесятых годов. Одним из первых примеров является американский эксперимент, в ходе которого на протяжении семи месяцев производилась съемка обыденной жизни американской семьи Лаудов (*Loud*); 300 часов отснятого материала было впоследствии транслировано в эфире. В 1989 году американский телеканал Фокс (Fox) запустил программу *Полиция* (*Cops*), в которой оператор сопровождает полицейский патруль на дежурстве, а отснятый материал монтируется в нечто похожее на телевизионные новости—рассказ о том, что на дежурстве происходит. Нетрудно догадаться, что некоторых событий скорее всего и не произошло бы, если бы рядом не было камеры. Жизни, застигнутой врасплох, или жизни «как она есть», в чистом виде не получается. В 1993 году в США было запущено еще одно подобное шоу *Реальные истории дорожного патруля* (*Real Stories of the Highway Patrol*). В 1999 году британский Канал 4 показал программу *Дом 1900 года* (*The 1900 House*), где документировалась жизнь семьи, которая в течение съемок жила в доме указанного исторического времени и использовала только предметы обихода и одежду, доступные семье среднего класса викторианской эпохи.

Тем не менее появление в 1999 году *Big Brother* произвело революцию. Основной особенностью нового шоу было то, что герои на протяжении своего участия в проекте не могли покинуть замкнутого пространства дома с садиком, где они жили, были обязаны постоянно носить на себе радиомикрофоны, не имели права пользоваться пишущими средствами и бумагой (и вступать в коммуникацию друг с другом таким образом), а главное—они были 24 часа в сутки под наблюдением открытых и скрытых камер, установленных снаружи и внутри дома, даже в таких местах как душ. Постоянное аудиовизуальное наблюдение и невозможность для участников вступить в коммуникацию, которую не заметили бы создатели шоу и которую нельзя было бы при желании показать зрителю, и объясняет название шоу, отсылающее нас к ситуации и фразе из романа Джорджа

Орвелла *1984*: «Большой Брат наблюдает за вами» ("Big Brother is watching you"). Шоу имело большой успех именно благодаря новаторской вуайеристской (в широком смысле слова) направленности, когда на экран выносились самые различные аспекты реального человеческого быта, которые нам обычно не видны и которые до тех пор не показывались ни на телевидении, ни в документальном кино. Шоу одновременно являлось и игрой навылет: участники еженедельно номинировали двух кандидатов на выбывание из своих рядов, а телевизионная аудитория решала, кому из них уходить из проекта. Последний оставшийся участник получил денежный приз. Владельцем формата была голландская фирма Endemol. Шоу впервые вышло в Голландии, но по-настоящему заговорили о шоу и о феномене Реалити-ТВ после запуска шоу в Великобритании в 2000 году, и его дальнейшего триумфального шествия, в первую очередь по англоязычному телепространству.

Историю Реалити-ТВ в России на настоящий момент можно разбить на четыре этапа.

Этап первый—этап «бытовизма» и вуайеризма (осень 2001 г.-весна 2002 г.)

На российском телевидении эпоха реалити началась 27 октября 2001 года с выходом первого выпуска шоу «За стеклом» на телеканале ТВ-6 (илл. 1-2-3). Шоу имело оригинальный формат, основанный на вольном соединении тематики двух западных шоу: *Big Brother* и скандального *Loft Story*, появившегося во Франции весной 2001 года. В специально отстроенном жилище в части фойе гостиницы «Россия» в буквальном смысле за стеклом, с 40 телекамерами, в том числе в душе (элемент *Big Brother*), оказались три молодых человека[5] и три девушки. Предполагалось, что участники «создадут пары», поскольку приз—квартиру в Москве--должны были получить на двоих оставшиеся после ряда голосований юноша и девушка (элемент *Loft Story*, правда там квартира была не в Москве). Шоу было абсолютно безсценарным, за исключением некоторых заданий, которые участники получали от невидимого режиссера (вариант Большого Брата) через громкоговорители—например, провести литературный вечер или дискотеку.

илл. 1
За стеклом. Лого.

илл. 2
За стеклом. Дискотека.

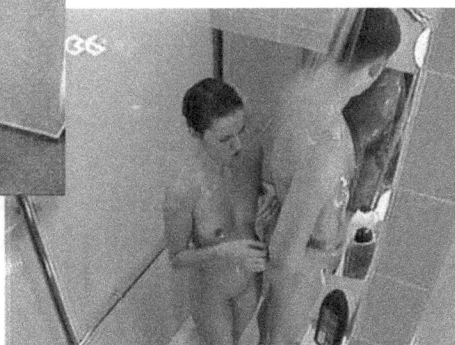

илл. 3
За стеклом. Душ.

Вуайеристская направленость шоу была задействована на всех возможных направлениях:

• прямые включения во время одной из телетрансляций (их было 3-4 в день),

• прямая 24-часовая трансляция происходящего в интернете,

• наличие в квартире прозрачной стеклянной стены — одностороннего зеркала, через которую участников можно было увидеть с улицы (существует мнение, что по длине очередь зрителей к «России» была сравнима с очередью в Мавзолей В. И. Ленина)[6].

Следует признать, что благодаря всему этому шоу максимально приближалось к заявленной передаче реальности и, вероятно, именно в этом и в том, что это происходило впервые, была причина его популярности.

Тем не менее, безсценарность и «бытовизм» не могли долго привлекать аудиторию, и создатели последующих шоу, очевидно, это понимали. В *За стеклом-2: последний бифштекс* участники были разбиты на две команды, каждая из которых обслуживала отдельный ресторан и боролась за посетителя и выручку; рестораны были настоящие и зрители могли прийти и вживую увидеть участников, а также поддержать их морально и материально, сделав заказ в ресторане. Шоу *Теперь ты в армии* поместило участников в казарму, но в целом к концу сезона 2001-02 года фантазия создателей реалити-шоу первого поколения начала иссякать, рейтинги шли вниз, и в итоге безсценарные бытовые вуайеристические шоу на российском телевидении сошли на нет. Именно в этом сезоне начался второй этап Реалити-ТВ в России.

Этап второй—шоу-конкурсы, построенные на импортных форматах (зима 2001-02—по наше время).

Второй этап характеризуется импортированием проверенных на западном телевидении медиа-продуктов (форматов). С содержательной точки зрения это были заранее отснятые на пленку соревнования или конкурсы, представленные в виде законченных отредактированных нарративов-телепрограмм. Первым российским шоу, основанным на купленном импортированном формате был «Последний герой» (илл. 4-5), показанный на ОРТ (оригинальное название *Survivor*, владелец формата Чарли Парсонз). Это шоу-соревнование, где две команды участников отправляются на отдаленные экзотические острова и живут в условиях приближенных к условиям, в которых оказался Робинзон Крузо (кстати предшественником формата было шведское шоу «Робинзон», автором которого также был Чарли Парсонз). В дополнение к рассказам о лишениях, которые терпят участники (отсутствие привычной еды и необходимость обходиться местной флорой и фауной, отсутствие жилья и необходимость его построить, опасность атаки ядовитыми

илл. 4
Последний герой. Лого.

илл. 5
Последний герой. Камеры в
ожидании события.

насекомыми, змеями и хищными животными), зрителю показывают экзотические полуспортивные соревнования между племенами и советы племен, в частности те, где проигравшее племя голосует за выбывание одного из участников.

При ближайшем рассмотрении нетрудно обнаружить, что шоу типа «Последний герой» вообще не относятся к сфере реалити, несмотря на то, что к ним применяют этот термин. Ни о какой реальности, застигнутой врасплох, или жизни «как она есть» не может быть и речи:

- Герои уже не находятся в замкнутом пространстве—доме или квартире, где они могли бы постоянно контролироваться камерами. Камер мало, стационарных камер постоянного наблюдения нет или почти нет.
- Нет и упора на подглядывание, за исключением некоторых кадров, которые показываются с явным расчетом на зрительское эротическое возбуждение.
- Большинство кадров снято камерой, которая оказалась

на месте именно потому, что там что-то должно было произойти (в первую очередь запланированные события—соревнования, советы племен—но также и просто какое-либо подготовленное позирование перед камерой).
- В ряде ситуаций случалось обратное—участник играл на присутствующую рядом камеру.

Таким образом, по сравнению с реалити-шоу первого поколения, можно отметить усиление постановочного элемента.

Усиление контроля создателей над текстом реалити-шоу можно проследить и на заключительной—монтажной, или редакционной, стадии:
- Между реальным временем происходящего и временем трансляции шоу в эфире существует очевидный хронологический разброс. Это особенно характерно для *Последнего героя*, где съемки происходят на географически отдаленных экзотических островах, но имеет место во всех шоу второго и более поздних поколений.
- Прямого теле- или интернет-эфира более нет, отснятый материал проходит отбор и монтируется в соответствии с повесткой дня создателей шоу.

В этих условиях, в отличие от шоу первого поколения, в первую очередь *За стеклом*, с его каналами прямого доступа к происходящему, создатели имеют возможность как выстроить сюжеты, не имеющие отношения к реальной цепи событий, так и повлиять на рейтинг героя, показывая его в выгодном или невыгодном свете, или вообще не показывая. Ощущение сконструированности и отсутствия соприкосновения зрителя с действительностью подчеркивается тем, что
- в начале шоу в сжатом виде показывают события предыдущих выпусков (что по отношению к реальности невозможно, это функция памяти: увидеть реальное событие можно только раз, остальное—его репрезентации),
- в конце показывают несколько кадров из следующей серии/выпуска (что опять-таки противоречит принципу реальности, так как реальность существует

лишь в настоящем, нельзя сегодня увидеть реальность будущую).

Реалити-шоу, таким образом, приобрело черты обычного телесериала.

Еще одним приемом, активно использующимся уже в реалити-шоу второго поколения, является product placement, т.е. размещение в кадре продукта рекламного спонсора программы и инкорпорирование его в действие, в сам текст программы. Этот прием получил широкое распространение еще в кинематографе, особенно в голливудском и недавно стал использоваться и в российском[7]. В *Последнем герое*, это в частности косметика фирмы Nivea и кофе Elgresso Gold. Конечно, Робинзону Крузо в свое время тоже достались какие-то предметы с большой земли, но прожил он на острове не 40 дней, а многие годы, и понятно, почему он изображается таким обросшим на картинках; ухоженности же участников игры можно позавидовать — особенно бросаются в глаза безупречные bikini lines и гладкие ноги участниц, отсутствие волос в подмышках всех участников и депилированная грудь мужчин. Загар, возможно, действительно от местного солнца. Как следует из титров в конце программы, где-то в кустах прячется скорая помощь, окончательно ставя под сомнение непосредственность только что показанного «экстрима».

Следующими заимствованными форматами стали близкие по содержанию британский *Pop Idol* и голландская *Star Academy*. Оба представляют модификацию традиционного телевизионного конкурса талантов (talent show). На основе первого было создано шоу *Стань звездой* (последующее название *Народный артист*) на РТР; на основе второго было запущено весьма успешное шоу *Фабрика звезд* (автор формата — уже упомянутый Endemol) на Первом телеканале. *Фабрика-1* транслировалась уже осенью 2002 года (илл. 6-7). Для шоу отбирается некоторое количество молодых талантов с опытом и без опыта работы на эстраде. Зрители становятся свидетелями бытовых моментов жизни участников (которые живут вместе под скрытыми камерами), а также того, как участников начинают обучать пению, танцу, сценическому движению и речи. Участники регулярно

илл. 6
Фабрика звезд. Лого

илл. 7
Фабрика звезд. Группа
«Фабрика» (1-й сезон).

готовят новые номера и еженедельно выступают с новой коллективной концертной программой (илл. 8); также регулярно
происходит отсев участников. В *Фабрике* впервые был опробо-
ван новый способ контроля над содержанием шоу, теперь уже
не на уровне монтажа, а на уровне вмешательства в сам конкурс: продюсеры шоу могли повлиять на итоги голосования,
дав «иммунитет» участнику, против которого проголосовали
товарищи, т.е. оставить его в шоу.[8]

Особенно интересна *Фабрика* тем, что она, как ни одно другое реалити-шоу второго и последующих этапов, преуспела
в маркетинге своих сопутствующих продуктов/товаров (илл.
9-10) и товаров рекламных спонсоров; таких, например, как

илл. 8
Фабрика звезд.
Еженедельный
телеконцерт.

илл. 9. *Фабрика звезд.*
Обложка компакт-диска.

илл. 10. *Фабрика звезд* и Мясное ассорти—пародия или эксплуатация?

косметика MIA--продукция рекламного спонсора шоу, как в виде отдельных объявлений во время рекламных пауз, так и в виде product placement (участники пользуются этой косметикой, иногда даже разыгрывают рекламные сцены с ней, а ведущие постоянно напоминают о рекламном спонсоре, «косметике для молодой кожи» MIA).

Шоу также производит и рекламирует следующие товары и услуги:

• копирайты на песенные хиты, исполняемые участниками шоу,

• мелодии звонков этих хитов («рингтоны») и картинки-заставки с изображением участников для мобильных телефонов,

илл. 11

Журнала *Yes - Фабрика звезд*.

- платное SMS-голосование для поддержки любимого участника,
- финальный концерт в московском спортивно-концертном комплексе Олимпийский,
- DVD с записью этого концерта,
- последующее концертное турне по России,
- видеоклипы,
- компакт-диски с песнями, прозвучавшими на шоу,
- журнал *Yes-Фабрика звезд*, на страницах которого рассказывается о событиях текущей *Фабрики* и о жизни выпускников предыдущих шоу (журнал одновременно является информационным спонсором шоу и информационным продуктом, за который потребитель платит деньги, а также способом дальнейшей рекламы ряда товаров—в первую очередь, спонсоров шоу) (илл. 11).

Одним из более поздних примеров импортирования форматов является шоу *Ты—супермодель* (канал СТС), являющееся российским вариантом американского шоу-конкурса *America's Next Top Model* (илл. 12-13-14). Первый выпуск шоу был показан зимой 2003-04 телесезона, второй—в январе-марте 2005 года. Рекламными спонсорами являлись вездесущая MIA и компания Rolsen, производящая «мультивизоры»--телевизоры с встроенным DVD-проигрывателем и игровой приставкой. Естественно, участники на протяжении шоу пользуются как «косметикой для молодой кожи» (слоган продукции MIA), так

илл. 12
Ты—супермодель. Лого.

илл. 13
Ты—супермодель.
Участницы кон-
курса.

илл. 14
Ты—супермодель. Жюри конкурса.

илл. 15
Ты—супермодель. Участница на
обложке журнала Cosmopolitan.

и мультивизором. Одна из фотосессий начинающих моделей проходит для компании MIA, другая—для журнала *Cosmopoli-tan*, одного из информационных спонсоров шоу (илл. 15).[9]

Так же, как и в других шоу-конкурсах содержание выпусков полностью контролируется:

- Передачи выходят в свет намного позднее реальных событий.

- Часовой выпуск (если исключить рекламу, остается около 45 минут) содержит в себе дайджест событий, происходивших в течение трех дней.

- Каждый выпуск, начиная со второго, начинается с напоминания, чем (т.е. выбыванием какой участницы) закончился предыдущий, и заканчивается кадрами из следующего выпуска.

Третий этап в развитии реалити-шоу связан с проектами канала ТНТ, и начинается с выходом шоу *Голод*, первый выпуск которого был показан 8 ноября 2003 года (илл. 16-17-18). Это этап сюжетной интеграции рекламного продукта.

илл. 16. *Голод*. Лого.

илл. 17. *Голод*. Интернет-сайт.

илл. 18. *Голод*. За обеденным столом.

Формальный конкурс (игра на выбывание) был построен по следующей схеме: участники—обитатели изолированного от внешнего мира дома—остаются без средств к существованию и должны разными способами зарабатывать себе на хлеб во время выходов в город;[10] единовременно в город выпускается только одна пара участников. Каждую неделю по результатам голосования телезрителей выбывает один участник. В добавление к камерам в доме и во дворе пара, выходившая в город, снабжалась нательными скрытыми камерами, чтобы зритель мог видеть происходящее глазами участников.

Что касается рекламного аспекта, в шоу была обильно использована техника размещения продукта и логотипов продуктов. Основными такими продуктами были:

- хлебные сухарики «Три корочки»,
- пельмени «Сам Самыч»,
- шоколадные батончики Snickers,
- бытовая электротехника Bork.

Участников постоянно подкармливали сухариками и батончиками, изголодавшись они могли за огромные деньги, взятые из финальной призовой суммы, купить продукцию линии полуфабрикатов «Сам Самыч». Электрочайник, микроволновая печь, плита и ряд предметов бытовой электротехники, не связанной с кухней, были производства Bork. Логотип Snickers был размещен, среди других мест, на рюкзаках выходящих в город, на баскетбольном щите и скейтборде, а «Три корочки» явились даже спонсором турнира по шашкам, в котором вместо фигур играли указанными сухариками, а победительница была награждена пожизненным бесплатным снабжением этими сухарями.

Итак, тематика шоу, его содержание--«голод», необходимость зарабатывать на еду--были тесно связаны с продукцией ряда его рекламных спонсоров—продуктами питания и бытовой, в частности, кухонной техникой, что уже отличает *Голод* от шоу предыдущих периодов.[11] Первая рекламная пауза начиналась с рекламы сухариков «Три корочки», слоган которых, «Сухарики «Три корочки» спасают от голода», перекликается с названием шоу, причем явно неслучайно: связь подчеркивается написанием слова **голод**—и в рекламе и в заставке шоу это белые буквы, подтекающие подобно буквам в названиях фильмов ужасов.[12]

Становится очевидным, что шоу специально разработано как редакционное окружение *для* продукции конкретных рекламных спонсоров. Более того, в шоу *Голод* граница между традиционной, формально выделенной рекламой и ее редакционным окружением минимизирована, а временами окончательно стерта.

• Апогеем стирания этой границы явилась съемка участниками шоу на любительскую камеру разыгранного по придуманному ими сюжету рекламного ролика тех же «Трех корочек». Ролик был показан непосредственно в тексте шоу, а не в рекламную паузу, и преподнесен зрителю тематически как один из продуктов творчества участников и отчет о том, как они проводили в очередной раз время.

В тот же сезон 2003-04 года по телевидению начали рекламировать мороженое «Золотой слиток»--брикет эскимо в золотистой упаковке. В феврале на ТНТ было запущено новое шоу *Двенадцать негритят*, название которого отсылало к роману Агаты Кристи, *Десять негритят*, где один за одним погибают приглашенные на виллу десять человек. Приз, обещанный оставшемуся в конце участнику шоу,—двенадцать слитков чистого золота. Участников же обильно кормили указанным мороженым которое оказалось рекламным спонсором шоу.

Четвертый этап связан с появлением на канале ТНТ шоу *Дом-2* в мае 2004 года (илл. 19). Это самое долгое реалити-шоу на российском телевидении и, возможно, в мире. Оно идет на ТНТ по настоящее время (август 2012 г.) (илл. 20).

В шоу есть как черты, присущие шоу предыдущих периодов, так и инновации. К старому относится размещение в шоу продукции спонсоров, которую можно увидеть в рекламе, например, мороженое «Ля Фам» и лапшу быстрого приготовления «Ролтон», цифровую камеру и цветной принтер «все в одном» от Hewlett-Packard. Шоу производит ряд побочных

илл. 19. *Дом-2*

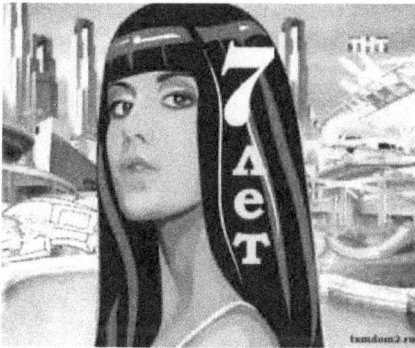

илл. 20
Дом-2. Семь лет шоу (2011 г.).

илл. 21
Дом-2. Шуточкая свадьба.

продуктов: гастроли участников, книги—воспоминания быв-
ших участников, журнал *Дом-2*; была выпущена настольная
игра. Мы опять встречаемся с необходимостью для участников
создавать пары (илл. 21), с редакционным контролем за ходом
шоу, который осуществляется за счет вмешательства в действие ведущих-участников (Ксения Собчак и Ксения Бородина)

илл. 22
Дом-2. Ведущие шоу--К. Собчак и
К. Бородина.

илл. 23
Дом-2. Обсуждение
событий дня.

(илл. 22), с использованием иммунитетов (осуществляется контроль за результатом голосования о выбывании участника – илл. 23). Присутствуют также:

- хронологический разнос событий и показа,
- редакционный монтаж,
- формат теленовостей в преподнесении дайджеста событий очередного выпуска в начале шоу и прощании со зрителями в конце.

Существенным нововведением явилась потенциально бесконечная продолжительность шоу. *Дом-2* не был закрыт в конце лета, как планировалось (и никто по сей день не получил обещанный дом, в отличие от первого шоу *Дом*, показанного летом 2003 г.). Официально было объявлено, что шоу не закрывается «по многочисленным просьбам телезрителей». Бесконечность действия обеспечивается использованием приема «крутящаяся дверь» (revolving door)—на смену выбывшим приходят новые участники (отсюда «зимовка», «первая весна» и т.д.). В этой ситуации возникает закономерный вопрос, получит ли кто-нибудь когда-нибудь давно уже построенный в подмосковье дом.

* * *

Реалити-шоу в массе своей развивались, таким образом, в следующих направлениях:
- от бесконтрольности к контролю (вплоть до изменения правил, как это случилось с *Домом-2*),
- от традиционных рекламных пауз до интеграции рекламы и рекламируемых продуктов непосредственно в редакционное пространство.

Почему это произошло? Очевидны, по крайней мере, две причины:

1. Медиум диктует свои условия. Телевидению нужен линейный нарратив, необходима композиция, что требует контроля за содержанием. Неслучайно здесь и использование в реалити-шоу, начиная со второго этапа, знакомых телезрителю форматов телесериала (дайджест событий предыдущего выпуска и анонс событий последующего) и новостей.

2. Вторая причина связана с рынком. Создателям шоу приходится контролировать содержание программы также и потому, что они должны делать выпуски более привлекательными для рекламодателей и особенно рекламных спонсоров. Это и достигается путем размещения продукции спонсоров в самом шоу и даже обыгрывания ее в сюжетных линиях.

В настоящее время программы российского Реалити-ТВ представляют собой сплав «реальности» (в виде показываемых псевдо-событий), «художественности» (в виде различных способов влияния авторов на события, а также отбора и аранжировки этих событий в определенный нарратив) и рекламы, связь между которой и текстом шоу откровенно стирается.

Notes

1   См. об этом подробнее в кн. Siegfried Krakauer, *Theory of Film: the Redemption of Physical Reality* (Princeton: Princeton University Press, 1997), 30-37.

2   Alan Williams, *Republic of Images: a History of French Filmmaking* (Cambridge, MA, and London: Harvard University Press, 2000), 28.

3   Например, в 15-м выпуске *Киноправды* (1923) за репортажем о демонстрации атеистов следует сюжет о молодом человеке, который заходит к себе комнату, снимает со стены икону и вешает на ее место антирелигиозный плакат. Позднее юношу показывают участвующим в комсомольском мероприятии. Постановочные эпизоды имеются и в *Шестой части мира* (1926).

4   См. Graham Roberts, *Forward Soviet! History and Non-fiction Film in the USSR* (London and New York: I.B. Tauris, 1999), 27.

5   Всего юношей было четверо, но они не находились в доме одновременно—четвертый пришел из запасных на место другого, оставившего проект по собственному желанию.

6   С.Л.Уразова. «Reality TV в России. Первый опыт телеклонирования». *Вестник московского университета*, Серия 10, *Журналистика*, 2003, No. 3, с. 69.

7   В фильме *Ночной дозор* (2004 г.) таким продуктом является кофе Nescafe. Если герои пьют или покупают кофе, то зрителю ясно дается понять, что это Nescafe. В фильме *Дневной дозор* (2005 г.) это автомобиль Mazda и пиво Старый мельник.

8   Этот прием стал особенно активно применяться на шоу *Дом-2* (см. о нем далее в статье), где путем предоставления иммунитетов ведущие добивались выбывания—по голосованию участников—тех, против кого изначально большинство не голосовало, иногда даже никто изначально не голосовал.

9   Другим информационным спонсором шоу был журнал *Антенна*.

10   Изначально частью сюжетной интриги было также то, что участников вывезли с завязанными глазами на самолете из Шереметьево в неизвестном направлении и некоторое время после приезда в дом они не знали, в какой стране находятся. После выхода в город первой пары стало ясно, что они находятся в Берлине, и интрига завершилась.

11   Влияние рекламы на содержание материалов среди которых она расположена (и соответственно влияние рекламодателей на редакционную политику) имеет место не только на телевидении и не только в пост-советской, рыночной России. Джеймс Карран отмечал это влияние как одну из ведущих тенденций в развитии британской прессы послевоенного времени, затронувшую, в первую очередь, качественную прессу. См. James Curran, "Advertising and the Press" in James Curran, ed., *The British Press: A Manifesto*. London: Macmillan, 1978.

12   Обычно буквы подтекают кровью, хотя в данном случае имитации крови нет. Идея, вероятно, заимствована по аналогии с фильмом о вампирах *The Hunger* (т.е. «голод») и последовавшим за ним мини-сериалом с тем же названием, но в ходе шоу вампирская тема не эксплуатировалась.

In Memory of Richard Stites: "I'm a Classic"

by Anton Fedyashin

In the southwest corner of plot 41 of the Helsinki Orthodox Cemetery, a black marble plaque succinctly reads in gold letters, "Professor Richard Stites 1931-2010." Weeping birch trees shade the gravestones and a stone wall guards the cemetery's serenity from the bustle of the city streets. Richard rests among the descendants of jeweler Karl Faberge and Russian painter Ilya Repin. While for many Russian émigrés this cemetery became the end of enforced postrevolutionary exile, for Richard Finland was a place of voluntary escape from the stifling heat of Washington, DC summers. It was also an academic haven. Since 1968 he came to Helsinki regularly to work in the Slavonic Collection of the National Library of Finland, whose spectacular collection and irreplaceable staff enabled him to conduct research for his books. In gratitude for his consistent support, in August 2010 the library hosted in his honor a conference organized by Professor Natalia Baschmakoff of the University of Eastern Finland.[1]

Having started out in Lycoming College in Pennsylvania, Richard taught at the International College in Copenhagen, Brown University, Ohio State University (Lima Campus), and in 1977 joined the History Department of Georgetown University, where he remained until his death. Although he published over one hundred and thirty articles and chapters, Richard repeatedly advised his students and colleagues to "write books, not articles," and he practiced what he preached. In addition to ten edited volumes, he wrote four books that became classics in their own time: *The Women's Liberation Movement in Russia*; *Revolutionary Dreams*; *Russian Popular Culture: Entertainment and Society since 1900*; and *Serfdom, Society, and the Arts in Imperial Russia*.[2] Quantity and quality went hand in hand—each one has appeared in paperback and will be used in university classes for years to come. He also co-wrote the textbook *A History of Russia: People, Legends, Events, Forces* with Catherine Evtuhov, David Goldfrank, and Lindsey Hughes.[3]

The breadth of his scholarship was impressive. He came to feel equally comfortable on both sides of the 1917 revolutionary divide when few scholars did so. Nor was geography an obstacle: one of his last and incomplete projects, provisionally titled *The Four Horsemen: Revolution and the Counter-Revolution in Post-Napoleonic Europe*, is a comparative study of the revolutions in Naples, Spain, Greece, and Russia during the 1820s. In reality, he was a European historian with a concentration on Russia, which he saw as an integral part of Western history. A proud Philadelphian (of which he regularly reminded everyone), he symbolized the best of the American spirit—an open and pragmatic mind. In exploring Russian and European history, however, he never expressed the condescension that one finds often among posterity and outsiders.

What makes Richard's books eminently readable is the balance that he struck between the complexity of the subject and the clarity of style that became his signature. Acutely attuned to historical polyphony, he relished the multiple layers of time, but wrote straightforwardly with a simplicity and fluidity that pulled the eyes along the page. His style made writing seem effortless, but those acquainted with his work ethic knew that it never was for him—he polished his texts tirelessly, yet never became infatuated with his own prose. One of Richard's favorite books in terms of style was A. J. P. Taylor's *The Origins of the Second World War*, although he disagreed with the author's arguments.[4] Richard wrote for the intellectually curious, but never forgot that a good history book ought to tell an absorbing story. He chose his topics accordingly. Writing for a wide audience, he nevertheless eschewed simplifying and popularizing difficult topics. Always keeping a critical

distance from his subjects, he treated them with an infectious enthusiasm that was just enough to inspire in readers the imagina-
tive empathy necessary to see the world from the perspective of
controversial figures—the heroine of *Women's Liberation Movement*,
Aleksandra Kollontai, is both flawed and magnificent. As he wrote
in *Revolutionary Dreams*, "by focusing on the utopian motif in the
emerging revolutionary culture (including those currents in the
revolution that were defeated), I hope to advance the study of this
remarkable phenomenon and to help humanize the subject which
has often been the analysis of an enemy."[5] Yet he never descended
into essentialism or apologetics.

There was something theatrical in his writing. Painting with
words, he recreated "the realm of the memory of the place," to
use his own words, on the visual as well as the intellectual plain.
"Especially admired was the 'dynastic zone': the shores of the
Neva and the Admiralty, the Kazan and Spassky districts, the royal
and grand ducal palaces, the grand cathedrals," Richard wrote in

Serfdom, Society, and the Arts. "Interspersed, as if on guard, stood government and military ministries and the barracks of the Guards Regiment."[6] Space itself became a primary source for him, and one always sensed an unfulfilled graphic talent for which Richard compensated in his writing. He walked the streets of which he wrote and on one occasion asked a guide to close the door and leave him for a few minutes in Vera Figner's Shlisselburg Fortress prison cell so that he could experience a fraction of solitary confinement. Upon encountering new buildings, he would startle his companions by asking abruptly, "Where's the north?" His graduate classes became walking tours of cities as he placed characters and events in specific temporal and geographical circumstances.

Richard openly expressed his dislike for "isms" and refused to be pegged. Yet he was an iconoclast from the start, as the subjects and temporal scope of his books demonstrated. One can say that he followed the "social turn," yet he walked his own path along which many trailed. He wrote about both high and low culture and he knew both well. He urged every graduate student to read Jeffrey Brooks' *When Russia Learned to Read : Literacy and Popular Literature, 1861-1917*, which he considered one of the best historical works precisely because it focused on ordinary tastes and uncovered modes of thinking that most historians overlooked.[7] Exploring Soviet popular culture, he attended the concerts of Alla Pugacheva and Valery Leontiev, to whom he lovingly referred as "Allochka" and "Valerochka," respectfully, of course. This respect for ordinary people and simple tastes also made Richard eminently approachable.

Fluent in all things he did, he was above all a congenial friend and colleague who turned hanging out in bars into an academic exercise. He approached living people with the same curiosity as his material. He rarely talked about his own research and preferred instead to ask questions. He was a consummate listener, which endeared him to his interlocutors—as did the occasional dirty joke. Yet, his informal demeanor never obscured the intellectual fire that burned within. Prussian in his discipline when working on his own projects, he always found time to read and comment on the work of others. It helped his students that he was always easy to locate, especially on Tuesday and Friday nights in Washington, DC. At the bar, he played an academic advisor with the same ease with which he broke into a song, which he often did. His expertise on the "woman question" manifested itself in many ways, the most important of which was his genuine respect for female scholars and graduate students. Time always went fast with Richard. The heavily attended memorial service hosted by Georgetown University in April 2010 became a testament to his influence on students and colleagues.

He treated historical scholarship not as a science, but as an apprenticeship that could only evolve with consistent practice. He believed that good writing resulted from rewriting, as many of his students (the author included) found out to their initial chagrin and ultimate gratitude. His love of performance contributed to his teaching style. He punctuated lectures on Soviet history with political anecdotes that sent waves of laughter through the classroom. His undergraduate assignments included voluntary "historical theater" performances in lieu of papers. "Let's face it," he used to say, "I should have been an actor." He was a great teacher too.

Helsinki changed when Richard injected his energy into this quiet northern capital, which became his unofficial summer office for over thirty years. Today, seagulls soar above the cemetery where he lies. Their shrill cries fade into whimpers often followed by staccato calls that resemble human laughter. Richard mixed erudition with humor effortlessly. Disciplined and rigorous in his scholarship, he never lost interest in the wealth of living material that surrounded him—his close friends, colleagues, and students. He knew how to get people into a theater, but also how to let them out. It is impossible to imagine anyone saying of another person "he reminds me of Richard," which is probably the greatest compliment to this masterpiece of humanity who will live in the hearts of those who knew and loved him.

Notes

1   I am greatly indebted to Professor Baschmakoff for inviting me to participate in this conference, from which many ideas for this obituary emerged. Conference details can be found at www.helsinki.fi/aleksanteri/english/news/events/2010/0802_stites.htm. A report on the conference can be found at www.kansalliskirjasto.fi/extra/bulletin/brief4.html.

2   Richard Stites, *The Women's Liberation Movement in Russia: Feminism, Nihilism, and Bolshevism, 1860-1930* (Princeton: Princeton University Press, 1978); idem, *Revolutionary Dreams: Utopian Vision and Experimental Life in the Russian Revolution* (New York: Oxford University Press, 1989); idem, *Russian Popular Culture: Entertainment and Society since 1900* (Cambridge,UK: Cambridge University Press, 1992); idem, *Serfdom, Society, and the Arts in Imperial Russia: The Pleasure and the Power* (New Haven: Yale University Press, 2005).

3   Catherine Evtuhov, David Goldfrank, Lindsey Hughes, Richard Stites, *A History of Russia: People, Legends, Events, Forces* (Boston: Houghton Mifflin, 2004).

4   A. J. P. Taylor, *The Origins of the Second World War* (New York: Atheneum, 1961).

5   Stites, *Revolutionary Dreams*, 4.

6   *Serfdom, Society, and the Arts in Imperial Russia*, 19.

7   Jeffrey Brooks, *When Russia Learned to Read: Literacy and Popular Literature, 1861-1917* (Princeton: Princeton University Press, 1985).

Contributors

Boris Briker teaches Russian literature, language, and culture and coordinates the Russian Program in the Global Studies Department at Villanova University. Growing up in Ukraine, he holds a PhD in Russian Literature from the University of Alberta, Canada. In his younger years he coauthored (with Anatolii Vishevskii) a collection of satirical short stories in Russian. Briker writes mostly on Russian literature and culture of the twentieth century and on popular humor. He has published widely on writers of the Soviet period, including Bulgakov, Babel, Ilf and Petrov, Aksënov, Iskander, and Bunin. Most recently, Briker has written on anti-Stalinist humor in Stalin's time. Currently he is working on a book, *Russian Satire and the Soviet State (1918-1940)*.

Robert Edelman, a native of Flatbush and a childhood fan of the fabled Brooklyn Dodgers (and shocked into recognition of reality by their 1957 move to LA), is Professor of Russian History and the History of Sport at the University of California, San Diego, where he has taught since 1973. His first two books were on pre-revolutionary Russian history: *Gentry Politics on the Eve of the Russian Revolution: The Nationalist Party, 1907-1917* (1980), and *Proletarian Peasants: the Revolution of 1905 in Russia's Southwest* (1987). Since then he has written two prize winning monographs on Soviet sport: *Serious Fun: A History of Spectator Sports in the USSR* (1993) and *Spartak Moscow: A History of the People's Team in the Workers' State* (2009). He is presently editing *The Oxford Handbook of Sports History* and is directing a multi-year project on sport in the Cold War for the Wilson Center for International Scholars. He has also worked in various sports reporting and journalistic capacities and as an adviser to several NBA clubs seeking talent from the former Soviet Union.

Anton Fedyashin is the Executive Director of the Initiative for Russian Culture and Assistant professor of History at American University in Washington, DC. He is the author of *Liberals under Autocracy: Modernization and Civil Society in Russia, 1866-1904* (Wisconsin University Press, 2012) and he is currently working on his next book project, *Shades of Gray: the Cold War and the Spy Novel.*

Boris Gasparov received his education in linguistics and musicology in Moscow. He continued his intellectual development in Tartu, Estonia, at the time when Yuri Lotman and others were making that university the world's center for original ideas about semiotics, linguistics, and literature. He emigrated to the United States in 1981 and taught at Berkeley for 11 years, before coming to Columbia where he is professor of Russian, co-chair and founder of the University Seminar on Romanticism, and a member of the Seminars on Linguistics and on Slavic History and Culture. His books range from Slavic medieval studies and comparative grammar to semiotic studies of oral speech, to Pushkin and his time, to Russian modernism and twentieth century poetry. Music remains deeply embedded in his teaching, scholarship, and personal life. His book, *Five Operas and a Symphony: Word and Music in Russian Culture* (Yale University Press, 2005), has received the ASCAP Deems Taylor award. Gasparov's ongoing projects include *Speech, Memory, and Meaning: Intertextuality in Every-Day Language*, and a book on the Early Romantic roots of modern theoretical linguistics.

David Goldfrank—Richard Stites's colleague for thirty-three years, and also a childhood fan of the Brooklyn Dodgers—is Professor of History and Director of Medieval Studies at Georgetown University His books include *The Monastic Rule of Iosif Volotsky* (1983, rev. ed., 2000), *The Origins of the Crimean War* (1994), *A History of Russia* (co-authors, Catherine Evtuhov, Lindsey Hughes, Richard Stites, 2003/4), and *Nil Sorsky: The Authentic Writings* (2008). His edited volumes include *Passion and Perception: Essays on Russian Culture by Richard Stites* (2010) and *Essays in Russian Monasticism = Russian His-*

tory 39.2 (2012). His current major project is a study cum translation of Iosif's *Prosvetitel'*.

Helena Goscilo is Professor and Chair of Slavic at The Ohio State University and writes primarily on culture and gender in Russia, secondarily on visual genres. Her publications in the last two years include *Cinepaternity: Fathers and Sons in Soviet and Post-Soviet Film* (co-ed., Indiana UP 2010), *Reflections and Refractions: The Mirror in Russian Culture* (*Studies in 20th and 21st Century Literature* 2010/2011), *Celebrity and Glamour in Contemporary Russia: Shocking Chic* (co-ed., Routledge 2011), *Putin as Celebrity and Cultural Icon* (ed., Routledge 2012), and *Embracing Arms: Cultural Representations of Slavic and Balkan Women in War* (co-ed., Central European UP 2012). Among her current projects are a volume preliminarily titled *Fame in Flight: Russian Aviation* and a collection of articles on *Moscow as Global City* (both with Vlad Strukov).

Anita Kondoyanidi holds her first Ph.D. in Literature and Literary Criticism. She is currently working on her second Ph.D. in Russian/ Soviet History at Georgetown University. Her dissertation title is "Disillusioned Prophet: Maxim Gorky and the Russian Revolutions, 1913-1936." Her articles have appeared in *The Russian Review* and *Revista de Instituciones, Ideas y Mercados* (*RIIM*).

Anna Lawton is Adjunct Professor at Georgetown University's School of Foreign Service, where she teaches courses in visual culture and film studies. Previously, she was an Associate Professor at Purdue University. She has published extensively in scholarly journals and contributed to collections of essays. Her latest book, *Imaging Russia 2000: Film and Facts,* received the CHOICE award as Outstanding Academic Title 2005. Other books include: *Before the Fall: Soviet Cinema in the Gorbachev Years* and *Vadim Shershenevich: From Futurism to Imaginism.* Edited volumes include: *The Red Screen: Politics, Society, Art in Soviet Cinema* and *Words in Revolution: Russian Futurist Manifestoes 1912-1928.* Lawton also served on the National Gallery of Art Advisory Film Committee and was Deputy Director of Public Information and Media Outreach with the US Information Service at the American Embassy in Moscow.

Pavel Lyssakov is Associate Professor, Faculty of Liberal Arts and Sciences, St. Petersburg State University (SPBGU). He graduated from SPBGU in 1986 and received a PhD in Russian Literature from Columbia University in 1998. Author of a number of articles on 19th and 20th century Russian Literature and editor of *Cultural Studies* (*Kul'tural'nye issledovaniia*, 2006, co-editor, Alexander Etkind), his research interests are Nikolai Gogol, Russian Modernist fiction, film, and mass media.

Stephen M. Norris is Associate Professor of History at Miami University (OH). He is the author of two books, *A War of Images: Russian Popular Prints, Wartime Culture, and National Identity, 1812-1945* (2006); and *Blockbuster History in the New Russia: Movies, Memory, and Patriotism* (2012). He is the co-editor of three volumes, two featuring contributions by Richard Stites, *Preserving Petersburg: History, Memory, Nostalgia* (2008); *Insiders and Outsiders in Russian Cinema* (2008); and *Russia's People of Empire: Life Stories from Eurasia, 1500 to the Present* (2012). He is currently researching and writing a biography of Boris Efimov

Lewis Siegelbaum is the Jack and Margaret Sweet Professor of History at Michigan State University. He has migrated from labor history to the history of consumption and material culture and from working on the Stalin era to the post-Stalin decades of Soviet history. He has published *The Politics of Industrial Mobilization in Russia* (1983), *Stakhanovism and the Politics of Productivity in the USSR* (1988), *Soviet State and Society between Revolutions* (1994), and *Cars for Comrades: The Life of the Soviet Automobile* (2008; Russian edition, 2011). Among his edited volumes are *Stalinism as a Way of Life* (2000, co-edited with A.K. Sokolov), *Borders of Socialism* (2006), and *The Socialist Car* (2011). He is engaged in a macro-project with Leslie Page Moch on migration in Russian political space across the twentieth century

Sergei I. Zhuk is Associate Professor of History at Ball State University. He is an author of *Rock and Roll in the Rocket City: The West, Identity, and Ideology in Soviet Dnipropetrovsk* (2010) and *Russia's Lost Reformation: Peasants, Millenialism, and Radical Sects in Southern*

Russia and Ukraine, 1830-1917 (2004). Formerly a Professor of American History at Dniepropetrovsk University in Ukraine, he completed a Ph.D. in Russian History at the Johns Hopkins University in 2002. He is currently writing a book on a social and cultural history of American studies in the USSR.

www.ingramcontent.com/pod-product-compliance
Lightning Source LLC
Chambersburg PA
CBHW020658270326
41928CB00005B/178